APR 1 3 2005

The Origins of
Modern Musical Criticism
French and Italian Music
1600-1750

Studies in Musicology

George Buelow, Series Editor

Professor of Musicology
Indiana University

Other Titles in This Series

The Origins of
Modern Musical Criticism

French and Italian Music
1600–1750

by
Georgia Cowart

RESEARCH PRESS

Produced and distributed by
UMI Research Press
an imprint of
University Microfilms International
Ann Arbor, Michigan 48106

A revision of the author's thesis,
Rutgers University, 1980

Library of Congress Cataloging in Publication Data

Cowart, Georgia.
    The origins of modern musical criticism.

    (Studies in musicology ; no. 38)
    Revision of thesis (Ph.D.)—Rutgers University, 1980.
    Bibliography: p.
    Includes index.
    1. Musical criticism—History and criticism. 2. Music—
History and criticism—17th century. 3. Music—History
and criticism—18th century. 4. Music—France—History
and criticism. 5. Music—Italy—History and criticism.
I. Title. II. Series.
    ML3916.C7 1981   780'.944   81-641
    ISBN 0-8357-1166-8   AACR2

For David

Contents

The Quarrel in the Context of Early Eighteenth-Century Criticism
Aspects of Seventeenth-Century French Classical Criticism:
    Philosophy of the Ancients
The Dispute Over Taste
Musico-Poetic Theory in the Sixteenth and Seventeenth Centuries
Lecerf's *Comparaison:* Classical Doctrine as Musical Criticism

Before Rameau
Lullistes and *Ramistes*
The War of the Buffoons

National Styles and Good Taste in Music in Britain and Germany

Britain
Germany: Transmission of the Quarrels Over French and Italian
    Music
Germany: Transmission of French Classicism
Good Taste and National Styles in German Musical Aesthetics

Musical Examples

Preface

Seventeenth-century quarrels over French and Italian music may be traced to the cultural rivalry between France and Italy during the Renaissance, and more immediately to the modern Italian style that dominated European music during the course of the century. Parallel though independent quarrels over the respective merits of ancient and modern music had their roots in Italian humanism and were developed as part of the larger battle between Ancients and Moderns in seventeenth-century France. These two scholarly disputes, finally converging in the early eighteenth-century controversy between François Raguenet and Jean-Laurent Lecerf de la Viéville, encouraged the growth of a modern critical outlook, for writers arguing the virtues of opposing historical and national styles were forced to posit standards by which aesthetic judgments could be formulated.

There has been no major discussion of this subject in the musicological literature beyond a German dissertation in 1947 which erroneously attributed Lecerf's *Comparaison* to the author of another book that included Lecerf's treatise. No attempt has been made to trace the quarrel between Lecerf and Raguenet to the seventeenth-century conflict between Ancients and Moderns, nor have musicologists delved into the wealth of treatises, growing out of that conflict, that discuss ancient and modern music in the critical language developed by contemporary literary critics. Further, the debt of eighteenth-century German musical thought to the earlier French quarrels has for too long gone unrecognized.

Many people have made this book possible. The most far-reaching debt of gratitude is to my parents, who have supported me in innumerable ways throughout my life. The original study was first conceived in a doctoral seminar taught by my advisor, Professor George J. Buelow. Special thanks are owed to all the members of that seminar, especially Stephen Machon, whose creative work in the areas of style and taste led me to the present topic. Alfred Mann, now at Eastman School of Music, Henry Kaufmann, Robert Moevs, Richard Chrisman, and C. F. Main at Rutgers, and Luise Peake at the University of South Carolina, also gave valuable advice. The librarians at the University of South Carolina and at the University of North Carolina-Chapel Hill were unfailingly helpful and courteous; I would like to thank especially Harriet Oglesby and Thomas Parkman at Thomas Cooper Library, and Rachel Frew at the music library, UNC-Chapel Hill. A tremendous debt is owed my husband, David, not only for his ready support and encouragement, but also for the example of his own polished prose and respect for good writing. Finally, the person to whom I remain most indebted is Professor Buelow, whose enthusiasm for teaching and scholarly research both inspired this undertaking and prevented it many times from faltering.

Acknowledgments

The author gratefully acknowledges the following sources of the musical examples. Examples 1-3: Théodore Gérold, *L'art du chant en France au XVIIe siècle* (Strasbourg, 1921; repr. ed., New York, 1973). Example 4: Lully, *Oeuvres complètes,* vol. 5 (Paris, 1932). Example 5: reprinted in Paul-Marie Masson, "Musique italienne et musique française: la première querelle," *Rivista musicale italiana* 19(1912):521–25. Example 6: Lully, *Phaeton,* in: *Chefs d'oeuvre classiques de l'opéra française* (Leipzig, 1880; repr. ed., New York, 1971). Example 7: Lully, *Oeuvres complètes*, vol. 10 (Paris, 1939). Example 8: G. and A. Bononcini, *Tre Cantate* (© 1974 Edizioni Curci s.r.l., Milan). Example 9: *Oeuvres complètes de François Couperin*, vol. 10 (Paris, 1933). Example 10: *Denkmäler der Tonkunst in Osterreich*, vol. 47 (Graz, 1960, Akademische Druck- u. Verlagsanstalt).

I

Early Comparisons of
French and Italian Music

Quarrels over the relative merits of both French and Italian music and ancient and modern music reached an important climax in the famous debate between François Raguenet and Jean-Laurent Lecerf de la Viéville during the years 1702–1706. This particular debate, which would give substance to further discussions by French musicians and intellectuals throughout the eighteenth century, had its origins in the stylistic differences that had become apparent as the Renaissance gave way to the Baroque in France. Such differences, highlighted by Cardinal Mazarin's introduction of Italian opera and by Jean-Baptiste Lully's development of a consciously French operatic style, may be traced indirectly to even earlier cultural divergences that had begun to manifest themselves as early as the sixteenth century.

The Renaissance

The French king Charles VIII's invasion of Italy in 1494 initiated a half century of Italian campaigns which, though futile in themselves, effected a formal introduction of the Italian Renaissance in France. From the courts of the defeated Medicis Charles brought scholars and artists, and his successor, Louis XII, enriched French libraries with precious manuscripts from Milan.[1] Even as French political dominance began to wane during the later years of Francis I's reign (1515–1547), cultural interchange between the two countries intensified as Francis's generous patronage drew such famous Italian poets and artists as Luigi Alemanni, Andrea del Sarto, Leonardo da Vinci, and Benvenuto Cellini.[2]

Paradoxically, the wars in Italy generated among the French not only an intense national pride, but also a certain envy of the assumed cultural superiority of the Italians. The military expeditions of Charles VIII and Louis XII inspired the circle of poets and chroniclers gathered at court to exalt the political and military—and by implication, moral—superiority of France,[3] while the humanist writers in this coterie began to campaign for an indigenous poetry based on a more general acceptance of the French language. One of these humanists, Lemaire de Belges, deserves particular attention, for his long poem, *La concorde des deux langages* (Paris, 1513),[4] prefigures in its use of allegory and comparative technique many later comparisons of French and Italian modes of expression.

The poem is divided into two parts: "The Temple of Venus," written in imitation of Petrarchan tercets, and "The Temple of Minerva," written in traditional French alexandrines. The juxtaposition points up the common assumption that, while the clarity and good sense of the French language are appropriate to the goddess of wisdom, only the more sensuous and "feminine" Italian language can properly describe the goddess of love. The author, however, refutes this generalization in his introduction,[5] and concludes the work by calling for an end to strife between the two nations and the two tongues and for a mutual appreciation for the other's merits.[6]

The French imitation of Italian poetry, especially that of Petrarch, continued throughout the sixteenth century.[7] Joachim Du Bellay, whose *Deffense et illustration de la langue françoise* (Paris, 1549) served as a manifesto of the group of poets known as the *Pléiade*, championed in that and other works the superiority of the pure French language against the Italianate poetry of Clement Marot and his defenders. In 1553 Du Bellay rails against the artificial and mannered poetry of the Italians in his "Elegie d'amour":

> I am not so subtle an artisan
> That with the language of a courtesan,
> False sighs and feigned tears,
> Show externally a distorted expression,
> Dissembling by means of artifice,
> For I am neither Tuscan nor Lombard.[8]

In "Ode contre les Pétrarchistes" he contrasts the pure poetical expression of former times to the flattery and deceit introduced by the Italians:

> Our good ancestors, who led us to this art,
> Never learned to speak like Petrarch,
> But conversed frankly with their ladies
> Without paint or make-up.
> But as soon as *Amour* became learned
> He who was French before,
> Became flattering and deceiving
> And of a Tuscan nature.[9]

Before Francis I, French pride had depended largely on superiority of arms, but the *roi chevalier*, by imitating the Italians' lavish patronage of the arts, gave to France a growing confidence in her own cultural heritage. The changing evaluation of France *vis à vis* Italy is reflected from an Italian point of view in Baldassare Castiglione's *Il libro del cortegiano* (Venice, 1528), in which two interlocutors, Lodovico, Count of Canossa, and Giuliano de Medici, argue whether the glories of France can ever compare to those of Italy. Lodovico declares that France will never excel except in military glory, but Giuliano maintains that if Francis succeeds to the throne, the general culture of France will equal her nobility in arms. Both agree that the French possess a moral valor which the Italians have lost.[10]

The Italian wars were officially ended in 1559 by Francis's successor, Henry II, who needed to turn his undivided attention to the struggle against the Huguenots and their efforts to bring the Protestant Reformation to France. Henry's marriage to Catherine de Medici, Lorenzo the Magnificent's daughter, insured a continuation of strong ties to Italy, however, and Italian influence increased with Catherine's power when she became queen mother and regent during the reigns of her three sons.[11] Resentment of Italian influence at court and on French culture grew with the increasing tension between Catholics and Protestants in France, and the Huguenots blamed the influx of Italian ideas, especially the political philosophy of Machiavelli's *Il principe* (Rome and Florence, 1532), for the deterioration of French morals and eventually for Catherine's role in the massacre of the Huguenots on Saint Bartholomew's Day, 1572.[12]

One Protestant writer, Henri Estienne, blamed Italians in France not only for French political and religious unrest, but also for the corruption of the French language. In his *Deux dialogues du nouveau langage françois italianizé* (Geneva, 1578),[13] he personifies the pure French tongue and its degradation in the respective characters of Celtophile (Lover of France), who speaks an elegant, simple French, and Philausone (Lover of Italy), whose efforts to ape the Italianate courtiers represent an amusing parody of fashionable court language.[14] An objective arbiter of the disagreement finally judges in favor of Celtophile, pointing out that the courtiers, being Italian, are in no position to act as paragons of French taste.

Estienne's *La précellence du langage françois* (Paris, 1579)[15] attempts a justification of the superiority of French to other modern languages. In his introduction, Estienne explains his concentration on the comparison between French and Italian, claiming that if he can prove the Italian language inferior, all other languages will easily take their place far below those two in quality. To illustrate popular support for his theory, he quotes an anonymous Latin proverb which would be taken up by critics for over a century: "Balent Itali, gemunt Hispani, ululant Germani, cantant Galli" (Italians dance, Spaniards groan, Germans howl, French sing).[16] The treatise proper, like the *Deux dialogues*, consists largely of technical linguistic analyses.

French criticism of the encroachment of the Italian language and culture seems not to have extended to the field of music until the seventeenth century, although French and Italian music interacted continually throughout the Renaissance. Composers as well as performers traveled freely between France and Italy, and both vocal and instrumental music underwent reciprocal influence. A continual interplay may be seen between chanson and madrigal at the time of the Italian campaigns; the works of Willaert, Verdelot, Festa, Arcadelt, Claudin, and Jannequin all draw heavily from both French and Italian musical traditions.[17]

Most of Francis's instrumentalists came from Italy,[18] and in 1529 Francis made Alberto Rippe, the celebrated Mantuan lutenist,[19] his *valet de chambre*. Rippe and other Italian lutenists helped to popularize Italian forms such as the villanella, madrigal, and canzona in France; a great number of these forms, including works by Lassus, da Rore, Vecoli, and Marenzio, may be found in French lute collections of the late sixteenth and early seventeenth centuries.[20]

Court entertainments at Fontainebleau grew out of the Italian tradition of *masquerades* and *pastorales*, and later in the century the *ballet de cour* developed from these entertainments with another infusion of Italian elements based on the tastes of Catherine de Medici and her court. The Piedmontese Baltazarini da Belgiojoso came to France in 1576, changed his name to Baltasar de Beaujoyeulx, and became Catherine's *valet de chambre*; his *ballets de cour* represent a second fusion of traditional French airs with diverse elements of the Italian *mascherate* and *intermedi*, along with dances of the Italian theater. Both the musicians and choreographers collaborating on his *Ballet comique de la reine* of 1581 were for the most part Italian, part of the circle of "foreigners" with which Catherine surrounded herself;[21] Ludovico Celler, in his study of the *Ballet comique de la reine*, comments that the work "owes its existence to the Italian spirit."[22]

The sixteenth century was, then, a period in which the French began to exercise themselves on the subject of Italian cultural superiority, yet without managing to identify Italian musical influence as grounds for controversy. The lack of critical reaction to the infiltration of the Italian musical style may perhaps be explained by the fact that musical criticism, especially the comparative evaluation of two different bodies of literature, had not yet reached the sophistication of literary and linguistic criticism, which had been finely honed by the humanist classical critics, and the concept of national style was slower to affect musical thought than literary. Also, differences in national style could more easily manifest themselves in literature and language than in music, for the spoken languages of France and Italy diverged more completely than their musical languages, which in the sixteenth century still continued to share the more universal Franco-Flemish idiom.

The Early Seventeenth Century

Marie de Medici, as wife of Henry IV (ruled 1589–1610) and regent during the minority of their son Louis XIII, continued the importation of Italian courtiers, writers, artists, actors, and musicians; politics were also Italianized by her Italian minister, Concini, who was so distrusted by the French public that he was arrested and murdered in 1617.[23] Italian political influence declined somewhat with the ascendance of Cardinal Richelieu in that year, but Louis XIII and his wife, Anne of Austria, shared Marie's passion for Italian culture and encouraged its continuation in France until mid-century when, after the deaths of Louis and Richelieu, Anne appointed the Italian Giulio Raimondo Mazzarino (Mazarin) as *premier ministre*.[24]

"Italianisme," as the French call the systematic imitation of Italian language, manners, and modes of expression, reached its height in the society of early seventeenth-century France.[25] An Italian, Catherine de Vivonne, marquise de Rambouillet, presided over the "blue room" of the Hôtel de Rambouillet, long regarded as the ultimate standard for elegance in social gatherings *à l'italien*.[26] Imitations of the Rambouillet salon abounded, and the aping of Italian manners became linked to the *précieux* element of society, especially the fashionable women of the *nouveau-riches*.[27] At their best, these women created a lively, intelligent milieu in which the arts and ideas could flourish; at their worst, they lapsed into the ridiculous posturing satirized by Molière in the play *Les précieuses ridicules* of 1659.

One of the cults fostered by Mme. de Rambouillet's salon was that of the cavalier Marino, the Italian poet who transformed the Renaissance style of Ariosto and Tasso into a new, mannered art full of conceits (*concetti*), syntactic distortions for surprise effects.[28] On an extended visit to France in the early part of the century, Marino was royally received by Marie de Medici and her minister Concini as well as by Mme. de Rambouillet.[29] His poetry, like the manners of the *salon bleu*, was the object of inept imitation by many Italian and French poets, and the great lengths to which Marino's French followers went to achieve bizarre effects caused an inevitable reaction by the classicists in the latter half of the seventeenth century.[30]

Marie de Medici and Henry IV patronized music as avidly as literature, and their marriage in 1600, the festivities of which included the *Euridice* of Peri and Rinuccini, marks an important date for the early history of opera. The librettist Ottavio Rinuccini, poet and nobleman, had special ties with the court of France and was rumored to be the unrequited lover of Marie.[31] He came to France shortly after her marriage in 1600 and was made *gentilhomme de chambre* to Henry IV; on frequent journeys between Paris and Florence in the early years of the century he was entrusted with important communications between the rulers of France and Tuscany.[32]

At the prompting of Rinuccini, Henry IV requested from the grand duke of Tuscany the "loan" of Giulio Caccini and his family; Caccini arrived in 1604 with letters of introduction to the minister Concini, who welcomed the family handsomely and introduced them at court. In a letter to the grand duke, Caccini describes this event, mentioning with satisfaction the enthusiastic reception of their performances of French, Italian, and Spanish songs.[33]

The impact of Caccini's vocal and compositional technique must be understood in light of the prevailing French vocal style associated with the *air de cour*. Since Ronsard and the *Pléiade*, music and poetry had been intimately linked in France, so much so that poetry was often considered incomplete without musical setting. Composers, still under the influence of *musique mésurée*, generally sacrificed a preconceived rhythmic structure in order to remain faithful to the rhythm of the verse, which often utilized a strict octosyllabic line or, even more frequently, the alexandrine structure of the twelve-syllable anapestic line.[34] This manner of setting focused interest on a smooth, graceful melody at the expense of harmony, counterpoint, and rhythm and produced an impression of ceaseless melodic movement which, though polished and charming, lacked the rhythmic variety and harmonic intensity of the Italians. The French style is exemplified in the early seventeenth century by Henry IV's *surintendant de musique* Pierre Guédron, whose *airs de cour* were widely admired, not only in France but also in Italy and other countries as well.[35]

One element almost nonexistent in the works of Guédron and his contemporaries, the repetition of text with melismas on the first statement, was quite common in the works of Caccini[36] (see Example 1). The use of short melismas was not inimical to the French style, but in general these were much less extended than in the Italian works (see Example 2). Finally, the Italian use of such ornaments as the *esclamazione* and the *trillo*, and such rhythmic figurations as those of the following example, contributed to a pathetic effect almost entirely lacking in French music (see Example 3).

The French had developed a style of singing which they considered appropriate to the constrained, delicate lines of the *air de cour*, and seem to have reacted to the passionate intensity of the Italians with mixed admiration and horror. A Mlle. Sandrier, who went to Italy to sing,

> returned to Paris seventeen years later, where she began to sing the Italian airs she had learned in Turin. She caused a sensation, which, however, was shortlived; several people concluded that she sang badly, for it was completely in the Italian manner, and she grimaced horribly; some even said she was having convulsions.[37]

In 1607 Jean-Baptiste Du Val, a Frenchman traveling in Italy, commented similarly on the singing he heard in Venice:

> . . . they sing well in their way, which one tastes for the first time without finding much pleasure, and finds it quite different from our own manner of singing . . .[38]

Pierre de Nyert, the French singer and pedagogue who accompanied the Duc de Créqui to Rome in 1623, returned to France to teach singing in a new way based on Italianate technique. His reforms, apparently successful because of their modification of the Italian method to the French taste, included the establishment of rules governing proper pronunciation and breathing and the introduction of a greater degree of ornamentation. According to Tallemant de Réaux, writing in the years 1657–1659:

> . . . de Nyert combined what was good in their manner of singing with what was good in ours; he created a new way of singing which Lambert practices today, and to which he perhaps adds a little. . . .[39]

In the same decade that de Nyert studied new ideas in vocal execution in Rome, the French gamba player André Maugars (c.1580–c.1645) visited that city in order to learn more of Italian performance practice as well as compositional technique. Maugars, one of the most celebrated gambists of his day, had spent four years in England where he served as musician to James I. After his return to France, he became known as the translator of Francis Bacon's *The Advancement of Learning*, and shortly thereafter, as musician to Cardinal Richelieu. Historians differ as to the reasons for Maugars' sojourn in Italy during the years 1635–1639, but most agree that his *Response faite à un curieux sur le sentiment de la musique d'Italie* (Rome, 1639)[40] was written with an eye to the favor of Richelieu.[41]

Maugars' treatise begins with a discussion of Italian sacred music, in which he finds more "art, learning [*science*], and variety" than in its

Example 1.　　Giulio Caccini. "Odi Euterpe il dolce canto," from *Le nuove musiche* (Florence, 1601. Courtesy of Burt Franklin, New York)

Example 2.　　Pierre Guédron. "Air," from Gabriel Bataille, *Airs de différents autheurs mis en tablature de luth* (Paris, 1608). Caccini. "Dovrè dunque morire," from *Le nuove musiche*

Guédron:

Caccini:

Example 3:　　Caccini, "Amor, io parto," from *Le nuove musiche*

French counterpart, along with more license.[42] This license, when taken with discretion, contrasts favorably with the strictures of French composers, who "bind themselves religiously to pedantic categories and think they have committed solecisms against the rules of art if they have one parallel fifth, or deviate however slightly from the mode."[43] The Italians, he says, make fun of French regularity, and see the rules in their proper light: as guidelines for beginners with lack of judgment, not as rigorous laws which hamper the working out of a fugue subject or the composition of a beautiful melody.

Maugars praises the divided choirs of Rome, each with its own organ, in the performance of motets, and describes in detail the Italian oratorio, a genre still unknown in France. He also admires the instrumental participation in sacred performances, mentioning in particular the organ, harpsichord, *lyre* (a type of viol), violas, and archlutes. The organist Girolamo Frescobaldi is the object of Maugars' most fervent accolades ("I have fallen insensibly into praise of this excellent man"),[44] and he is careful to point out that, due to the greater importance of improvisation in Italy, Frescobaldi cannot be judged on the basis of his printed works alone, but must be heard in actual performance. With regard to improvisation, Maugars proudly notes that such talents were not expected of him as a Frenchman, but that the Italians were amazed to find that he also could improvise well.

As an instrumentalist, Maugars enthusiastically reports the esteem accorded to instrumental music by the Italians, in contrast to the greater emphasis placed on vocal music by the French. The Italians say, according to him, "that a single man can thus produce more beautiful inventions than an ensemble of four voices and that it [instrumental music] has charms and licenses which vocal music does not."[45]

Italy's vocal music, however, seems to have made an equally great impression on Maugars. A fervent devotee of the art of the castrati, he admires not only their singing, but especially their dramatic talents. Most of Maugars' description of Italian singers, however, is devoted to one in particular, the beautiful and gifted Leonora Baroni,[46] who was later to cause such a sensation in France under the auspices of Mazarin. Of a concert given by Leonora with her mother and sister, Maugars exclaims, "I forgot my mortal condition and believed myself to be already among the company of the blessed."[47]

On a more analytical level, Maugars describes Italian singing as more animated than the French, with more ornamentation of the melodic line. He recommends that French singers have more commerce with the foreigners in order to improve their style and offers as an example the

French singer de Nyert, "who has combined so well the Italian method with the French that he has received the applause of all informed gentlemen."[48] He also advises French composers to emancipate themselves from their pedantic rules and to visit Italy as he has done. He admits, finally, that in some areas French music assumes superiority: though Italians compose marvelous sacred music, the French excell in *airs de mouvement*; Italians play the organ "very knowledgeably" ("*très-scavamment*"), the French "very agreeably" ("*très-agréablement*"). No nation can compete with the French in the instrumental airs, ornamentation, and particularly in the natural songs and instrumental dances of the ballets. In conclusion, Maugars states for the first time in simple terms what would become a cliché in future quarrels over French and Italian music: "that we sin in deficiency, the Italians in excess."[49] And his solution foreshadows that of later writers and composers when he suggests a type of composition "which would have their beautiful variety without their extravagance."[50]

From the early seventeenth century, most comment on the contrast between French and Italian music and performance practice comes either from French travelers in Italy, such as Maugars, or from the correspondence of French and Italian writers. One of the most important figures in the dissemination of information about Italian music in this period was Giovanni Battista Doni (1594–1647), a scholar and music theorist who had traveled to France as legate to the pope, Ottavio Corsini. Doni may have met the French theorist Marin Mersenne (1588–1648) at that time, for an extensive correspondence arose between the two in the following years.[51] In his letters to Mersenne, Doni described contemporary Italian music and musical thought, and much of Mersenne's discussion of the subject in his *Harmonie universelle* (Paris, 1636–1637) may be traced to the information so transmitted.

Most of Doni's correspondence with Mersenne centered around the studies of ancient music in which he was involved,[52] but many opportunities also arose for comments on the contemporary music of France and Italy. In 1636 Doni sent to Mersenne Monteverdi's famous lament from the opera *Ariadne*, declaring it the best example of a piece in this genre. He comments favorably on the librettist, Ottavio Rinuccini, but complains that Monteverdi, though a good musician, is a man of little intelligence, lamenting that, unlike in ancient times, composers are not always men of distinction. As for the music of the French, Doni criticizes it mostly for its excessive restraint:

> For instead of making their melody varied and artificial, they mostly make it simple and trivial, as one can see by the number of notes that never move away from one chord. However much your musicians feel obligated to continue in this style, it seems

to me that they have the opportunity to perfect and change it. . . . And I am assured that if your princes would go to the expense, and time permitted it, this would succeed enormously.[53]

Mersenne, apparently avid for news of Italian music, had already received another letter on the subject in the previous year (1635) from another Frenchman traveling in Italy, J. J. Bouchard. Bouchard's letter from Rome gives some indication of the controversy raging over French and Italian music, even at this early date:

As for what you ask concerning whether Italian music is better than French, this is a great controversy here. Our Frenchmen who come find Italian music disagreeable, and the Italians consider ours ridiculous and of no account. If you wish to know my opinion, I will say that, for artifice, knowledge, and forcefulness of singing, for quantity of musicians, principally castratos, Rome surpasses Paris as much as Paris surpasses Vaugirard. But for delicacy, and *una certa leggiadria e dilettevole naturalezza* [a certain lightness and delightful naturalness], the French surpass the Italians by far. . . . The French are more suave and agreeable, the Italians more learned and astounding.[54]

Mersenne, engaged in the composition of his *Harmonie universelle* in these years, undoubtedly incorporated the reports of both Doni and Bouchard. Basing his evaluation of the two styles on their ability to depict and communicate the passions, he finds that French music, "tranquil, voluptuous, and languishing," cannot compare with Italian, which expresses anger, fury, spite, and the other passions "with a violence so extraordinary that one thinks [the singers] to be touched by those very affections which they represent in song." French singing, on the other hand, is content to flatter the ear with "never-ending sweetness" completely lacking in energy.[55] Mersenne states his belief that French composers are capable of the passionate intensity witnessed at Rome and Florence, and urges that they overcome their timidity in order to compose truly dramatic music.

Like Maugars, Mersenne recommends that French composers and performers visit Italy in order to learn the Italians' manner of singing as well as their general knowledge of music. While not all aspects of Italian music are praiseworthy, Frenchmen can learn from certain admirable traits such as the Italian recitative, which is more animated than the French; French musicians surpass only in coquetry, never in vigor. Though the French do not wish their music to be as dramatic as Italian opera, Mersenne suggests that they incorporate what is good in Italian music into their own, accommodating the exclamations of the Italians to their own sweetness, and the pathetic quality of the Italians to their own clarity of expression. After discussing the innovations of Peri and Caccini, Mersenne closes with an obvious echo of Doni's letter cited above:

> But our musicians are, it seems, too timid to introduce this manner of recitative in France, although they are as capable of it as the Italians, if anyone would encourage them by meeting the expenses required by such an undertaking.[56]

The openness of Mersenne and Bouchard to the music of the Italians was not shared by the majority of their countrymen at mid-century. Testimony to the superiority of French music is given by the French man-of-letters Ismael Boulliaud, who finds the Italians lacking in capacity for singing and inflection,[57] and by Michel de Marolles, who includes a discussion of French music in his *Mémoires* (c. 1657; first published Amsterdam, 1755). Marolles enumerates the well-known composers and performers of his day, including Guédron, Boisset, Lambert, Mersenne, Gaultier, Chambonnières, and du Mont, and insists upon the worth of French music in comparison to the Italian, "even though it is not as noisy, and has more sweetness; but these do not seem to be qualities which would render it inferior."[58]

These scattered opinions from the first part of the seventeenth century reveal a growing awareness of, and response to, the differences between French and Italian musical styles. In essence these differences amounted to the contrast between opera and *air de cour*, for at this time opera was associated exclusively with Italy and generally considered unsuitable to the French temperament, both because of the French distaste for sung drama and of the difficulties involved in setting the unwieldy poetic structure of the French language.[59] Contemporary writers perceived the real contrast between Italian and French music to be one of purpose: Italian opera attempted to move the affections, often by violent means, while French song sought rather to touch the emotions in a more delicate manner.[60] Thus, by mid-century Frenchmen felt a growing pride in a French musical style which, distinct from the Italian style, was able to reflect their own national temperament.

The Period of Mazarin

It was Cardinal Mazarin (1602–1661) who, as Anne of Austria's powerful *premier ministre* during the decades of the 1640s and 1650s, sought to introduce Italian opera in France. As a child, Mazarin had been educated by the fathers of the Oratory of St. Philip Neri during the early years of the seventeenth century, and later attended a Jesuit college in Rome.[61] After serving the powerful Colonna family in his youth, Mazarin entered the service of the cardinal Antonio Barberini in 1632. By the 1630s, Rome had overshadowed Florence as a center for opera, and the Barberini family were making their mark as lavish patrons of this art.[62] Mazarin, who participated in the production of Stefano Landi's *Sant'Alessio*, which opened the Barberini theater in 1632, must have learned in this milieu not only the new developments in musical theater, but also the workings of musical patronage at its most magnificent.[63]

In 1639 Mazarin entered the service of the French King Louis XIII and his minister Richelieu, and became minister in his own right after the deaths of Richelieu in 1642 and of Louis in 1643. He lost no time in creating a musical establishment in Paris based on that of the Barberinis in Rome; Leonora Baroni arrived in 1644,[64] and soon afterwards the famous castrato Atto Melani, who was to act as secret agent for Mazarin during the years 1648–1649.[65] By 1646 the Barberini family had been forced by its political enemies to seek refuge in France,[66] and Mazarin's plans for Italian opera were furthered by the importation of their retinue of Italian singers, composers, and stage designers. With respect to the future of opera in France, perhaps one of the most important arrivals was that of the master machinist Giacomo Torelli (1608–1678), who had been sent to Anne by the Duke of Parma.[67]

The year 1645 saw Italian entertainment begin in earnest at the French court. In February an unidentified Italian comedy was performed, and in December of the same year the court witnessed *La finta Pazza*, a play by Giulio Strozzi with music by Francesco Sacrati and sets by Torelli.[68] Like the later performance in 1654 of Carlo Caprioli's *Nozze de Peleo e di Teti*, this work was received coolly except for the general amazement at Torelli's machinery. The revival of Francesco Cavalli's *Egisto* in 1646 was also received with little enthusiasm.[69]

During this period, political opposition to the policies of Mazarin grew, and a coalition known as the Fronde prepared for the series of civil wars which would disrupt the government of France from 1648 to 1653. Besides their complaints concerning Mazarin's general management of affairs, much of the *frondeurs'* antagonism stemmed from their anti-Italian sentiments and their resentment of the intrusion at court of the Italians imported by Mazarin.[70]

The opposition to Mazarin's introduction of Italian opera constituted the first real anti-Italianism in music in France, and that opposition was largely political. Luigi Rossi's *Orfeo*, the elaborate musical entertainment that Mazarin produced in March 1647, had the unexpected effect of consolidating public opinion against Mazarin on the eve of the civil wars.[71] *Frondeurs* and churchmen united in outcries against the opera, supposedly because of the inferior music and unseemly plot, but in actuality more for purely political and personal vendettas against Mazarin. What was finally taken up as a veritable battle-cry among Mazarin's detractors was the enormous sum of money spent on the production. This was exaggerated out of all proportion and the French public, burdened with the highest taxes yet levied in France, began to point accusingly to the costly pleasures of the court. Guy Joly wrote in his *Mémoires* in 1648 that the opera had cost over five hundred million *écus*, and that this enormous sum, "excessive and superfluous," proved that the affairs of state were not so troublesome that Mazarin could not have spared them if he wished.[72] Nicolas Goulas' *Mémoires* include an even stronger complaint:

> Everyone is appalled at the horrible expense of the Italian machines and musicians who have come from Rome at such great expense, for it is necessary to pay for them to come back and forth and to be supported in France. There are twelve or thirteen castratos and some women, one of whom [Leonora Baroni] has the reputation of selling her beauty in Italy.[73]

During the actual wars of the Fronde, Torelli was imprisoned and persecuted, and Rossi and Melani forced to flee.[74]

Public distaste for Mazarin and his Italian operas is clearly evidenced by the songs and pamphlets, collectively called *Mazarinades*, written during the period of the Fronde. The most famous of these, written by an anonymous author in 1651 and called simply "La Mazarinade," includes a reference to *Orfeo* as "this beautiful ballet, this handsome but unhappy Orpheus/Or rather, this Morpheus who put everyone to sleep."[75] Another *Mazarinade*, written in prose as a "Letter from a priest sent to M. le prince de Condé, at St. Germain-en-Laye, containing the truth of the life and manners of Cardinal Mazarin," resembles a modern-day scandal sheet in its denunciation of Mazarin's connections with the Italian singers:

> Who doesn't know what cost France has paid for the singer-comedians that he brought from Italy, among whom was a woman of ill fame [Leonora Baroni] whom he debauched in Rome in order to insinuate himself into the good graces of Cardinal Antonio? All of this during the war, when people were pressed to contribute to the subsistence of the armies; and the blood of the poor was used to make the Cardinal Mazarin laugh . . . proving to all the world that he has no other religion than that of Machiavelli. . . .[76]

It was against this background that Jean-Baptiste Lully came to Paris in 1646, one year before *Orfeo* and two years before the outbreak of civil war. In his teens during these wars, Lully came of age, like Louis XIV, at a time when French resentment of Italian domination of politics and the arts had reached its peak. Brought to Paris at fourteen to serve in the household of the Duchesse d'Orléans, Mlle. de Montpensier, Lully entered the service of the king in 1652 when his patroness was exiled for her Italian sympathies.[77]

Far from beginning his career strictly as a composer of French music, Lully had composed Italian cantatas, airs, and duos for Mlle. de Montpensier. Under Louis, his duties entailed the composition and direction of the instrumental symphonies and dances of the *ballets de cour*, but in fact he interpolated many Italian airs, dialogues, trios, and choruses among the French vocal portions of the ballets, composed by Cambefort, Boësset, and Lambert, in order to please Mazarin and the queen mother, who enjoyed Italian vocal music. The young king was also enamoured of Italian airs, and in the years following the Fronde assembled a group of Italian singers under the direction of the composer Carlo Caprioli. These singers performed musical interludes in the ballets, and beginning with Lully's *Dialogue italien de la Guerre avec la Paix* in 1655, brought Lully to the public attention with their performances of his Italian vocal pieces. From the years before 1657 only one French air can be attributed to Lully.[78]

Only the libretti remain for Lully's earliest ballets. These reveal several typical Italian numbers: a comic Italian recitative in the *Ballet des bienvenues* (1655), written to celebrate the marriage of Mazarin's niece; a chorus of allegorical figures representing the "passions of love," along with an Italian lament in *Psyche* (1656); and an Italian air sung by the character Venus as well as an Italian serenade sung in dialogue in *La galanterie du temps* (1656).[79]

The earliest extant ballet music by Lully is a scene from his *Amor malato* (1657) to a libretto by Francesco Buti, Rossi's librettist for *Orfeo*.[80] Its comic Italian recitative was a great success with the Parisian audience proving that, handled correctly, the Italian style could be successfully adapted to the French taste. Indeed, the ballet was so well received that the French composers and anti-Italian faction at court attempted to counter its appeal by producing a completely French ballet a month after its performance. Though their *Plaisirs troublés* failed to surpass Lully's Italian ballet in its success, the controversy between French and Italian supporters put an end to the composition of purely Italian ballets at court, and from this time until the death of Mazarin in 1661, the Italian style existed only alongside the French.[81]

This stylistic juxtaposition may be seen in Lully's next ballet, *Alcidiane* (1658). The work begins with an early example of Lully's French Overture, and ends with an Italian finale. It includes numbers in French and Italian; at one point a rhythmically straightforward "Marche ital-

ienne" metamorphoses into a more delicately ornamented "Marche française"[82] (see Example 4).

Lully's portrayal of the French and Italian styles becomes self-conscious to the point of parody in his *Ballet de la raillerie* of 1659. Besides
an eclectic mixture of French and Italian numbers, the work contains a
famous dialogue between two allegorical figures representing French and
Italian music. In response to *Musique italienne*'s question, why she is so
offensive, *Musique française* answers that her songs are too extravagant.
Musique italienne retorts by labeling *Musique française* "languid and
sad." "But do you consider your long, boring embellishments any better?" asks *Musique française*. "I sing more strongly because I love more
strongly," challenges *Musique italienne*, but *Musique française* has the
last word: "My manner of singing expresses my languor better, for when
sadness truly touches the heart, the voice is less shrill."[83]

French music's languid, monotonous character is mimicked by the
use of slow harmonic rhythm and long note values (see Example 5a). And
Musique italienne's coloratura passages are humorously exaggerated (see
Example 5b). The word "death" ("*morte*") gives rise to the conventional
Italian use of chromaticism (see Example 5c).

Lully's Italian and Italian–French ballets reflect in a humorous and
witty manner the crisis of French music at mid-century during the up-
heavals of the Fronde and the rule of Mazarin.[84] The Italian minister's
importation of opera had emphasized the discrepancy between Italian
music and French taste, while instilling in the French a desire for a national style that would stand as a true equal to the Italian operatic style,
thus symbolically rendering France the cultural and political peer of Italy.
Lully's early ballets reveal his genius for synthesizing elements of Italian
opera and French *ballet de cour* in a genre suitable to the French temperament, but the completion of this synthesis was not to come about
until the later, more orderly years of the Sun King's reign.[85]

The Year of Transition: 1661

The year of Mazarin's death, 1661, was a turning point in the history of
France, for it also marked the beginning of Louis XIV's personal reign
and a number of resultant changes in the cultural tone of the French court
and society. Louis, having learned the dangers of foreign political influence in the wars of the Fronde, carefully chose his ministers from among
the ranks of the *bourgeoisie*, a segment of society traditionally patriotic
and anti-Italian.[86] French anti-Italian sentiment, kept in check after the
defeat of the Fronde and Mazarin's return to power, asserted itself anew
upon his death.

Example 4.   Lully. "Marche italienne" and "Marche françoise" from *Alcidiane*
(Courtesy of *Revue musicale*, Editions Richard Masse, Paris)

Example 5a.   Lully, Dialogue between *Musique française*
and *Musique italienne*, from *Ballet de la raillerie*

Example 5b.   Lully, Dialogue between *Musique française*
and *Musique italienne*

Example 5c.   Lully, Dialogue between *Musique française*
and *Musique italienne*

The effects of Mazarin's death on music were immediate. Fouquet, a nobleman who had attained great power and wealth as superintendent of finances under Mazarin, was arrested in September of 1661, having in August entertained the king so sumptuously that his finances were called into question.[87] The designer Torelli, who had participated in the entertainment, was banished, and the castrato Atto Melani, whose political intrigues were uncovered in a search of Fouquet's papers, was also obliged to seek refuge in Italy. From this time forward, the Italian musical establishment began to lose its secure position at the French court, and gradually disbanded over the course of the next decade.[88]

In May 1661, Lully became the king's superintendent of music upon the death of Cambefort. His *Ballet de l'impatience*, composed in collaboration with the French writer Benserade and the Italian Buti, and performed in July 1661, is generally considered his farewell to the *goût italien*; from this time he set about becoming a French composer, and soon came to be regarded and prized as such by the king, the court, and the public.[89] Lully reinforced this image by securing papers of naturalization in December 1661, and shortly thereafter made his position impregnable by marrying the daughter of the most popular composer of the previous generation, Michel Lambert.[90]

The year 1661 also saw the publication of the first extended pro-French comparison of French and Italian music, a letter written by Pierre Perrin (1620–1675), librettist and producer of the *Pastorale d'Issy*, which had been set to music by Cambert and performed in 1659.[91] The letter,[92] which sets forth a list of Italian operatic abuses and demonstrates how Perrin's *Pastorale* corrects them, indicates to what extent Perrin and Cambert had composed their work as a formula designed to appeal to the critics of Italian opera.

As a librettist, Perrin comments first on the use of ordinary poets and dramatists in Italian opera, rather than "poet–musicians" who understand how to create verses appropriate for musical setting. Because there is so much intrigue, plot complication, and dialogue in their works, the Italians must resort to a chant-like recitative style, whereas Perrin has composed his pastoral entirely of scenes purely for singing and for the expression of the passions.

Concerning performance practice, Perrin's criticism of the Italians is that heard most commonly from French musicians: the Italians take too many liberties, their ornaments are too frequent and affected, and their manner of singing, while expressing the passions admirably, strikes the French as being rather vulgar. Perrin claims to have chosen singers for his *Pastorale* who have been taught by the finest French masters to sing in a "finer, more fashionable" manner which is also more regular and reasonable.

Perrin contrasts his opera's length, an hour and a half, with the six or seven hours' duration of Italian operas, and boasts that whereas their individual numbers continue for fifty or sixty lines, his last only ten or twelve, thereby lessening the tedium of a single voice and producing greater variety. Perrin's work is also arranged so that no one or two singers have an inordinate share of the singing, and the variety of voices is enhanced by a variety of ritornellos and symphonic pieces.

The use of the Italian language is criticized by Perrin not only for its incomprehensibility to the French but, more fundamentally, for its use of bizarre figures of speech and transpositions of syntax. Perrin discloses a rumor that the librettist Buti had suggested to Mazarin that they produce a work in French for the Parisians, to which Mazarin replied that Italian music was meant not to please the public, but only the king and queen and himself, who understood and enjoyed Italian. Perrin's drama, on the other hand, is written in a "pure" French which eliminates all archaic and distorted syntax and presents a "beautiful and natural expression of the passions."[93] The use of castrati, "the horror of women and the laughing-stock of men,"[94] constitutes the final cause for Perrin's complaint. He recommends the intimate atmosphere of Issy, where his *Pastorale* was performed, and praises the natural demeanor of his actors and actresses.

In sum, Perrin's letter is not so much a criticism of Italian opera *per se* as an analysis of its lack of success in France and a plea for a type of musical drama more suitable to the native French sensibility.[95] While the *Pastorale d'Issy* may hardly be called a French answer to the magnificent operas of Rossi and Cavalli, and while Perrin's viewpoint is anything but objective, still his proposals struck to the heart of French artistic pride and focused the desire for a clearly defined French national style.

The Late Seventeenth Century

After 1661 the tenor of French culture and thought became imbued with greater pride in national achievements and more scepticism of Italian domination in the arts. In literature, the critics were forging a classical doctrine to oppose to the art of ornaments and conceits, and the opinions of a generation of writers[96] were summarized for posterity in the critical works of Nicolas Boileau (1636–1711). Boileau urged his countrymen to shun the tasteless extravagances of the Italians in favor of the purity and simplicity of the French masters, and his *Art poétique* (Paris, 1674) became the Bible of French classical criticism.[97]

As in literature, French musical opinion in the late seventeenth century began to turn towards native music and musicians. The final debacle for the Italian faction at court came with the performance of Francesco Cavalli's *Ercole amante* on February 7, 1662. Cavalli, aware of the differing tastes of the French, endowed his opera with more dramatic coherence, a greater emphasis upon ballets and machinery, elaborate costumes and sets, and simpler harmonic and melodic figurations. The music itself was lost, however, amid the loud conversations of those spectators who did not understand Italian, and as with Cavalli's *Xerxes* (1654), which had been performed in Paris in 1660, only the external trappings of the opera appealed to its French audience.[98]

The main reason for French disapproval of *Ercole*, however, as in the case of Rossi's *Orfeo*, was political. Colbert, who as minister of finance had become Louis' most powerful official, preferred French music to Italian, and his opinions were seconded by other members of the new government. The image of Lully as champion of French music was taking root in the minds of the public, and the ballets he composed for *Ercole amante* evoked admiration at the expense of the vocal music; in fact, the opera was generally called a "ballet" in France.[99]

Through the remainder of the decade, Lully continued to forge a personal dramatic musical style in his collaborations with Molière in the *comédies-ballets*, while Perrin and the composer Cambert sought to establish a French national opera. In 1671 the *Académie d'Opéra* was founded, and inaugurated with a performance of their *Pomone*, followed in 1672 by another pastoral by Cambert, *Les peines et les plaisirs d'amour*, to a libretto by Gabriel Gilbert. From the few remaining fragments of these pastoral works, James Anthony evaluates Cambert's music as "well on the way to the creation of a French recitative which, if less concerned with textual elements than that of Lully, is more genuinely musical."[100]

As is well known, Lully secured the royal privilege in 1672 from Perrin who was imprisoned for bankruptcy and, doubtless having realized through the efforts of Perrin and Cambert the potential of the French language for use in opera, began to create a national French music drama. His pastoral of 1670, *Les fêtes de l'Amour et de Bacchus*, had succeeded the ballets as a step in the fusion of the French and Italian styles, but his *Cadmus et Hermione* of 1672 may be considered the first real synthesis of the two into a truly French operatic style.[101] While earlier comparisons between French and Italian music had contrasted Italian opera to French airs, ballets, or pastorals, discussions of French and Italian music from this period onward would oppose French opera to Italian and, more specifically, Lully's operatic style to the Venetian style of Cavalli, Cesti, Stradella and, later, Alessandro Scarlatti. Lully was undoubtedly influenced by his exposure to Cavalli's operas performed in Paris, and his melodic and scenic structure owe a great deal to the Italian master. Through the 1670s and 1680s, however, Italian composers moved toward lighter texture and increasing importance of the aria at the expense of the recitative, and, as Lully's operas began to exhibit a stylistic unity based on the tastes of his patron, the differences between the French and Italian styles became more marked.[102]

As the name *tragédie-lyrique* implies, the French opera of Lully was taken more seriously as drama than the Italian opera, and the libretti by Quinault were more tightly constructed than the loosely organized melodramas of Buti and his Italian successors.[103] The comic scenes for which Lully had shown such an aptitude in his early ballets were entirely expurgated from the *tragédie-lyrique*, the serious purpose of which was the same as the classical tragedy of Racine: an Aristotelian catharsis intensified by the musical and rhetorical heightening of the vocal declamation.

Lully's new type of recitative,[104] perhaps the most striking characteristic of his style, exactly paralleled the innovations in theatrical declamation in late seventeenth-century France. Racine's son described this type of speech as a "kind of singing," and Racine himself is quoted as having instructed the actress La Champmeslé to cover ranges of an octave or more.[105] Lully's recitative, with its complex notation and strictly syllabic orientation, follows the natural speech patterns in a manner that fulfills the operatic ideal of a "heightened speech" perhaps more successfully than any other musical style.

Lully's airs, developed from the *air de cour*, differed from the Italian arias in their brevity, narrow range, and conservative harmonies. They contained fewer long coloratura passages, but more single-note ornamentation, such as trills and passing tones. They often tended toward dance rhythms and binary form, usually eschewing the more highly developed *da capo* form favored increasingly in Italy. Other features of Lully's airs include more static basses and slower harmonic rhythm than their Italian counterparts, with a more diatonic orientation of melody and harmony.

The one area in which French opera was never equalled by the Italian, even in the opinion of the most ardent Italian advocates, was in the *divertissement*. Lully brought the French chorus, ballet, and *symphonie* to a peak of perfection, and these elements were enhanced by the most sumptuous costumes, machinery, and stage sets. The chorus, almost nonexistent in Venetian opera by the 1640s, was considered one of the finest aspects of Lully's *tragédie-lyrique*. It is used for dramatic effects in underworld or magic scenes, and almost always adds weight to the spectacle of the climactic finale. Usually homophonic, the chorus may be varied through the use of polyphonic texture, as well as through the occasional use of unaccompanied or double-chorus scoring.[106]

In creating a French musical style from these materials, Lully acted as a servant of an established French taste, based on pride in restraint and order, a love of the ballet, and a desire that the mental, visual, and aural senses be equally satisfied. As shown above, concessions to this French taste had been made by Cavalli when composing operas for Paris, and Perrin and Cambert had catered to the French taste in their pastorals. But it was not until Lully's series of *tragédies-lyriques* from 1673 to 1687 that a real operatic style was created to coincide with the temperament of his audience, and particularly of his patron. Most late seventeenth-century opera critics take pride in this French operatic style created by the Florentine, and find its classical restraint superior to the extravagances of the Italians.

One of the first comparisons of the French and Italian musical styles after the establishment of the *tragédie-lyrique* is the letter "To the Duke of Buckingham upon Operas," written ironically by one of France's most inveterate opera-haters, Charles Margaretel de St.-Denis, Seigneur de Saint-Evremond.[107] St.-Evremond had been banished from France as a result of the same investigation that had incriminated Atto Melani in 1661 and, writing in England, became one of the century's wittiest and most astute literary critics. Although all opera for him destroys the rationalism and "good sense" he finds in true tragedy, his remarks on the subject of French and Italian style are perceptive.

St.-Evremond respects poets more than musicians, and comments that the librettist, rather than the composer, should control the opera, but he makes an exception for Lully, "who knows the passions better, and enters further into the heart of man, than the writers themselves."[108] He praises Lully's genius for "a hundred different sorts of music," and states that no other style of recitative is as well understood or as varied as his. Italian recitative, on the other hand, is tedious, "an awkward use of music and speech";[109] even the Italians themselves wait impatiently for the arias which come all too seldom.

As for performance, French singing is, according to St.-Evremond, infinitely superior to Italian. He finds Italian singing exaggerated; rather than sing, they laugh, sob, exclaim, weep, and roar. He sees this exaggeration as a violation of good taste, and says:

There is no nation that produces greater courage in the men, more beauty in the women, nor more spirit in both sexes. One cannot have everything, and where so many good qualities are so common, the lack of good taste is no great misfortune.[110]

Repeating the old maxim, "Solus Gallus cantat," St.-Evremond remembers the preference of Luigi Rossi for French singing, quoting him as saying that "to make fine music, Italian airs must come from a French mouth."[111]

St.-Evremond compares the French appropriation of Italian machines with the German appropriation of French modes and customs:

> . . . as if we would atone for the fault of being prevented in the invention, we carry
> to excess a custom which they introduced. . . . In truth, we cover the earth with
> deities, and make them dance in troops.[112]

St.-Evremond closes by advising others to keep silent on the subject of opera if they would not have their taste impugned, but restates his opinion that, as preposterous as the premise of opera may be, no one performs within its limitations as well as Lully and Quinault.

As in earlier years, a valuable source for late seventeenth-century comparisons of French and Italian music is provided by the journals of French travelers to Italy. In 1680 the Frenchman Limojon de St.-Didier described Venetian opera in *La ville et la république de Venise* (Amsterdam, 1697), comparing the superiorities of that nation's music with those of his own. He describes the Italian theaters as magnificent but badly illuminated, and finds the machines inferior to the French. He mentions the common Italian practice of the exit aria, an artifiical means of drawing applause at the end of a scene, and notes that it succeeds so well that one hears "a thousand Benissimo's," as well as vulgar and ridiculous catcalls from the gondoliers to the female vocalists.

The usual French complaint concerning deficiencies of the libretto is included, St.-Didier maintaining that the four-hour operas would not seem so long if the dramatists were more conversant with the rules of the theater. Also suffering in comparison with French opera are the ballets, whose dancers seem to have lead in their shoes. In favor of the Italians, however, St.-Didier, in contrast to St.-Evremond, finds the Italian singing "languishing and touching," calling the Venetian castratos and women singers the finest in Italy. He praises the orchestra, which synchronizes with the voices with great precision, and admires the Italian arias (*chansonettes*).

St.-Didier's impressions are confirmed by another traveler, Maximilien Misson, writing eight years later.[113] He also writes unfavorably of external operatic trappings, including costumes, dances, machines, and stage illuminations. While admitting that the Venetians have some good performers and some beautifully composed arias, he is distracted by the excessive ornamentation ("they dwell many times longer on one Quavering, than in singing four whole lines") and the *recitative secco* ("they run so fast, that it is hard to tell whether they sing or speak, or whether they do either, or both together"). He speaks slightingly of the castratos who "suffer themselves to be maimed in order to have finer voices," and deplores the buffoonery and "bawdy" which is expressed in the most explicit terms: the gondoliers, he says, are admitted free to applaud and shout like madmen. The seven opera houses in Venice are frequented, Misson assumes, simply because men have nowhere else to entertain themselves, and the operas are so long that the end is expected only a quarter of the way through.

A more analytical, historically oriented treamtent of French opera in relation to Italian is given by Claude François (père) Ménestrier in *Des représentations en musique anciennes et modernes* (Paris, 1681).[114] Ménestrier addresses himself to the prevalent view of the French language as unsatisfactory for operatic treatment, and credits Perrin with the first preception that French texts could be used to express the most "beautiful" and "tender" sentiments. Faced with the problem of the unwieldy alexandrine invariably used in the theater, Perrin had understood the necessity of shorter, more naturally varied lines and had, therefore, fashioned the poetry of his pastorals in a manner admirably suited to musical setting. By combining some of the "manner" of Italian opera with the more natural, simpler beauty of the French language, Perrin had created something neither strictly Italian nor French, but "more agreeable than either."[115] In his own time Ménestrier knows of no Italian composer who can surpass Lully.

Although most comparative criticism of opera in this period favored the French style established by Lully, a couple of isolated attacks on his music appeared during the period of his greatest fame. The first was a letter written in 1677 to Pierre de Nyert from his friend Jean de la Fontaine, the poet and fablist.[116] La Fontaine addresses Nyert as the inventor of the art of singing, and reminisces fondly on the period of Rossi's *Orfeo*, recalling with nostalgia the beautiful singing of Atto Melani and Leonora Baroni. He sees Lully in 1677 as a composer who, having exhausted his talents, repeats the material of earlier works and retains his power only through the favor of the king.[117]

In 1688, the year after Lully's death, François de Callières wrote a literary parody, *La guerre des anciens et des modernes* (Paris, 1688), which depicts Lully's arrival in the underworld.[118] He is preceded, however, by an Italian musician who acquaints Orpheus with the differences between the music of Italy and France. The latter's operas contain good symphonies, excellent ballets, a few agreeable airs and dancing tunes with a lively rhythm, but on the whole the operas are long and tedious, and

the Italian musician cannot understand why the French pay good money
to hear the same thing fifty times over in the course of an evening. The
female singers are either inaudible or shrill, and the male singers cannot
compare with Italian castratos, but the complacent French deserve this
indifferent singing, for they pay Lully more to provide bad singers than
the Italians pay to hear the finest voices of Venice. The noise level is so
high for the size of the theater "that few people leave the theater after
three hours attendance without a headache, and frequent yawning."[119]
Yet this audience, desiring to be fashionable, does not dare to oppose
those of no taste by refusing to attend these performances. And Lully,
composing for profit rather than glory, does not take care to polish his
works, and thus mixes mediocre passages with "admirable scraps." Another cause of Lully's indifference is his absolute authority in the realm
of French opera, making the librettist subject to the musician,

> . . . whereas the musician ought to humor the poet's ideas, only employing his art
> to heighten the force of the expression, and adding new vigor by sounds appropriate
> to the particular subject of the poet's passions in such pieces as are proper to be
> sung.[120]

This assortment of essays, treatises, poems, satires, political pamphlets, travelers' journals, and musical pieces documenting the French
reaction to differences between their music and Italy's issues from the
most unusual variety of sources. What the commentators do have in common, however, is the attempt to understand and explain a phenomenon
only dimly perceived in seventeenth-century musical thought: style. The
international Franco-Flemish style had only begun to break into distinctive national styles in the course of the sixteenth century, and only in the
seventeenth century did these styles become a source of self-conscious
pride, especially in France and Italy, and to a somewhat lesser extent in
Germany.[121] Further significance lies in the fact that, inasmuch as these
early gropings towards comparative descriptions do constitute stylistic
analyses, they also constitute the early beginnings of modern musical
criticism. Significantly, at least four of the early writers (Perrin, St.-Evre-
mond, La Fontaine, and Callières) were important literary figures; since
opera was at first regarded more as a literary, dramatic genre than as a
musical one, it was natural that literary criteria for excellence and techniques of analysis should be transferred to opera and eventually to other
types of music.

II

The Quarrels Between
Ancients and Moderns

The quarrels between Ancients and Moderns in the sixteenth and seventeenth centuries came about as pride in modern progress and national identity began to conflict with a long-unchallenged belief in the superiority of the art, literature, and philosophy of the ancient world. On the whole the Ancients wished to preserve the artistic standards established in antiquity, and the Moderns wished to create new standards based on originality and creativity.[1] The change in thinking brought about by the challenge of the Moderns coincided with the decline of rigorous education in the classical languages and literatures, and with the growth of a larger middle class less trained in these humanist disciplines. The most dramatic evidences of this change may be found in seventeenth-century France, where the quarrel between Ancients and Moderns was officially opened in 1635, but already the ground for the quarrel had been laid and many of its issues defined in late sixteenth-century Italy. In both countries, complaints against the tyranny of the rules began within the sphere of literary criticism and spread to the related fields of music and the fine arts.

Italy in the Late Sixteenth Century: Ancients and Moderns in Literature

The controversy began with the literary quarrels of the late Italian Renaissance, the greatest of which took place over three works: Dante Alighieri's *Divina commedia* (1307–1321), Ludovico Ariosto's *Orlando furioso* (1502–1532), and Giovanni Battista Guarini's *Il pastor fido* (1590).[2] Though only the last of these was a strictly contemporary work at the time of the quarrels, all three were considered "modern" in that they deviated from the models set by Homer, Virgil, and the Greek tragedians. Invariably the quarrels involved a comparison of a modern and an ancient work, and invariably the standards to be accepted or refuted, interpreted or adjusted, were those of Aristotle's *Poetics*.[3]

The publication in 1548 of Francesco Robortello's commentary on Aristotle, *In librum Aristotelis de arte poetica explicationes*,[4] may be regarded as having divided the *cinquecento* into two halves, the first under the influence of neo-Platonic and medieval rhetorical traditions, the second under the almost absolute domination of the critical theories of Aristotle. When the literary debates gathered momentum in the 1560s, reverence for the *Poetics* had become so universal that most of the participants interpreted Aristotle's precepts to serve their own purposes. The Ancients, as "orthodox" Aristotelians, regarded any departure from the letter of Aristotelian law as anathema, while the Moderns, as "liberal" Aristotelians, viewed the *Poetics* as a collection of principles applying to new forms and styles of literature as well as old.[5]

Representative of the more conservative philosophy is the *Arte poetica* (Venice, 1563) of Sebastiano Minturno. Criticizing the defenders of the modern poet Ariosto, Minturno denies their authority in comparison with that of Aristotle and the other ancient theorists. If the art taught by Aristotle is true, Minturno insists, there can be no other truth:

> For truth is one; and that which is true once must be true always and in every age, nor does the difference in times change it. . . . Thus the change in times, appearing later, will not make it possible that we should treat in poetry more than one single matter, and of proper magnitude, with which all the rest fits and is joined with verisimilitude and reason.[6]

The Moderns grew more bold as the century reached its close. In *De gl'heroici furori* (Paris, 1585),[7] the philosopher Giordano Bruno declares pleasure to be the end of poetry and music its essence. Discarding all rules of plot, rhetoric, and genre, he praises the originality of genius and declares that invention, rather than imitation, should guide the poet. Similarly, Agostino Michele, in his *Discorso in cui si dimostra come si possono scrivere le commedie e le tragedie in prosa* (Venice, 1592), argues for modern usage against ancient dogma, and maintains that music, painting, and poetry should change as all other things change. Citing the successful development of these arts in the sixteenth century,[8] Michele delves into the *Poetics* anew to demonstrate that even Aristotle assumed the growth and evolution of genres.

Renaissance Quarrels over Ancient and Modern Music

The second half of the sixteenth century saw the merits of ancient and modern music debated in a series of quarrels which were at least as stormy as those over ancient and modern literature.[9] The participating music theorists, unlike their literary counterparts, tended to remain within the bounds of humanist thought in their desire that music should emulate the models of antiquity; however, because of the lack of such models, their quarrels were occasioned more by differences over methods of imitating ancient music than by differences over the desirability of such imitation. All Ancients, then, in their overall outlook, these writers fell into two general categories: the conservatives, who defended Franco-Flemish polyphony as the fulfillment of ancient ideals, and the progressives, who wished to restore a monophonic style which they saw as the true practice of the ancient Greeks.

The call for reform had originated not with musicians but with humanist scholars and churchmen who pointed to the wonderful effects of the music of antiquity and asked why the music of their own time could not move its listeners in the same manner. Finding their answer in the inability of sixteenth-century counterpoint to serve as a clear vehicle for the communication of a text, these writers decried the complexities of the Franco-Flemish style. Typical are the complaints of the Cardinal Jacopo Sadoleto in his *De pueris recte instituendis* (Venice, 1533), an influential work on education:

> What correctness or beauty can the music which is now in vogue possess? It has scarcely any real and stable foundation in word or thought. If it should have for its subject a maxim or proverb, it would obscure and hamper the sense and meaning by abruptly cutting and jerking the sounds in the throat—as though music were designed not to soothe and control the spirit, but merely to afford a base pleasure to the ears, mimicking the cries of birds and beasts, which we should be sorry to resemble.[10]

In the second half of the sixteenth century, proposals for a reinstatement of the actual compositional principles of ancient Greek music sparked the quarrels between reformers and defenders of the *status quo*. The earliest of these quarrels, between Nicola Vicentino (1511–c.1576) and the Portuguese theorist Vincenzo Lusitano, had as its central issue Vicentino's theory that the ancient Greek genera—diatonic, chromatic, and enharmonic—should be revived as a means of textual expressiveness in contemporary polyphony; Lusitano opposed Vicentino's theories, as well as his chromatic compositions, as a threat to what he considered the pure diatonicism of the ancients. A formal debate between the two musicians in 1551, won by Lusitano, was later described by Vicentino in his *L'antica musica ridotta alla moderna prattica* (Rome, 1555), as well as by Ghiselin Danckerts—one of the judges of the debate—in his *Sopra una differentia musicale*.[11]

Comparisons of ancient and modern music continued in the discussions of the Florentine Camerata gathered around Count Giovanni Bardi during the years from 1560 to 1591 or 1592.[12] Bardi, a wealthy patron of music and literature, desired to effect a musical renascence that would correspond to the humanist revival in literature and the other arts.[13] In 1572 he and another member of the Camerata, Vincenzo Galilei (1520–1591), began to correspond with the humanist philologist Girolamo Mei (1519–1594)[14] in Rome; Mei's letters, which attempted to disprove the use of polyphony among the ancient Greeks and to reconstruct the monophonic form of their music, provided a fresh stimulus for the study and imitation of the music of antiquity.

In order to understand the challenge brought by Mei and Galilei to the defenders of sixteenth-century polyphony, it is necessary to understand the aesthetic philosophies underlying the quarrel. Like the literary critics of the late Renaissance, the musical theorists who argued the merits of ancient and modern music based their arguments on varying interpretations of the aesthetic theories of Aristotle. At the heart of musical Aristotelianism was the passage in the *Poetics* that likens music to poetry as an imitative art.[15]

A conservative interpretation of this passage may be observed in Gioseffo Zarlino's *Istitutioni harmoniche* (Venice, 1558).[16] Zarlino sees music as the imitation of a subject chosen from nature, and he considers standard four-part counterpoint as symbolic of the four elements of nature. He admires in Franco-Flemish polyphony the imitation of the text by a fugal subject, and of the subject by the contrapuntal lines; and he praises music in this style—particularly that of Adrian Willaert—for its literal imitation of specific words as well as its more pervasive imitation of the general sense and mood of the text.[17]

While Zarlino uses this Aristotelian theory of imitation to justify the Franco-Flemish style as a realization of the ideals of the classical past, the more progressive theorists—led by Mei and Galilei—use the same theory to justify their call for reform. As a student of Piero Vettori, whose translation and commentary on the *Poetics* had appeared in 1560,[18] Mei had witnessed the turn to the more scholarly, scientific Aristotelian studies of the late sixteenth century, and his musical writings reflect the influence of this literary outlook. In his letters to Bardi and Galilei, Mei not only interprets the meaning of imitation as applied to music and the other arts, but also relates this interpretation to the Aristotelian concept of catharsis, the purging of emotions through the production of such emotions in the listener.[19] According to Mei's theory, only the ancient practice of monody can achieve a true imitation of the text, thereby producing the appropriate emotions in the audience.[20]

Galilei, who had begun his musical study as a pupil of Zarlino, was gradually persuaded through his correspondence with Mei to regard the work of his former teacher as sincere but superficial, and to desire a more thoroughgoing interpretation of the doctrine of imitation. The preface to his *Dialogo della musica antica e della moderna* (Florence, 1581), which commends Zarlino and the other conservatives for having sought to rescue music from medieval darkness, continues:

> That part which they understood and appreciated, they brought little by little to its present condition. But it does not seem to any who are intelligent, according to what can be learned from countless passages in the ancient histories and in the poets and philosophers, that they restored it to its ancient state, or that they attained to the true and perfect knowledge of it: this may have been due to the coarseness of the times, the difficulty of the subject, and the scarcity of good interpreters.[21]

Galilei goes on to praise Mei for having brought the understanding of ancient music to its perfection, and declares the purpose of his *Dialogo* to be an application of Mei's theories to the creation of an affective modern musical style. Emphasizing the analogy between music and rhetoric, Galilei, following Mei, advocates the return to pure melody as a means of recapturing the mysterious ancient affections.

The treatise proper contains a more severe denunciation of Zarlino, whom Galilei seems loath to forgive for having misrepresented Franco-Flemish polyphony as the fulfillment of ancient musical precepts. Galilei criticizes Zarlino and the contrapuntists for imitation of text only in the narrow sense of word-painting, and insists that the imitation of true human nature—that is, human emotions—can only be achieved through a more comprehensive expression of the text by means of the monodic style.[22]

At the turn of the century, a friend of Zarlino, Giovanni Maria Artusi, published a treatise which initiated perhaps the most famous of all controversies setting the music of the past against that of the present: *Artusi overo della imperfettione della moderna musica* (Venice, 1600), with its attack on the music of the well-known composer Claudio Monteverdi (1567–1643).[23] By 1600, monody and the new concerted style had replaced Franco-Flemish polyphony as "modern music" or the *stile nuovo*; this new style, exemplified in the works of the monodists, Monteverdi, and his contemporaries, was characterized by the free treatment of dissonance and a general disregard for the traditional rules applying to sixteenth-century counterpoint. Artusi, however, ignores the new premises upon which modern music is based and attempts to judge Monteverdi's works according to Zarlino's rules for counterpoint, which he sees as the embodiment of ancient precepts.

Monteverdi, undaunted by Artusi's criticism, seized the opportunity to issue a manifesto proclaiming a new practice (the *seconda pratica*) which would include the possibility of a variety of styles:

> Being in the service of this Serene Highness of Mantua, I am not master of the time I would require: nevertheless I wrote a reply to let it be known that I do not do things carelessly, and as soon as it is rewritten it will appear with the title *Seconda pratica overo perfettione della moderna musica*, at which some will wonder, not believing that there is any other practice than that taught by Zarlino. But let them be assured that, concerning consonances and dissonances, there is a different way of considering them from that already determined which defends the modern manner of composition with the assent of reason and sense.[24]

This new practice, according to a gloss on the letter by the composer's brother, seeks to fulfill rather than to destroy the ancient ideals, for its primary aim of seeking textual expressiveness is one advocated by the ancients.[25]

Monteverdi's position was to receive an endorsement and further elaboration toward the middle of the century by Marco Scacchi, an Italian theorist living in Warsaw. In his *Breve discorso sopra la musica moderna* (Warsaw, 1649), all music is classified as *musica antica* or *musica moderna*, the first always employing the same style, the second employing two practices and three styles. In the first practice, harmony is mistress of the text, in the second, text is mistress of the harmony; and the three styles are those of the church, chamber, and theater.[26]

The quarrels over ancient and modern music in Italy held great significance for the future of musical thought. Their outcome, like that of the literary quarrels, was a recognition of stylistic multiplicity: in literature, the styles and genres introduced by modern poets were granted validity alongside the accepted forms of the ancients, and in music the theoretical base was broadened to include the coexistence of *musica antica* and *musica moderna*.[27]

The new tendency to treat music and literature under a common critical rubric had its origins in Florentine intellectual circles. Besides the Camerata, the most important of these was the *Accademia degli Alterati*, in whose discussions of literature and philosophy we find important subsidiary treatments of music.[28] Of the literary figures included among its members, a number were also musical amateurs: Count Bardi, patron of the Camerata; Ottavio Rinuccini, librettist of the operas *Euridice*, *Dafne*, and *Arianna*, and his brother, Alessandro, distinguished poet and orator; Lorenzo Giacomini, literary theorist and translator of certain Aristotelian passages on music; and Agostino del Nero, an amateur singer whose correspondence with Mei on ancient music was later studied by the theorist Giovanni Battista Doni.[29]

All of the timely aesthetic questions were debated within this group. Discussions of Aristotle's *Poetics* occupied a six-month period in 1573, and the agenda of 1574 included the topic of poetry as imitation. In 1586 Lorenzo Giacomini gave a discourse on Aristotelian catharsis which, influenced by the work of Mei, relates Aristotle's dramatic theories to musical aesthetics.[30] Another member, Giulio del Bene, made a speech proposing the transfer of music from the old quadrivium, where it had stood alongside arithmetic, geometry and astronomy, to the trivium, where it takes a place with the linguistic arts of grammar, rhetoric, poetics, and dialectic.[31]

The quarrels over ancient and modern literature had entered the *Accademia degli Alterati* in 1573, when its members had debated the worth of Dante's *Divina commedia*,[32] and in 1583 the Alterati enlisted as vigorous supporters of their compatriot Ariosto during the quarrel surrounding his *Orlando furioso*. Count Bardi served as spokesman for the literary Moderns on Feburary 24, 1583, and his defense, based on the lyricism of Ariosto's poetry, abandons the traditional criteria for excellence in poetry. Maintaining that "those verses will be the best which will have the best rhythm and the best sound, and consequently will be the most musical, hence the most singable," he points to professional settings of Ariosto's *Orlando* such as those by Gian Domenico da Nola, as well as to the simpler settings sung spontaneously in the courts and in the streets, as proof of the poem's intrinsic musicality.[33]

Bardi, a member of both the *Accademia degli Alterati* and the Camerata, was an important figure in the new relationship between music and literature. The convergence of the two may be seen in the statements above in defense of Ariosto, as well as in his *Discorso sopra la musica antica, e'l cantar bene* (c.1580),[34] which had been the first of the musical documents to issue from the Camerata. Influenced by Mei's correspondence, the treatise denounces Franco-Flemish polyphony, emphasizing textual supremacy and the affective quality of the modes. Bardi's forward-looking musical theory is supported by a modernist position in the Dante quarrel, then at its height; the *Discorso* contains no less than five references to the "divine poet Dante," and ends with a quotation of Dante's indictment of the ignorant—presumably an allusion to those who disagree with Bardi's own views.

The polemical spirit seems not to have reached France in the sixteenth century, although ancient and modern music were discussed there among humanist circles. The most important of these circles was the group of poets known as the *Pléiade* who, like the members of the Camerata, wished to bring about a renascence of the ancient concept of musico-poetics. The greatest poet of the *Pléiade*, Pierre de Ronsard

(1524–1585), believing ardently in a close union of poetry and music, developed poetic procedures which he felt would render poetry apt for musical setting.[35]

Ronsard's original position on the issue of ancient and modern music might be compared with Zarlino's, for though he defers to the "divinity" of ancient music, he does not set it above the polyphonic style of his own time. In the dedication to his *Livre des mélanges* published by Le Roy and Ballard in 1560, he justifies contemporary polyphonic music by maintaining that inspiration may occur at any moment in history:

> Moreover, the divine inspirations of music, poetry, and painting do not arrive at perfection by degrees, like the other sciences, but by starts, and like flashes of lightning here and there, appear in various lands, then suddenly vanish. And for this reason, sire, when some excellent worker in this art appears, you should guard him carefully, as something so excellent that it rarely appears. Among those who have arisen within six or seven generations are Josquin Desprez, a native of Hainaut, and his disciples Mouton, Willaert, Richafort, Jannequin, Maillard, Claudin, Moulu, Certon, and Arcadelt, who in the perfection of this art cedes nothing to the ancients, from being inspired by his Apollo Charles, Cardinal of Lorraine.[36]

In a revision of this dedication for the edition of 1572, Ronsard has been persuaded by the music of Lassus that Franco-Flemish polyphony may not only equal the music of the ancient Greeks, but may even surpass it:

> And now the more than divine Orlando, who like a bee has sipped all the most beautiful flowers of the ancients and moreover seems alone to have stolen the harmony of the spheres to delight us on earth, surpassing the ancients, and making himself the sole marvel of our time.[37]

If Ronsard can be compared with the conservative musical theorists of Italy in his approval of contemporary polyphony, another member of the *Pléiade*, Antoine de Baïf (1532–1589), may be compared with such writers as Mei and Galilei in his advocacy of a more radical return to the music of antiquity.[38] Baïf created the *vers mesurés à l'antiquité*, which followed the quantitative patterns of classical poetry, and he helped to found the *Académie de poésie et musique* (1570), an institution whose goal was a union of the two arts.[39]

Just as Mei largely determined the direction that Florentine musical thought would take, a French humanist, Pontus de Tyard (1521–1605), strongly influenced Baïf and the *musique mesurée* that grew out of this French Academy. Tyard and Baïf shared the *Pléiade*'s belief in the unity of word and tone, but they went beyond their colleagues, joining the Florentines in viewing this union only as a means toward the arousal and control of the passions, not as an end in itself. Tyard, inspired by neo-Platonic rather than Aristotelian thought, even went so far as to declare the union of poetry and music a mystical symbol for an initiation of the soul into the first stages of its unification with God.[40]

Thus in France, as in Italy, ideas concerning ancient and modern music were developed not so much by professional musicians as by laymen who wished to see poetry reunited with its sister muse. The humanists' desire to unite poetry and music helped to bring music into the realm of the linguistic arts of the old trivium rather than the numerical disciplines of the quadrivium, thus opening the way for the seventeenth-century inclusion of the musical subjects within literary discussions, and the eventual transfer of literary critical techniques to music.

Ancients and Moderns in Seventeenth-Century France

Efforts by seventeenth-century Frenchmen to assess their culture through a comparison with that of ancient Greece and Rome had roots in Renaissance humanism. But as the French began to evaluate the splendors to which their country had attained during the magnificent reign of Francis I (1515–1547), they also began to grow suspicious of their previous awe before the long-lost glories of two essentially foreign cultures. Self-confidence grew as poets, artists, and scientists of the *grand siècle* continually seemed to surpass the achievements of their predecessors; the idea of progress[41] gradually began to supplant the idea of decadence, and the Moderns began vigorously to assert not only their equality, but even their superiority, to the men of ancient Greece and Rome.

Although the seventeenth-century phase of the quarrel between Ancients and Moderns is generally associated with French polemicists, it should be noted that the Italian *moderni* and *antiquari* also continued their quarrels during the course of the century. In fact, the immediate stimulus for the beginning of the quarrel in France was probably the work of an Italian poet, historian, philosopher, and diplomat, Alessandro Tassoni, whose *Pensieri diversi* (Modena, 1612)[42] gave a new turn to the quarrel. Though a few iconoclasts had dared to suggest that modern literature could rival ancient, none had approached the scathing denunciation of the ancients that Tassoni put forth in the twenty-seven chapters which he devoted to that subject. These chapters are distributed according to three categories: the speculative sciences, the active sciences, and the arts. Central to each is Tassoni's theory that the sciences and arts all show a gradual—though not uninterrupted—progress toward perfection. The early seventeenth century sees, according to this theory, the culmination of a steady development begun in ancient Greece, interrupted in the Middle Ages but continued in the fifteenth and sixteenth centuries.

France took up Tassoni's quarrel when Jean Baudouin, one of the founding members of the *Académie française*, translated Tassoni's work into French.[43] Shortly thereafter, on February 20, 1635, another Academician named Boisrobert delivered a diatribe against the ancients to the Academy, that bastion of classical tradition; this gauntlet flung before the defenders of antiquity is generally considered the formal opening of the quarrel in France.[44]

Two years later, in 1637, appeared a decisive work, not only for the quarrel of Ancients and Moderns, but also for the general direction of French seventeenth-century thought: René Descartes' *Discours de la méthode*.[45] Descartes prided himself on having forgotten what he had read, and he taught the seventeenth century to distrust antiquity as the humanists had taught the sixteenth century to admire it. What he presented in the *Discours* was not a body of knowledge, but a way of investigating which stressed the investigator's rational faculties at the expense of his dependence upon authority:

> The first [rule] was to accept nothing as true which I did not know clearly to be so: that is, carefully to avoid precipitation and prejudice; and to understand in my judgments nothing more than what was presented so clearly and so distinctly that I could have no occasion to doubt it.[46]

The radicalism of this statement can be understood only in the context of the strength of the classical tradition in early seventeenth-century France. Education was almost exclusively centered on the study of the classics, and all new works were judged strictly on the basis of ancient standards. The University, so influential on each new generation of writers and thinkers, instilled in its students a kind of rigidified and unimaginative humanism, so that modern thinking in effect amounted to a reaction against one's education.[47]

By the second half of the century, however, the tastes of Louis XIV and his court had created a milieu in which a renewed classical outlook could flourish. As a parallel to the social and political order reestablished by Louis after the wars of the Fronde, a unified aesthetic code was sought to illuminate the special brand of French classicism developed by the poets, dramatists, and artists of late seventeenth-century France.[48] Such a code was found in the Aristotelian doctrines of the Italian Renaissance, and was applied to French literature in a series of critical works culminating in the *Art poétique* (Paris, 1674) of Nicolas Boileau-Despréaux, the leader of the Ancients in these years. The *Art poétique* advocated clarity, moderation, reason, and imitation of nature; its influence was powerful, extending as far as Alexander Pope's *Essay on Criticism* (London, 1711).[49]

Boileau and the Ancients found their most formidable opponents on the Modern side in two brothers named Perrault: Claude—physician, architect, scientist, and musical theorist; and Charles—minister of building to the king, poet, and creator of the famous volume of fairy tales *Ma mère l'oye*.[50] Claude Perrault was the first to receive the sardonic excoriation of Boileau's pen. Apparently, he had once been unsuccessful in treating an illness of the famous critic, and Boileau, in the *Art poétique*, speaks at length of a physician, "celebrated assassin," who finally leaves to Galen this "suspect science" in order to become an architect.[51]

Charles Perrault, later to become the most celebrated leader of the Moderns, entered the controversy between Ancients and Moderns only with a certain timidity. His *Critique de l'opéra ou Examen de la tragédie intitulée Alceste ou le Triomphe d'Alcide* (Paris, 1674) was published anonymously in the same year as Boileau's *Art poétique*, and was directed toward a faction of Ancients who had accused Lully's librettist Pierre Quinault of having transformed Euripides' *Alceste* into a grotesque modern travesty. Members of this cabal, led by Boileau and the playwright Jean Racine, tried to persuade Lully to choose another librettist, but Perrault came to his old friend Quinault's defense.[52] In supporting the fashionable modern drama which Quinault represented, Perrault's *Critique* declared, with some reservations, the superiority of the Moderns:

> I readily admit that the ancient authors have more genius than those of our day for the description of the things of nature, the sentiments of the heart and whatever concerns expression. But, in works of the mind, there are other things to be observed, such as propriety, order, economy, distribution and arrangement of all the parts, all of which demand an infinite number of precepts which cannot be discovered except by a long succession of experiences, of reflections and commentaries; it is possible that the most recent centuries have the advantage in these kinds of things because they have profited by the work and study of those who preceded them. . . .[53]

Several years passed after the *Critique* during which little was heard from either side. Charles Perrault, apparently occupied with politics, published no more for the Modern cause for thirteen years. But on January 27, 1687 he reopened the quarrel when he delievered to the Academy a short poem which quickly became a *succès de scandale*. Entitled *Le siècle de Louis XIV*,[54] the poem opened with the following lines:

> Beautiful antiquity was always worthy of veneration
> But I have never thought it worthy of adoration.
> I see the ancients without bending my knee,
> They were great, it is true, but only men like us;

And one can compare, without being unjust,
The century of Louis XIV with that of Augustus.[55]

Perrault went on to discredit the ancient authorities in science and history, Aristotle and Herodotus, and included detailed descriptions of modern inventions to demonstrate the scientific superiority of the modern age.

The years from 1687 to the end of the century saw the height of the quarrel. The Moderns by this time had gained a definite initiative; they had become powerful in the Academy and popular with the *monde galant*, especially its women, who were less rigorously trained in the classical tradition. Torrents of literature issued from both sides, and the debate was enlivened by the active participation of the highly influential journals of the day. On the whole, these shapers of society (especially the *Mercure galant*) tended to favor the cause of the Moderns, though some attempted to remain neutral (for example, the *Journal des savants*).[56]

It was again Charles Perrault who produced, shortly after his appearance at the Academy, the classic statement of the Moderns' position in the first book of his *Parallèle des anciens et des modernes* (Paris, 1688).[57] This work, an extensive comparison of ancient and modern accomplishments, favored the moderns in almost every field. In the sciences, Perrault obtained information from the astronomer Constantin Huyghens to reveal the accomplishments of modern times; as for literature, he amplified his previous statements that nature is equally generous to all men, and that men of his day have the opportunity to build on and surpass ancient knowledge.

Perrault's book won the approval of the public through the clarity and attractiveness of its language and format. A series of dialogues portrays three well-characterized figures: a profound and articulate *abbé* (spokesman for Perrault's own ideas), an unimaginative *président* (a conservative booby who is immediately converted on every point by the *abbé*'s intelligence), and a rash young *chevalier*, who has the correct basic (modern) opinions, but who has not thought them through sufficiently. In the four dialogues published between 1688 and 1697, these characters compare in detail ancient and modern examples in such fields as architecture, sculpture, painting, rhetoric, poetry, astronomy, geography, navigation, war, philosophy, music, medicine, gardening, and even cooking.[58]

Perrault sent a copy of the third dialogue (on poetry) to Boileau, who responded with his *Réflexions sur Longin* (Paris, 1694). In this study of the *Treatise on the Sublime* by the ancient rhetorician Longinus, Boileau emphasizes the constant admiration of generations through the centuries as the strongest argument in favor of the ancients; in refuting the *Parallaèle*, he details with disdain Perrault's ignorance of classical literature.

But six years later, in a letter written in 1700,[59] Boileau ended his quarrel with the century when he conceded to Perrault that seventeenth-century France could indeed compare favorably with ancient Greece, at least in the genres of tragedy and romance and in the areas of philosophy, architecture, and modern sciences; he climaxed this dramatic reversal with the admission that the age of Louis XIV may be considered not only comparable but even superior to the most famous ages of antiquity.

The Musical Quarrels of Ancients and Moderns in the Seventeenth Century

The French controversy over ancient and modern music seems to have grown directly from the larger Italian and French literary quarrels as well as from the quarrels of the Italian music theorists. The Italian literary Moderns, seeing the superiority of modern music as a corollary to the superiority of modern literature, brought the peripheral musical quarrels into the mainstream of critical thought; this development, foreshadowed in the work of Agostino Michele,[60] was brought to fruition in the Italian work that sparked the quarrel between Ancients and Moderns in France, Tassoni's *Pensieri diversi*.[61] Tassoni, perhaps reasoning that the self-evidence of the superiority of modern music would bolster his tirade against all things ancient, concluded his work with a chapter on "Musichi antichi e moderni,"[62] which enlarged upon his general thesis that all the arts have progressed from the rudeness of ancient times towards an apogee of perfection in the seventeenth century.

After a preliminary survey of ancient music in which Tassoni displays his knowledge of early sources, mainly the works of Plutarch and Plato, he presents three major premises to support his argument for the superiority of modern music: modern stringed instruments have more strings, thereby producing a more harmonious sound; modern music is more elaborate (*artificioso*) than ancient; and modern music has the advantage of a developed system of notation, because of the invention of the staff by Guido d'Arezzo. After citing a list of the miraculous effects that ancient music was known to have had, Tassoni counterattacks with rival accounts of modern musicians, for instance, the ability of the harpsichordist Cosimo Bartoli to soothe distracted minds at the court of Pope Clement VII. Tassoni goes on to name some of the geniuses of composition in his day, including Ferdinando Cieco, a blind musician and theorist who was able to compose in his mind elaborate four-part counterpoint, and Carlo Gesualdo, the Italian madrigalist who brought to music new miracles of invention.[63]

An opposing defense for the music of the ancients may be seen in the Italian humanist Giovanni Battista Doni's *De praestantia musicae veteris* (Florence, 1647).[64] Doni refutes the views of Tassoni in his first dialogue, where Charidorus, defender of ancient music, claims that although the "ingenious" Alessandro Tassoni has censured the ancients in his treatise, still all the splendors of counterpoint in modern times could not rival ancient music in the results they produced in their listeners.

Doni may be considered a member of the small but important "anti-monody" minority of those reformers wishing to restore the music of the ancients.[65] The character Charidorus propounds Doni's own position that ancient music, polyphonic like modern music, may be considered superior by virtue of the effects it wrought; his opponent Philoponus brings forth proofs that ancient music was monodic and therefore inferior. Philoponus' argument is in fact based on the writings of such authors as Mei and Galilei, who believed ancient music to have been monodic.[66] He demonstrates as evidence for monophony among the ancient Greeks the avoidance of thirds and sixths, which were dissonant in Pythagorean tuning; the popularity of the chromatic and enharmonic *genera*; and the absence in Greek sources of any mention of those "most artificial" types of composition, including fugues and canons. Charidorus replies that thirds and sixths may have been dissonant in theory, consonant in practice; the *genera* were never completely "pure"; and the presence of polyphonic instruments such as organs attests to polyphony of some sort even it it were not described in treatises.

Doni's treatise not only brings together the literary and musical quarrels of Ancients and Moderns in Italy, but also represents a link with France, for it was dedicated to Mazarin, the Italian cardinal who ruled France during the minority of Louis XIV. Doni had visited France in 1621, and had returned to Rome to serve the Cardinal Antonio Barberini;[67] Mazarin, also in the employ of the Barberini family in this period, may well have known Doni in Rome. The preface to *De praestantia musicae veteris* credits Mazarin with bringing the Italian heritage of the glory of ancient Greece and Rome to France. Referring almost certainly to Luigi Rossi's *Orfeo*, performed in Paris in the same year as Doni's treatise, Doni mentions the Roman and Florentine musicians who had gone to France to introduce that country to musical drama.

Doni's ideas were also disseminated in France by means of his voluminous correspondence with the French theorist Marin Mersenne which, extending through the second quarter of the seventeenth century, provides a rich source of information on musical thought in France and Italy during this period. Through Doni, Mersenne learned of the work of Mei and

Galilei,[68] and Doni relates his own views on ancient music in passages such as the following:

> You ask my opinion of the ancient music of the Greeks, which, from what I can tell, seems to have been excellent in every way. . . . Not that I believe everything that is said about its potency and the admirable effects that were accomplished through its power. In this I make the distinction between the effects recounted of the music of Timotheus[69] and his age, which I take for true, and the music of the more remote past, which I do not believe to have cured the plague, etc., as it has been said. Also, I believe that the ancients were more disposed to be moved by music, for several reasons that can be argued, although I believe that almost as much could be accomplished today, if the faults of modern music were corrected and the ancient manner revived.[70]

Mersenne's *Quaestiones celeberrimae in Genesim* (Paris, 1623), which provides summaries of the various views on ancient music, and includes Mersenne's own enthusiastic description of the characteristics of Greek music, may have been influenced by the theories of Doni. The treatise also includes information on ancient organs obtained from the organist Jean Titelouze, who had included a more iconoclastic opinion of ancient music in a letter to Mersenne in 1622:

> . . . since that time [antiquity] music has changed so much with taste, that I believe if we heard the best music of their time, it would seem unbearable to our ears. For example, have I myself not seen music change so much in thirty years that certian counterpoint which is common and even seems good was earlier criticized even by those who make use of it today?[71]

Outside the circle of Mersenne and his correspondents, little was written on the subject of ancient and modern music in the early years of the seventeenth century in France. An isolated attack on modern music was made by the theorist Antoine Parran[72] in his *Traité de la musique* (Paris, 1639); this work, a conventional counterpoint treatise, included a section "on the effects of music." Chapter Four of this section, on "the admirable effects of the modes," opens with the following words·

> I will take this opportunity to complain justly and reasonably, for anyone who wishes to listen, of the lack of effects of the music of our time; or to put it more clearly, the bad effects that it most often produces and the lack of good ones. We know that in ancient times music produced the most marvelous effects, as for example, we read about Clytemnestra, who being left alone by Agamemnon who sent to the siege of Troy, was kept chaste and immaculate by the Dorian song of a musician, who was left with her to guard her against the lascivious advances of Egisto: but having lost her sweet and faithful guard, she lost immediately the gem of her chastity.[73]

It was not until 1680 that a major work on the subject of ancient and modern music was published. In that year, just before the resumption of the literary hostilities, Claude Perrault (Boileau's "celebrated assassin" who had now turned to architecture and physics) included in his *Essais de physique* (Paris, 1680) a treatise on acoustics entitled *De bruit*, in which he discusses the physical properties of sound. As an appendix to this treatise, he includes a chapter called "De la musique des anciens." Of the French critiques of ancient music in the seventeenth century, this is the most learned, its erudition being lightened by a *galant* dialogue which serves as introduction.[74]

The narrator of this dialogue, arriving early to obtain a seat at the opera *Les amours d'Apollon et de Climène*,[75] overhears a discussion of the merits of ancient and modern music by two partisans named Paleologue ("love of ancient things") and Philalethe ("love of truth"). Paleologue, a gray, wasted man, moves the audience gathered around by his rhetorical talents, while Philalethe, though less entertaining, persuades more by logical reasoning than by affected discourse.

Paleologue proclaims the superiority of Italian opera to French, but Philalethe contradicts him, saying that he has read about a purely French opera performed in France almost a hundred years earlier, before the invention of Italian opera.[76] Paleologue is sure that it must have been a sorry spectacle, for "the same difference between the divine and inimitable things of Antiquity seen in earlier times, and all that our century is capable of producing, exists in all the arts and sciences between the Italians and the French."[77]

Philalethe takes issue with the argument of Paleologue that more importance lies in the invention or creation of a thing, maintaining that sometimes its perfection is of more value. Distinguishing good taste (*bon goût*) from good sense (*bon sens*), he goes on to insist that taste develops through the centuries, just as a child's taste gradually changes from milk to wine; works by Homer were highly esteemed simply because of the primitiveness of taste in his time, and because of the lack of anything superior with which they could be compared. He then gives two reasons why the Ancients esteem old works so highly: not to be obliged to praise the works of their competitors, and to appear more intelligent than other critics, who are unable to appreciate the virtues of ancient art.

Just before the opera begins, Philalethe mentions a friend who, prompted by an earlier work vaunting the infinite superiority of the music of antiquity, has completed a treatise proving that polyphony did not exist in the music of ancient times. Paleologue responds that no one, regardless of how ignorant he considers the ancients, could go so far as to accuse them of ignorance of counterpoint.

After the opera, whose ravishing music, scenery, and libretto have deeply moved all present, the author of the treatise on ancient music, Aletophane, happens to appear. He has just come from an after-dinner gathering at which he has converted three passionate Ancients to his side, and Philalethe beseeches him to make Paleologue a fourth. Aletophane, however, maintains that his treatise is not so much a polemic as simply a proof that ancient music did not reach the perfection of modern music because the ancients did not use counterpoint; he will let that argument stand for itself.

The treatise proper is largely based on an examination of the ancient works of Aristoxenus, Euclid, Plutarch, Ptolomy, Alypius, and Gaudentius, as well as the later, medieval works of Cassiodorus, Martianus Cappella, and Boethius. The case for the monophony of Greek music is supported by four main arguments: 1) that no rules exist for polyphony in the ancient sources; 2) that the most beautiful intervals—thirds and sixths—were proscribed; 3) that a close examination of the term *symphonia* shows it to be only the practice of different voices singing one melody in different octaves; and 4) that the accounts of the marvelous effects of ancient music do not necessarily attest to the excellence of that music, just as men who have never seen Negro women from the kingdom of Ardres are bound to imagine something more exotic than real.

Perrault repeats Tassoni's argument that modern instruments have more strings than ancient, thereby creating a more harmonious sound and making counterpoint possible within a wider range. Another proof for the superiority of modern music is the fact that the ancients discouraged too great a sweetness in their music, fearing that it would soften their people.[78] The most general and pervasive argument is that the music of the ancients was of necessity primitive, "a noise befitting the infancy of the world." Perrault quotes Biblical passages illustrating the tumult and confusion of voices and instruments in the time of Moses, and concludes:

> . . . there is more reason to attribute an invention to enlightened men, in a polite, knowledgeable century rich in marvels, than to a barbarous and rude century, such as that in which some believe that this invention [polyphony] was born.[79]

There are several indications that Perrault's treatise was written as a rebuttal to the defense of ancient music in Doni's *De praestantia musicae veteris*. Allusion had been made to such a work in Perrault's preface, where the character Philalethe introduces the treatise of "Aletophane" in the following manner:

> He says to me that having some knowledge of music and desiring to know how that of the ancients could be compared to ours, he stumbled across a work whose author

maintained that the music of the ancients was infinitely more beautiful and perfect than ours and that if anyone thought otherwise it was only through ignorance of the end of this music.[80]

As if to refute Doni's treatise, Perrault's work treats almost all the same issues from an opposite point of view. Both treatises are based preponderantly on philological studies of ancient sources, with such terms as *symphonia* explicated to serve respective "monodic" and "anti-monodic" purposes. Philalethe ("Lover of truth"), the protagonist of Perrault's treatise, comes to the aid of the Modern underdog in Doni's treatise (Philoponus, "Lover of labor"), strengthening almost every point of his argument for the monophony—and thus inferiority—of ancient music. Finally, Palelogue's statement that any French opera must have been a sorry spectacle, since the same difference exists between ancient and modern music as exists between Italian and French, echoes Doni's dedication to Mazarin, which says that Italy, in introducing opera to France, has brought to France the superior heritage that Italy had inherited from the ancients.[81]

The year 1687 marked two important events in the war between Ancients and Moderns. The appearance of Charles Perrault before the Academy in that year sparked a renewal of hostilities between the two camps, and the death of Jean-Baptiste Lully in the same year brought his works to the attention of the critics as representative of the modern French style. These events led to the publication, in 1688, of four important documents, two from the side of the Moderns and two from that of the Ancients.

Both the works by Ancients are satires, one on the quarrel between Ancients and Moderns itself and the other on the personal foibles of Lully. The first, François de Callières' *Histoire poétique de la guerre nouvellement déclarée entre des anciens et des modernes* (Amsterdam, 1688), was not only an immediate success throughout France, but was also translated into English and gave Jonathan Swift the idea for his *Battle of the Books*, a similar satire on the English phase of the quarrel between Ancients and Moderns.[82]

The events in Callières' book take place just after Perrault's reading of *Le siècle de Louis le grand*, as Ancients and Moderns prepare for war on Parnassus just as they do in the Academy. The Ancient forces are led by Homer and Virgil, their Modern opponents by the French playwright Corneille and the Italian poet Tasso.[83] After a mighty and heroic battle, Apollo mediates a diplomatic peace: Homer will be called the Prince of Poets, and Corneille and Racine will be known as the French Sophocles and Euripides. Perrault's poem will retain for eternity the name "poem of discord," but its poet will receive the praises of Parnassus for its style, which pleases Apollo.

The section on music takes place in the underworld, where the imminent arrival of Lully, the recently deceased modern composer, throws his ancient counterparts—Orpheus, Amphion, and Arion—into a "strange fright." Orpheus fears being overshadowed by Lully, for though he himself caused beasts to follow him, Lully is followed and admired even by polite men. But an Italian musician who has also recently arrived from the other world is able to inform Orpheus:

> Do you think . . . that the greatest part of those men who follow Lully so eagerly know any more about music than the beasts that followed you? And don't you believe they are greater beasts than yours to continually carry their money to his opera only to hear the same thing fifty times over?[84]

This Italian musician goes on to inform Orpheus of several aspects of French opera which would remain critical fodder for partisans of Italian opera throughout the next century.[85]

When Lully finally arrives, he demands an audience with Orpheus. This he used to ridicule Orpheus and the time-honored legends of ancient music. Praising his ancient rival for having moved the infernal shades in order to retrieve his wife, Lully proceeds:

> But after having seriously considered what you had done, and of the dangerous consequences of such an enterprise, you fortunately looked back, contrary to Pluto's commands, thus depriving her of reaching the light. One could not more easily acquire the reputation of good husband and great musician, without being troubled with the inconvenience of a wife . . .[86]

Lully proposes to Orpheus that, instead of making war, they should form a partnership and produce an opera which will profit both, using Parnassus for a theater, Pegasus for a flying machine, and the Muses for performers. In considering the orchestra to be used, Lully inquires about a certain ancient flutist, known to have inspired the chastity of Clytemnestra when she had found herself under the duress of a seducer's wiles. Lully makes a wry twist on this famous example of the miraculous effects inspired by ancient musicians:

> For my part . . . I must confess my works have had an opposite effect, and that I have labored successfully to corrupt my century; however, they deserve no less applause, since we both attained our desired ends.[87]

Orpheus, amazed at Lully's proposal, answers that the ancients work for glory and not money, whereupon Lully, calling them a parcel of fools, turns a somersault and exits.

Antoine Bauderon de Senécé's *Lettre de Clement Marot à Monsieur de S****, the other satire of 1688, is aimed more at the personal roguery of Lully than at the modernism of his style, but the work as a whole reinforces the position of Callières in its denunciation of Lully's music as well as of his personal habits. In the preface, the author declares his alignment with the Ancients, and proceeds to create the account of a mysterious letter from the deceased poet Clement Marot, describing Lully's triumphant entry into the underworld. In this account Orpheus and the other ancient musicians follow Lully's procession with respect and admiration, for they see their own glory magnified in the lesser achievements of modern composers; other modern composers, however, resenting Lully's success, absent themselves.

Lully is informed that he must appear before the queen of the underworld to undergo judgment which will lead either to immortality or to exclusion from the Elysian Fields. A speech is made in Lully's defense by the creator of the *Ballet comique de la reine* of 1581, Balthasar de Beaujoyeux, whose career as an Italian musician in France had paralleled Lully's; both of humble birth, they "similarly chose to elongate their names to match the aggrandizement of their fortunes, one to *le seigneur* Balthazar de Beaujoyeux, the other to *le sieur* Jean-Baptiste de Lulli."[88]

Speaking against Lully are a variety of ancient and modern poets and musicians. The ancient poet Anacreon complains that Lully should not be honored since the real creator of opera is its poet, not its musician. Pierre Perrin[89] testifies that, having studied the faults of the Italians for twenty years, he himself would have brought good taste to France if it had not been for Lully. The playwright Molière protests that, after collaborating with him to produce the *comédies-ballets*, Lully claimed all the credit for himself. Orlando Lasso testifies that Lully was a distinguished composer—if one is distinguished by breaking all the rules; and the later Italian composers Luigi (Rossi) and Giacomo Carissimi accuse Lully of plagiarism, Rossi requesting that the compositions stolen from him be saved when the rest of Lully's works are condemned.

Finally, Lully is brought before the last judge, *Bon Goût* (Good Taste). An excerpt from Lully's opera *Athys* is played and found only mediocre by this mighty judge; a second excerpt, the *sommeil* scene from *Armide*, puts him straight to sleep. But this reaction is interpreted by his helpmate *Raison* (Reason) as approval of the work; interpreting the aesthetic of the affections to suit Lully's purposes, she declares that a work that is intended to express sleep can do no better than to cause sleep in its listeners. "Thus we see for the first time," concludes Sénecé, "an equitable judgment rendered by a sleeping judge."[90]

On the Modern side, the year 1688 saw the publication of Bernard le Bovier de Fontenelle's *Digression sur les anciens et modernes*, a popular work which dealt a crucial blow to the Ancients. In the portion of this treatise devoted to music, Fontenelle praises modern music as a tribute to the progress of the arts. Citing opera as a new genre which has produced a new genius, Lully, he also mentions the *chanson* as an older genre which, instead of perishing in modern times, has blossomed: "and I maintain that if Anacreon had seen them [chansons], he would have sung them more than most of his own."[91]

The final important publication of the year 1688 was Charles Perrault's *Parallèle*, the most comprehensive statement of the Moderns' cause.[92] His discussion of music, however, only appeared in the fourth of the series of dialogues, published in 1697. The construction of this dialogue bears some resemblance to the preface of Claude Perrault's treatise on ancient music: the intelligent *abbé* (Perrault) is not unlike the character of Philalethe, while the stupid *président* shares the naiveté of Paleologue in not imagining the ancients so backward as to have been ignorant of polyphony. Like his brother, Charles Perrault bases his argument for the superiority of modern music on the fact that ancient music was monophonic, and he cites his brother's treatise as proof of this:

> If you doubt it, you need only to read the treatise that Mr. Perrault of the Academy of Sciences has written on the subject, and you will be fully persuaded. This treatise is at the end of the first volume of his *Essais de physique*, and is entitled *De la musique des anciens*.[93]

Charles Perrault offers only one additional proof that the ancients may not have known polyphony: the fact that most nations even in the seventeenth century know only monophonic music. Being a man of the world, he is able to quote friends who have witnessed the use of monophonic music in such countries as Turkey and the Orient. As for the marvelous accounts told by the Greek poets, they are nothing but "figurative expressions which poetry uses to show that there are no men so wild or stupid that they are not moved and tamed by the charms of music."[94]

The quarrel between Ancients and Moderns had several important results. One was a more historical orientation to the study of music,[95] for in order to contrast the music of the present with that of the past, it was necessary not only to return to primary sources in order to obtain accurate historical information, but also to organize this material into chronological categories representing historical periodization. Moreover, just as the quarrels over French and Italian music had produced an awareness of national style, the quarrels between Ancients and Moderns produced an awareness of historical style, and as the way gradually cleared for the tolerance of both ancient and modern music, so did the necessity grow of recognizing a stylistic multiplicity that could comprehend both. This recognition also extended to the difference between what we know as Renaissance and Baroque music, for the conservative critics of *musica moderna* had considered this modern Baroque style as a contrast not only to the Franco-Flemish contrapuntal style, but also to the ancient ideals that the Renaissance style supposedly fulfilled.

From the beginning, there was a vague awareness of a connection between the quarrels over historical and national styles, though attempts at drawing parallels were crude. Generally, modern France and Italy were pitted against ancient Greece and Rome, but occasionally the lines were redrawn, and Italy was seen as the heir to the ancient splendor of Greece and Rome, while France was considered the modern newcomer to musical and literary culture. Since the seventeenth-century quarrel between Ancients and Moderns arose in part out of the newly found confidence of the French nation, it was natural that spokesmen for France should announce their country's equality not only to ancient Greece and Rome, but also to Italy—the country which, during the splendid achievements of the Jesuit Counter-reformation, all of Europe saw as a model for polite emulation if not for outright imitation.

This explanation provides a logical framework, in Claude Perrault's treatise, for Philalethe's espousal of the Italian cause in conjunction with his Ancient outlook. Callières, an Ancient, praises Italian opera at the expense of French in his allegory; such sympaties also explain the league of Orpheus and the Italian musician in that work, in spite of Lully's own attempts to form an affiliation with Orpheus. Lully himself, as the quintessential modern composer, receives praise from Modern critics such as Fontenelle, and blame from the Ancients, culminating in the parody of Sénecé. Ironically, the tables would turn completely in the eighteenth century, when Lully's operas would become the Ancients' classic model by which all "modern" works would be judged.

III

The Quarrel Between
Raguenet and Lecerf

In spite of Lully's monopoly of French opera, Italian music was not suppressed altogether in late seventeenth-century France. The dispersal of the Italian troupe after the wars of the Fronde had been gradual, and both professional and amateur musicians had continued to frequent the private perfomances held at the Parisian home of the Italian opera star Anna Bergerotti.[1] The Dutch astronomer Constantin Huyghens maintained contact with these musicians, especially the singer Pierre de Nyert, and his correspondence attests to a lively exchange of Italian music between Holland and France.[2] Likewise, the correspondence between René Ouvrard, *maître de musique* at the Sainte Chapelle, and the abbé Claude Nicaise in Dijon reveals a circle around Ouvrard in Paris that circulated manuscripts of Italian works and kept abreast of new developments in Italian sacred music.[3]

The poet Serré de Rieux, writing in 1734, dedicated a chapter of his long poem, *Les dons des enfants de Latone*,[4] to the then widely discussed issue of French and Italian music. In relating how a French "*goût sçavant*" was formed in imitation of Italian music, he describes the activities of another *afficionado* of Italian music, Nicolas Mathieu, the curé of the church of St. André des Arts during the years 1681–1706:

> This intense ardor caused by the example [of Italian music]
> Formed the *goût sçavant* which Paris saw develop,
> Our songs, enervated by a faded languor,
> Took new vigor from its strong character,
> It seems that all the art of Italy
> Was accommodated and reconciled to ours.
> The curious zeal of a pious amateur
> Attracted these motets to France,
> And they, forging a new path for our vocal music,
> Served as models for our nascent composers.[5]

A note to the text[6] describes the activities of Mathieu and relates the names of the most important Italian composers heard at St. André: Rossi, Cavalli, Cazzati, Carissimi, Legrenzi, Colonna, Melani, Stradella, and Bassani;[7] the poem continues with a description of the Italianate influence on the style of certain French composers such as Charpentier, Lalande, Campra, Clerambaut, Leclair, and Bernier.[8] Michel le Moël, who has published an inventory of the works in Mathieu's possession at his death, shows that his collection contained sacred works by all these Italian and French composers.[9]

Because of Lully's domination of the opera, Italian enclaves during this period fostered mostly sacred music. Marc-Antoine Charpentier, one of the most Italianate of the French composers, had studied in Rome with Carissimi, and brought the Roman oratorio style to France.[10] The many French churchmen making the customary pilgrimage to Rome were struck by the grandiose style of Roman church music, and transmitted their enthusiasm to the communities in which they ministered.[11]

By the turn of the century, general interest in Italian music had intensified in France; 1699 saw Ballard's first *Recueil des meilleurs airs italiens*, as well as André Campra's Italian opera *L'Orfeo negl'inferni* (a part of his larger work *Le carnaval de Venise*), and in 1701 Arcangelo Corelli's Opus 5 was first published in Paris.[12] Sebastien Brossard's *Dictionnaire de musique* (Paris, 1701) also appeared at this time, and included a "Traité de la manière de bien prononcer les mots italiens," which states, "Never has there been more taste and passion for Italian music than exists now in France."[13]

Brossard's entry for the term "style" holds interest for the present study because it evinces an early awareness of the differences between French and Italian music, as well as between ancient and modern music, as stylistic distinctions:

> In music, we call it [style] the manner of each particular way of composing, or performing, or teaching, and all of these will differ according to the genius of the composer, the country and nation, as also matter, place, time, subject, expression, etc. Thus one speaks of the style of Carissimi, of Lully, of Lambert, etc., the style of the Italians, the French, the Spanish, etc. The style of gay and joyous music is very different from the style of grave or serious music; the style of church music is very different from the style of music for the theater or chamber; the style of Italian compositions is piquant, flowery, expressive; that of French compositions is natural, flowing, tender, etc. From this come diverse epithets for distinguishing all these different characters, as the ancient and modern style; the Italian, French, German style, etc.[14]

The eighteenth-century quarrels between proponents of French and Italian music began with a short pamphlet by a musical dilettante, François Raguenet, the *Parallèle des Italiens et des Français en ce qui regarde la musique et les opéra* (Paris, 1702).[15] The abbé Raguenet, born in Rouen in 1660, had studied church law in his native city before moving to Paris, where he became a doctor at the Sorbonne and a member of the French Academy. As tutor to the nephews of the Cardinal of Bouillon, in 1698 he accompanied the cardinal on a journey to Rome, where he studied enthusiastically the masterpieces of Italian art and music. Upon his return to Paris, he published a description of Roman painting, sculpture, and architecture, *Les monuments de Rome* (Paris, 1700), which was widely read and earned for him the title Citizen of Rome, an honor which had been granted to no Frenchman since Michel de Montaigne. Apart from his writings on music, Raguenet also published biographies of Oliver Cromwell (Paris, 1691) and the Vicomte de Turenne (Paris, 1738), an *Histoire abrégée de l'ancien testament* (Paris, 1708), and *Syroës, histoire persane* (Paris, 1692), all of which found favor with the French public and went through many printings. Of Raguenet's later life little is known; his death in 1722 was attributed by one eighteenth-century author to suicide.[16]

Raguenet's *Parallèle*, written just after his *Monuments de Rome*, resembled that work in its fervid enthusiasm for Italian culture. Although Raguenet fashioned the treatise as an objective comparison between French and Italian opera, his strong preference for the Italian quickly asserts itself. While conceding to the French the quality of their libretti, choruses, dances, costumes, recitatives, and violin technique, he finds even more to admire in the Italian boldness of melody, variety of affections, ingenuity of stage design, and the greater intrinsic musicality of the Italian language itself. He also favors the Italian manner of singing and acting, and comments particularly on the marvels of the Italian castrati.

Raguenet's title imitated Charles Perrault's *Parallèle des anciens et des modernes* (Paris, 1688–1697),[17] one of the most popular and influential treatises to issue from the quarrel between Ancients and Moderns. Raguenet, in naming his book after that of a famous Modern and in praising the new, "modern" Italian style then at the height of fashion in France, thus aligned himself with the Modern cause. The work was approved for publication in January 1702 by another well-known Modern, Bernard le Bovier de Fontenelle, who added a special word to his official governmental *Approbation*:

> By order of *Monseigneur le Chancelier* I have read the present manuscript, and I believe that the printing of it would be most agreeable to the public, provided that it be capable of openmindedness.[18]

The common membership of Raguenet and Fontenelle in the French Academy may have brought them together as colleagues; at any rate, the popularity of the *Parallèle* may be attributed in part to Fontenelle, one of the most respected arbiters of taste in French society at this time.[19]

Raguenet's initiative was first taken up in March 1702 by the *Journal des savants*,[20] the oldest and most prestigious forum for intellectual debate in France in this period. The critic, in the sarcastic tone which was to characterize many of the documents of this quarrel, strongly denounces the substance and style of the *Parallèle*. One is tempted to think at first, he says, that Raguenet is praising French opera at the expense of Italian opera. But then we find that the Italians surpass the French in distorted melodies, bold irregularities, and all those things with which until now the French have reproached the Italians. The French have always accused the Italians of sacrificing the expression of the text to the harmony, and the pleasure of the spirit to that of the ear. But now, the journalist continues, it seems that this reproach is not at all justified and that no one in France has the slightest idea of Italian music, for the author assures us that it is in expression that the Italians excel. Furthermore, the style of the treatise is so elevated and poetic that the same could be said of Raguenet as of the Italian musicians, that he abandons himself to his ecstasy.

Reflecting the division of the public in the matter of musical taste, an opposing opinion of the *Parallèle* appeared in July of the same year in the *Memoires de Trévoux*,[21] the influential journal founded in 1701 by the Jesuits. Its critic justifies his detailed summary of the treatise on the basis of its extreme novelty and importance and, admitting that Raguenet's style could be less lively in places, he defends the quality of his writing as the mark of an enchanted admirer of Italian music. Perhaps as an allusion to the critical review in the *Journal des savants*, he closes by quoting Fontenelle's claim that the treatise would please the public, "provided it be capable of openmindedness."

After this review, two years passed before the appearance in 1704 of Jean-Laurent Lecerf de la Viéville's *Comparaison de la musique italienne et de la musique française*,[22] an answer to Raguenet's *Parallèle* and the principal manifesto for the superiority of French music. Lecerf, born in Rouen in 1674 (fourteen years after Raguenet), had received a Jesuit education under the Père de Tournemine, a celebrated scholar whose essays appeared regularly in *Memoires de Trévoux*. In 1696 Lecerf inherited from his father the title of Keeper of the Seals of the Parliament of Normandy, the only duties of which entailed presiding at Parliament two days a week. The remainder of his time he devoted to pursuing his intellectual interests, carrying on an assiduous correspondence with Tournemine and other Jesuit scholars, and writing poetry and essays for the *Memoires de Trévoux*. His critical pieces included explications of Lucian and Virgil, and a rather intriguing "proof that Alexander was not poisoned."[23] The work which most enhanced his reputation during his lifetime was a letter written in verse to the père Bouhours, a distinguished classical literary critic, on the return of his health after an illness; he later wrote an epitaph on Bouhours' death.[24] According to his brother,[25] Lecerf's relentless intellectual exertions soon exhausted his health, and he died in 1707 at the age of 33.[26].

An amusing, if vindictive, personal sketch of Lecerf is given later in the eighteenth century in the biography of Fontenelle, the writer who had affixed his *Approbation* to Raguenet's *Parallèle*. Fontenelle's opinion of Lecerf, as transmitted by his biographer, gives us a glimpse of the personalities and personal vendettas that undoubtedly played a major role in the quarrel:

> I hardly know any writings more strong, bitter, and malicious than those which Mr. de Freneuse published on this occasion. He was only an amateur, and not an artist; but he was the most passionate amateur. Extreme in everything, he pursued his studies with the same ardor and the same excess; hence his death at such an early age. Mr. de Fontenelle, who saw him in Rouen, and later in Paris, said to me that if anyone, through extreme spirit and sensibility, ever merited the name of a lunatic, an absolute lunatic, a lunatic in the head as well as in the heart, it was Mr. de Freneuse.[27]

Lecerf had apparently written his rebuttal to Raguenet soon after the appearance of the *Parallèle*, but waited for two years before publishing it, thinking that another champion might step forward to defend French music.[28] When the *Comparaison* was finally published, it consisted of three dialogues presenting Lecerf's ideas in a digressive though entertaining style, and a letter to a M. de la ***, in which the author *qua* author discusses his dialogues and explains their content.

The characters of the dialogues include a chevalier, Lecerf's spokesman, and a marquis and his wife whom the chevalier happens to meet at an opening performance of Campra's *Tancrède*. This takes place in a provincial town (presumably Rouen) in 1702, just after the publication of Raguenet's *Parallèle*, which the characters have all been reading. The marquis and marquise, representing the fashionable *gens du monde* sympathetic to Italian opera, are enlightened by the chevalier in the three dialogues, during which the characters peruse a copy of the *Parallèle* and discuss it point by point.

The main purpose of the dialogues is the presentation, in the mouths of Lecerf's characters, of detailed arguments which oppose the broader and more general comparisons of Raguenet. Because of the characters' amateur status, Lecerf refrains from having them discuss the more intellectual aspects of the issue, and the additional letter serves as a vehicle for Lecerf's own assessment of the question as a *savant*. In it he draws up a sketch of his aesthetic creed, which essentially amounts to approbation of natural (French) music and censure of affected (Italian) music. This creed is based on the literary theory of the seventeenth-century classical critics, especially Bouhours and Boileau, who attack Italian literature for its artificiality and affectation; by equating Italy's music with its literature, Lecerf prepares the reader for his own eventual application of classical literary theory to musical criticism.[29]

Whereas the critical reception of Raguenet's *Parallèle* had revealed a divided audience for that work, both the *Journal des savants* and the *Memoires de Trévoux* hailed Lecerf as a patriot who had stepped forward to uphold the honor of France. The favorable review in the *Journal* (August, 1704)[30] proved consistent with its previous dismissal of the *Parallèle*, but the sudden reversal of the *Memoires* (November, 1704)[31] may be explained by Lecerf's Jesuit connections and his ties with the journal itself. This article, in fact, names Lecerf as author of the *Comparaison* in spite of the fact that the work itself was from the first published anonymously.[32]

The author of the article, while mentioning the dialogues of the *Comparaison*, analyzes in much greater detail the more systematized aesthetic positions set forth in the letter. He comments particularly on the similarity of Italian poetry and music and on the correspondence of their descriptive terminology, discusses the problematical opposition of a French national taste to an Italian national taste, and traces Lecerf's theories of artistic imitation to those of Aristotle. On the whole, the review succeeds impressively in extracting Lecerf's most important points and in relating them to current critical concerns.

In 1705 Lecerf published a second edition of the *Comparaison*,[33] one which included in addition to the original a second part containing another three dialogues, a letter to Mme. D***, and a collection of lyrical verse. Lecerf's preface to the new edition reveals a transformation of the work from a straightforward refutation of Raguenet's *Parallèle* to a greatly expanded dissertation on the aesthetics, criticism, and history of music:

> I have often thought that, although we have in our language enough treatises on music, we have none that enters into a discussion of the beauty of our music. There are only treatises concerned with mechanics and craftsmanship, if I may say so; treatises which teach the rules in a dry manner, and of these none teaches us how to feel the esteem we ought to have for compositions in which these rules are observed. None leads *honnêtes gens* to judge as a whole the worth of a symphony or air. I believe there would be some merit and some glory in being the first to write a treatise of this nature.[34]

As in Part I, a letter to a supposed personal friend of the author summarizes the contents of the second three dialogues and helps to clarify the author's purpose. In Part II the letter addressed to Mme. D*** presents an appeal to her and her friends not to succumb to the artificial pleasures of Italian music. The question of taste again arises, and Lecerf, possibly in response to the critic of the *Memoires de Trévoux*, attempts to define good and bad taste, and to distinguish between national and individual taste.

Lecerf mentions in this letter a rumor that Raguenet has completed a defense of the *Parallèle*, and the fourth dialogue of the *Comparaison* anticipates possible objections that Raguenet might raise. The fifth sets forth a history of music and opera, and an account of Lully's life as told by the chevalier. The sixth dialogue opens with a lengthy refutation of the treatise of Claude Perrault, *De la musique des anciens*,[35] which had condemned ancient music in favor of modern. Lecerf takes the side of ancient music, and from its supposed characteristics derives a set of "eternal" standards applicable to all music. These standards, which include clarity, proportion, and expressiveness, then form a basis for a "Treatise on Good Taste" which completes the sixth dialogue, and Part II of the *Comparaison*.

Raguenet's *Défense du Parallèle des Italiens et des Français en ce qui regarde la musique et les opéra*,[36] printed in 1705 after the appearance of Lecerf's Part II, answers only the first three dialogues and the first letter of the *Comparaison*. The style of this treatise is more overtly polemical than that of the *Parallèle*,[37] and the tone one of indignation if not outrage. Raguenet refutes some points successfully, but does not respond at all to the larger issues introduced by Lecerf in Part I and further developed in Part II. While Raguenet's first-hand knowledge of Italian opera gives him a certain advantage, he lacks an overall view of the question in the terms Lecerf had proposed, and the writing remains amateurish.

The *Défense* received a mixed critical response. The reviewers of both the *Journal des savants* and the *Memoires de Trévoux* summarize the work, giving Raguenet credit for certain details but finding him lacking in scholarly sophistication. The journalist of the *Memoires* (May, 1706) desires that the complex issue of national taste be clarified and that the questions raised by Lecerf be answered with more authority.[38] The critic of the *Journal* (December, 1705),[39] reversing the previous position of that periodical, is more sympathetic to Raguenet's side of the argument if not to Raguenet himself. He quotes with approval the contradictions Raguenet had juxtaposed from the *Comparaison* as well as several examples of faulty grammar on the part of Lecerf, and ends by stating that "after all, we are not perhaps completely convinced that French music is better than

Italian; one could only wish that the good cause [that of Italian music] were in better hands."[40]

The third and final portion of Lecerf's *Comparaison* (Brussels, 1706)[41] contains a formal response to Raguenet's *Défense du Parallèle* in which Lecerf responds as much to the critic of the *Journal* as to Raguenet. In a tone of ironic politeness he counters the assertions of "M. l'Abbé et M. le Journaliste," labeling the latter "a Modern, a disciple of M. Perrault," and "an Italian in all things with all his heart."[42] He accuses Raguenet and the journalist of caviling at details while neglecting the larger issues, and devotes a large portion of his response to the question of Ancients and Moderns, attempting to defend Lully as an "ancient" because of his upholding of the ancient standards.[43] Much of his wrath is directed towards Fontenelle and the Moderns in general.

Besides the response to the *Défense*, Part III of the *Comparaison* also includes essays on sacred music and on the Italian composer Bononcini and fragments of an opera libretto written by Lecerf. In the essay on sacred music Lecerf sets out the ideal qualities of a music master, of sacred music itself, and of its performance according to the standards established in the "Treatise on Good Taste"; he then compares the sacred music of France and Italy according to those standards.

The final portion of Part III and of the *Comparaison* as a whole, the "Eclaircissement sur Bononcini," applies Lecerf's previous criticism of Italian music to a specific composer and specific works. Lecerf chooses Bononcini as the Italian composer currently most in vogue with the "fickle Parisians," their "*dieu des cantates*."[44] Besides commenting at random on various works, Lecerf isolates the cantata *Arde il mio petto amante* for a more detailed analysis. He examines its text, harmony, melodic structure, and other technical aspects, finding some beautiful details but an overall disregard for the rules and for good taste. Finally, bringing the quarrel once again to the comparison of ancient and modern music, Lecerf ends the work by challenging Raguenet to defend modern music against his attack in the *Comparaison*.

Raguenet, presumably left with no further defenses of Italian, or modern, music, remained silent, and the focus of the quarrel shifted to a growing animosity between Lecerf and the *Journal des savants*. This had begun with the comparatively sympathetic critique in the *Journal* of Raguenet's *Défense*, for which Lecerf had accused the critic of biased reviewing due to modernist and Italian sympathies. Not surprisingly, then, the next installment of the quarrel issued, in May 1706, from "M. le Journaliste," whose review of Parts II and III of the *Comparaison* is both unfavorable and somewhat unfair.[45] He sarcastically quotes Lecerf's weakest points out of context and accuses Lecerf of using the musical quarrel as an indirect means of attacking Fontenelle and the Moderns. The review is brief, and the effect of the whole one of summary dismissal.

In Lecerf's answer to this review, a short pamphlet entitled *L'art de décrier ce qu'on n'entend point, ou le médecin musicien: Exposition de la mauvaise foi d'un extrait du Journal de Paris* (Brussels, 1706), he identifies the critic as a M. Andry, a physician with few qualifications for reviewing such a work as the *Comparaison*. In the opening paragraphs of *Le médecin musicien* Lecerf maintains that Raguenet, after writing the *Défense*, called upon Andry to arbitrate the quarrel. Andry then, according to Lecerf, reviewed the *Défense* favorably and the *Comparaison* unfavorably,[46] and, after the publication of Parts II and III of the *Comparaison*, wrote the infamous review which Lecerf ironically describes as the "eternal proof of his probity and genius."[47] Andry apparently denied writing the first and admitted to the second:

> He denied strenuously having written the first review [of the *Défense*] and attributed it to M. Pouchard, thinking to use to his purposes the name of a dead man: he nobly boasted of this work [the review of the *Comparaison*] because all of the *Monsieurs* his colleagues were in a condition to protest if he attributed it to them.[48]

An enquiry into the editorial organization of the *Journal des savants* yields data consistent with Lecerf's half-humorous accusations. Since its inception, a single editor had headed the journal, but in 1702 its activities had been divided into several different categories, each directed by a well-known scholar. The division for mathematics and "general erudition" was headed by Fontenelle, that of languages and literature by the classical scholar Julien Pouchard, and that of medicine and physics by Nicolas Andry, Lecerf's *médecin musicien*."[49] Pouchard's death in 1705[50] coincided with a general trend towards a centralization of power under Andry, resulting in an expansion of the physics and medicine division over the next few decades.[51]

Lecerf's pamphlet points out Andry's lack of credentials for discussing "true beauty in music."[52] Lecerf calls Andry an incompetent judge and the *Journal* an unjust tribunal, and declares that if Andry ever writes a treatise on good taste in pills he will have his revenge. For the rest, Lecerf presents a thorough analysis of the review, indicating a large number of misquotations and quotations misleading out of context. Through this refutation of detail, he manages to call into question both Andry's credentials and critical methods.

The question as to whether Andry had actually written the two articles was left unanswered by the long defense appearing in the *Journal* (August, 1706) as a review of *Le médecin musicien*; the author defends the journal itself and its reviewing policy rather than the specifics of the two reviews "supposedly" by Andry.[53] After emphasizing the difficulties of the reviewer placed between the public expecting judgment and the author expecting praise, the article enumerates the qualities expected of a journalist: an objectivity set above his own personal interests and taste, an absence of personal injury or justification, and a search for dialectical truth which can be brought to light in quarrels such as the present one.

Such a dialectical truth was never established by Lecerf or Raguenet, but a reconciliation of sorts did grow out of a literary quarrel which ran parallel to the musical quarrel. This began in 1703, when the Marquis of Orsi published a critique of an earlier book, the père Bouhours' *La manière de bien penser dans les ouvrages de l'esprit* (Paris, 1687). Bouhours, a Jesuit cleric and popular Ancient critic, had used in that work the criteria of clarity of thought and simplicity of language to criticize the affected language, conceits, and hyperbole of modern Italian writers, especially Torquato Tasso (1544–1595). Orsi's book, *Considerazione sopra un famoso libro franzese, intitulato La manière de bien penser . . .* (Bologna, 1703), constitutes an attempt to defend the writers of Italy by proving Bouhours' imperfect knowledge of Italian literature and his poor choice of examples drawn from that literature.

Bouhours, who had died in 1702, had left a group of able defenders in his students, several of whom had become writers for the *Memoires de Trévoux*. In a four-part review (*Memoires*, February, March, April and May issues, 1705), these writers summarized Orsi's book and refuted its major points. Orsi, who had originally dedicated his book to Mme. Anne Dacier (1654–1720), the noted Greek scholar and translator, responded by publishing a series of letters which he had written to her during the summer of 1705 (published in Bologna, 1705). While these arguments seldom rise above mere quibbling, a larger moral is drawn from the quarrel in the review of Orsi's letters found in the *Journal des savants* (May 24, 1706). This review, the first real attempt at compromise, deserves to be quoted at length:

> As to the questions regarding various thoughts and expressions of Italian authors, we must state generally that the same difference which divides the connoisseurs in music on Italian and French taste, is found also between the Père Bouhours and M. Orsi, over *La manière de penser dans les ouvrages de l'esprit*. We must also state that there is nothing in composition that one cannot learn either from the authority of example, or that of the grammarians: what is the most difficult and most essential is the application of those examples and precepts, and that is what depends on taste, concerning which it is difficult to reconcile men, each one thinking to have the best taste. . . . That of the French and that of the Italians is not always the same. In France, Tasso is never placed at the side of Virgil or Homer; the rest of our judgments can be traced to that one. In Italy, critical opinion is different, and quarrels on the

subject will not be ended easily. The war will continue: but it cannot help but be useful to both sides. The reproaches of French writers can prevent the Italians from becoming too involved in the fire or the ingenuity of their imagination. But the contact with Italian authors can also perhaps contribute to bringing some of that fire and ingenuity to French works . . . .[54]

In summary, we may say that an investigation of the reviews of the *Journal des savants* and the *Memoires de Trévoux* brings to light an extensive body of literature which places the quarrel between Raguenet and Lecerf in a new perspective: the journals, rather than simply reporting the debate, actually helped to shape it. The necessity of stating the contentions of both parties and of assessing the implications of the quarrel led to increased involvement and participation of the journals in musical affairs; and it was the journalists who, in criticizing both sides and in bringing forward possible compromises, managed to suggest the possibility of a "*goûts rèunis*" and to foreshadow the eventual critical synthesis of the opposing viewpoints in the quarrel.

IV

Raguenet and Lecerf and the Development of Musical Criticism

Their Quarrel in the Context of
Early Eighteenth-Century Criticism

The treatises of Raguenet and Lecerf brought to the field of music two opposing aesthetic views which would continue to be debated throughout the century. Raguenet, advocating not only Italian music but also the modern style, bases his critical judgment on his own subjective appreciation of that style. Lecerf, seeing French culture as a tradition to be maintained against the invasion of Italian bad taste, bases his critical judgment on a strict set of objective standards supposedly derived from the music of the ancients. In a century which witnessed the consolidation of earlier critical thought into coherent aesthetic systems, the value of the quarrel between Lecerf and Raguenet lies in its clear delineation of two clashing philosophies which together would form the foundations of modern musical criticism.

Most writers on musical criticism[1] agree that critical thought in the modern era consists of 1) the evaluation of specific musical works, and 2) the explanation of these works to an audience. The term itself originated from the Greek *krineín*, to judge or discern, and the critic is most generally understood as a person who tells his audience what he thinks is good and why. His means of determining quality may range from subjective personal impressions to objective standards and rules, but most criticism of value falls somewhere between these two extremes. The modern critic is also a shaper of taste whose guidance helps to form public opinion; his audience consists primarily of informed amateurs—concertgoers and readers of periodicals—who look to the informed opinion of an expert.

Musical criticism so defined scarcely existed before the modern era, when the rise of a middle class provided the sociological basis of an amateur audience. Any clear perception of the critic's judicial responsibility was rare before the eighteenth century, and until then we find almost no mention of judgment except in the most widely scattered sources. Interestingly, however, the issue had been raised in antiquity; a rather penetrating discussion is included in the treatise *De musica*, attributed to Plutarch (46–120 A.D.)[2] This author defines a true musician as possessing judgment as well as skill; one who plays the Dorian mode, for example, without judgment of its nature and proper use has no real knowledge of music. Judgment is therefore a knowledge of what is proper and improper, both in the construction of a composition and in the function for which it is intended. It is based on one of two faculties, sense or intellect:

> Pythagoras, that grave philosopher, rejected the judging of music by the senses, affirming that the virtue of music could be appreciated only by the intellect. And therefore he did not judge music by the ear, but by the harmonical proportion, and thought it sufficient to fix the knowledge of music within the compass of the diapason.[3]

Concern with musical judgment ceased almost entirely in the Middle Ages and Renaissance.[4] Even the sixteenth and seventeenth centuries, so rich in literary debate and critical thought, saw little critical activity in the field of music. In this period, however, the growth of a new kind of practical criticism in literature provided a model for later musical criticism. The humanists' adulation of the classics had led to the reinstatement of more strictly aesthetic, rather than philosophical and theological, artistic criteria; the humanist author, in attempting to imitate the external forms of antiquity, was obliged to immerse himself thoroughly in the problems of form and beauty, to know which classical authors were worthy of imitation and why.[5] This application of concrete critical judgment of particular works continued in the quarrels over ancient and modern literature, for the necessity of defending one body of works over another led to a concerted attempt to appraise the values of both.

The efforts of the humanists, especially the groups which formed around Bardi in Italy and the *Pléiade* in France, to effect a renascence of the ancient concept of musico-poetics helped to render music susceptible to the same types of criticism as literature—especially the hybrid genre of opera which itself developed as a result of their theories. Like the humanists in literature, the musical humanists found it necessary to compare modern music with their ideas of what ancient music had been, and out of this comparison the critical faculty of judgment grew. Though the music of antiquity was virtually unknown to sixteenth- and seventeenth-century writers, its assumed characteristics served as standards—albeit artificial ones—by which contemporary music could be judged. And as the eternal validity of these standards began to be questioned, new methods of critical apprehension were sought. In reality, the debate between Ancients and Moderns represented a dialectic between the subjective and objective modes of criticism, for partisans of antiquity declared the necessity of rigorous application of immutable laws derived from ancient music, while the Moderns championed a greater emphasis on individual taste and the subjective response of the listener.

In the late seventeenth century, a few attempts had been made to equate the literary quarrel between Ancients and Moderns with the musical comparisons of French and Italian music. At that time Lully was embraced by the Moderns as one of their own, and Italian music—no longer in vogue since the death of Mazarin—fell almost by default into the opposite camp.

Any attempt, of course, to equate either Italian or French music with ancient music was ultimately futile, since both were legitimate modern styles. Nevertheless, there was a tendency throughout the seventeenth and eighteenth centuries to consider as modern only the style that was the most *à la mode*, relegating music of the recent past to comparison with ancient music. Thus, as the seventeenth century drew to a close, the operas of Lully took on the aura of tradition, while the Italian "sonatas and cantatas" that were invading France[6] inherited the designation of modernity. Also, as patterns emerged from desultory comments on French and Italian music in the seventeenth century, the French preference for the intellectual moving of the passions through clarity, naturalness, and a grasp of the artwork as a whole began to seem more consistent with the ancient ideals than the Italian preference for sensual moving of the passions through greater attention to sonority, variety, and dramatic effect.

Aspects of Seventeenth-Century French Classical Criticism:
Philosophy of the Ancients

The use of objective standards as criteria for excellence had crystallized during the course of the seventeenth century in the works of the French classical critics, many of whom participated as Ancients in the quarrel of Ancients and Moderns.[7] Paradoxically, it was these French classicists who continued the Renaissance Italian tradition of critical commentary on Aristotle's *Poetics*, while seventeenth-century Italian authors generally embarked on greater freedom from authority and greater recognition of individual genius.[8]

The earliest figure of importance in French classical criticism was François de Malherbe (1555–1628), a poet, prosodist, and grammarian who effected a trend toward the purification of the French language of its foreign terms, a greater emphasis on clarity and regularity, and greater attention to the actual craft of composition.[9] Soon afterwards, Jean Chapelain (1595–1674)[10] and Jean-Louis Guez de Balzac (1597–1654)[11] introduced the critical concepts and aesthetic theories of the Italian commentators on Aristotle, the most important of whom was Ludovico Castelvetro.[12] Through these French popularizers of the Italian commentaries, Aristotelian aesthetic theories became central to French classicism; their impact in France my be seen in endless discussion of artistic imitation and of the formal rules of tragedy.

The name most universally associated with French classical criticism is that of Nicolas Boileau-Despréaux (1636–1711) who, without contributing significant new material, codified the doctrine of reason, clarity, and Aristotelian imitation propounded by his predecessors. Boileau, as unofficial leader of the Ancients, argued for the rule of authority and for the imitation of antique models, and his *Art poétique* (Paris, 1674), written in terse, epigrammatic style, became a favorite source of quotation for later critics.[13]

The père Dominique Bouhours (1628–1702) also helped to forge the doctrines of French classicism. Bouhours had taken vows as a Jesuit in 1662, and his important book *Les entretiens d'Ariste et d'Eugène* (Paris, 1671) was banned because of its attacks on the Protestant stronghold of Port-Royal. The purism of Bouhours' theory is clearly seen in his masterpiece, *La manière de bien penser dans les ouvrages de l'esprit* (Paris, 1687), which attacked unclear thinking and writing in any form, but especially as found in modern Italian authors. Bouhours' influence on his contemporaries was powerful and lasting, for he taught many early eighteenth-century thinkers, including the founders of the *Mémoires de Trévoux*.[14]

One question often raised in discussions of French classicism is the extent to which it was influenced by Cartesian philosophy. Because of a similar emphasis on reason and clarity, Boileau's *Art poétique* has been called the *Discours de la méthode* of French poetry, but Boileau's dependence upon authority diametrically opposes Descartes' faith in the individual's reasoning powers.[15] Though Descartes' rationalistic philosophy undoubtedly reinforced the classicists' belief in universal reason, the origins of classical rationalism should be traced rather to earlier Italian criticism; in particular, Marco Girolamo Vida, in his *De arte poetica* (c.1517), had adumbrated a rationalistic method of criticism in the early sixteenth century.[16]

The rule of reason, growing out of Renaissance critical thought, forms the cornerstone of seventeenth-century French classical doctrine. Critical means of judging literature and the arts all begin with the determination of a work's conformity to reason, a method receiving general approbation and universal application in the late seventeenth century.[17] The term itself, more than any other, permeates the criticism of the era, but it is also accompanied by more specific words defining its various functions. The general term *raison* possesses connotations of an abstract philosophical essence, while the expression *bon sens* signifies the eternal intellectual capacity for the apprehension of truth. *Jugement* (judgment) and *bon goût* (good taste) serve as the two specifically critical uses of *raison*, *jugement* referring to the application of reason to the evaluation of particular objects in the external world, and *bon goût* referring its more systematic and universal application to a larger body of works.[18] Finally, *bon esprit*, often (but inadequately) translated "wit," refers to the application of *raison* to social intercourse; Bouhours calls it "*bon sens* which sparkles."[19] The flexibility of these definitions is demonstrated by Roger de Bussy-Rabutin, a late seventeenth-century critic, who states:

> For myself I consider *bon sens* and *jugement* to be the same. Madame de Coligny prefers that *bon sens* concern thoughts and expression, and *jugement* their practical application. . . . We all believe that *bon sens*, *raison*, and *bon esprit* are the same thing.[20]

Another characteristic associated with reason and *bon sens* is the idea of moderation and emotional restraint. Here the French classicists' disapproval of modern Italian literature finds a place in critical doctrine, for the Italians' extravagance is seen as the opposite extreme of *bon sens*. The conjunction of the ideas of reason, *bon sens*, and moderation are opposed to the Italian aesthetic in a well-known passage from Boileau's *Art poétique*:

> Flee this excess, and leave to Italy
> The shocking folly of all this artificial brilliance.
> Everything should aim at good sense: but to attain it
> The way is slippery and painful to follow;
> For if one departs even a little he is lost.
> Reason often has no alternative to the straight and narrow path.[21]

Boileau was not the first French classical theorist to condemn Italian excess. As early as 1640, Jules de la Mesnardière, in his *La poétique*, had urged French poets to search for the diamonds of ancient Greece and Rome, rather than the "enamels" of modern Italy or the "glass" of modern Spain.[22] Bouhours, in his dialogue "Le bel esprit,"[23] maintains that true beauty is found in simplicity and naïveté, and that too much brilliance is worse than not enough. "Mon dieu!" exclaims one of his characters upon hearing this:

> . . . how you delight me, says Eugene, in excluding from the ranks of *bels esprits* those writers of *beaux mots* and pretty phrases; these imitators and monkeys of Seneca; these Mancinis, Malvezzis, and Loredanis, who are always running after brilliance and *vivezze d'ingegno*, as they say in their language! For, to tell you the truth, I cannot stand them, and it is difficult enough to put up with Seneca himself, with his perpetual witticisms and antitheses.[24]

If reason was the goal of the French classicists, the means toward this goal was the application of the ancient precepts, especially those established by Aristotle in the *Poetics*.[25] The following passage, from René Rapin's *Réflexions sur la Poétique d'Aristote* (Paris, 1674; quotation from English translation of 1705) reflects the common tendency to blame the Italians for following their own imagination rather than the ancient precepts:

> . . . for unless a Man adhere to Principles, he is obnoxious to all Extravagancies and Absurdities imaginable: Unless he go by Rule, he flips at every step towards Wit, and falls into Errors as often as he sets out. Into what Enormities has Petrarch run in his *Africa*; Ariosto in his *Orlando furioso*; Chevalier Marino in his *Adonis*, and all the other Italians who were ignorant of Aristotle's Rules; and followed no other Guides but their own Genius and capricious Fancy?[26]

Of all the ancient precepts to be followed, the most important is Aristotle's dictum that art should imitate nature.[27] The seventeenth-century interpretation of the natural has little to do with nature in the literal sense; rather it posits—in the concept of *belle nature*—an ideal of classic simplicity, purged of all coarseness, ugliness, complexity, and artifice. Bouhours applies this definition to the process of thought:

> . . . something which is not at all affected nor farfetched, which the nature of the subject presents and which is born out of the subject itself. I mean to say a simple beauty, without paint or artifice, such as the ancients described true eloquence. One could say a natural thought could come to anyone; it would seem to be in one's head before he ever read it.[28]

Just as the idea of reason is reconciled with the authority of the ancients in classical doctrine, so is the imitation of nature linked directly to the imitation of the ancients. If the dictates of reason are universal and unchanging, then the same standards of judgment should apply to ancient and modern works. What the ancients wrote conforms to the ideals of nature, simplicity, and rationality so perfectly that in imitating them, one imitates not only nature, but nature purged of all its flaws.[29]

It was, of course, this imitation of the ancients and respect for authority that aroused the enmity of more progressive critics, initiating the quarrel between Ancients and Moderns. However, in attacking the admiration of the Ancients (the classical critics) for the literature and critical precepts of ancient writers, the Moderns actually called into question the entire body of classical doctrine. Instead of an absolute scale of values, they proposed a relative one, and instead of reliance on universal reason, they proposed reliance instead on individual taste.[30]

The Dispute over Taste

Since the time of the humanists, critics and artists had been concerned with the aesthetic problems of determining what was beautiful in the work of the ancients, and of imitating that beauty in their own time. As seventeenth-century artists and writers began to contemplate the creation of new works of art no longer based on the ancient models and critical formulas, the use of taste as a tool for determining quality became more and more crucial. As we have seen, the classical critics tended to see *bon goût* as the critical faculty of reason, while the Moderns (who were often writers and artists who wrote criticism to justify their own iconoclastic works) saw taste as a more personal phenomenon, that which pleases an individual at a particular moment or a country in a certain historical period.

Although the concept of taste appears from time to time in works of the Italian Renaissance,[31] it was the French classical critics who made it a real part of aesthetic theory. One of the first references, in 1645, is by Balzac, who writes to a friend, "Since you have a taste for (*goûtez*) my last works, and you have extremely good taste. . . ."[32] From the beginnings, good taste was equated not only with reason and *bon sens*, but also with antiquity. Chapelain, who speaks of "the good taste of antiquity,"[33] also states, "It is not possible that pleasure can be contrary to *bon sens*, unless it is the pleasure of depraved taste."[34]

In the second half of the seventeenth century, writers began to elaborate a distinction between two kinds of taste, the first associated with personal inclinations or feelings, the second with correct judgment according to the absolute standards dictated by reason. Critics complain that men are guided less often by reason and *bon sens* than by fashion or feelings. St.-Evremond states:

> The reason [that one may be approved one day and derided the next] is that men rarely judge by the strong advantages given to them by *bon sens*, but rather by fashion, whose applause is as soon over as the fantasy with which it originated.[35]

Jean de la Bruyère defines good taste as the ability to sense perfection in a work of art, especially those arts in which mediocrity is "disastrous": poetry, music, painting, and public discourse. He draws a distinction between feeling and taste:

> There is more vivacity than taste among men; or to state it more clearly, there are few men in whom strong feeling is accompanied by a sure taste and good judgment.[36]

This distinction, far from remaining in scholarly obscurity, seems to have served polite society as a parlor game, for in 1673 Madame de la Fayette writes to Madame de Sévigné that she has been engaged in an after-dinner conversation concerning whether certain persons have more taste or more feeling. "You have more feeling than taste," she says, "and M. de la Rochefoucauld too, and also myself, though not as much as you two."[37]

François de la Rochefoucauld, the well-known author of *Maximes*, responded to this comment with the first extended essay on taste, "Du goût" (c.1674), which opens with the statement, "Some persons have more feeling than taste, and others more taste than feeling."[38] The difference in the two is:

> . . . the difference between a taste which attracts us to something, and a taste which enables us to discern the true quality of a thing through the use of the rules. One can like a comedy without having a taste sensitive enough to judge it well, and one can have a taste good enough to judge the comedy without liking it.[39]

For La Rochefoucauld, taste may be variously defined; however, he believes there is only one *good* taste, that which is based on reason and good sense:

> In all these differences in taste, which we have enumerated, it is very rare, and almost impossible, to find the kind of good taste which knows the true worth of everything, which always recognizes quality . . . .[40]

The père Bouhours, in his *La manière de bien penser*, draws an identical distinction between *goût* and *bon goût*: calling taste "nothing but a certain relationship between the feelings and the objects presented to them,"[41] he defines good taste as an "instinct of right reason,"[42] which immediately appraises its object correctly. Bouhours also applies this difference to the quarrel over French and Italian literature. Eudoxe, the character who espouses the French classical outlook, criticizes an Italian passage for its strained metaphors, finding them contrary to the rules. Philanthe, however, defends the passage:

> Every nation, [replied Philanthe], has its own taste based on feeling as well as on beauty, custom, and all the rest.

> As if the justice of sense, retorted Eudoxe, were not of all languages, and what was bad in itself ought to pass for good in any country among reasonable people![43]

It was not until the following century that any compromise would be found between eternal reason and relative taste, but such a compromise is foreshadowed in a statement by another critic, the abbé de Villiers, who states in 1675:

> There is in a work of art that which depends on reason, and which never varies in any way, and that which is the province of taste and custom, and which is appropriate to each epoch and each nation.[44]

In the quarrel between Ancients and Moderns, the Moderns, discarding altogether the idea of universal good taste based on the rules, insisted on the superiority of individual taste in judging contemporary works of art. This position is stated by Charles Perrault in his *Parallèle*:

> I have found faults both in Homer and in Virgil that are not found in the moderns: for politeness and good taste, which are perfected with time, have rendered untenable an infinity of things which were allowed and even praised in the works of the ancients. You will see no poem in this century in which it is difficult to tell what the subject is, as in the *Iliad*, or where the action is imperfect, as in the *Aeneid*.[45]

Charles Perrault's brother Claude brought to musical discussions the idea of the superiority of modern taste. Like Charles, Claude Perrault uses the term *goût* to mean relative taste: taste, unlike good sense, improves through the ages, and thus modern music is superior to ancient.[46]

Musico-Poetic Theory in the
Sixteenth and Seventeenth Centuries

As we have seen in Chapter Two, it was the sixteenth-century humanists who, through their desire to unite music and poetry, effected the entry of music into the linguistically-based trivium rather than the numerically-based quadrivium. Bardi, Mei, Galilei, Ronsard, and Baïf had seen music as an inseparable complement to poetry, subject as such to poetry's rules, and musical humanists, stimulated by the research of the literary theorists, began to bring literary criteria to the study of music.

Authority for the combination of literature and music under the same critical standards was found primarily in the work of Plato, Aristotle, and Horace. Though not as influential in the seventeenth and eighteenth centuries as it had been in the early Renaissance, Plato's discussion of music and words in *The Republic* continued to serve as emphasis on the importance of the text in a musical setting: "The melody and rhythm," he says, "will depend upon the words."[47] Horace, in his *Ars poetica*, made analogies among the arts of poetry, painting, drama, music, and dance, and supplied the oft-quoted phrase, "*ut pictura poesis*": poetry should be as painting, that is, representative of nature.[48] The most important basis for the application of poetic theory to music, however, came from the passage in Aristotle's *Poetics* which stated:

> Epic poetry and Tragedy, Comedy also and Dithyrambic poetry, and the music of the flute and of the lyre in most of their forms, are all in their general conception modes of imitation. They differ, however, from one another in three respects—the medium, the objects, the manner or mode of imitation, being in each case distinct.[49]

Another Aristotelian concept carried into seventeenth-century dramatic theory, and later into musical theory, was that of *katharsis*—the purgation of the emotions (passions) of pity and fear. The classical critics of the seventeenth century enlarged upon this definition by speaking generally of a purgation of all the harmful passions, of which pity and fear were the most powerful.[50] This aim was complemented by the rhetorical ideal, derived from Quintilian, Cicero and Horace, of moving the passions in order to "instruct and delight,"[51] and in the latter part of the century with the more scientific, physiological inquiries of Descartes into the *passions de l'âme*.[52] Practical outgrowths of this theory occurred simultaneously in tragedy and opera in the later seventeenth century.

Racine appears to have introduced a greater emphasis on the rhetorical combination of word and tone in his production of his own plays, having his actors declaim their lines in a manner somewhere between song and speech.[53] The result of such declamation undoubtedly had much in common with the recitative of Lully, shaped so carefully to the anapestic Alexandrine and indeed modeled on the declamation of the famous actress Champmeslé.[54]

Thus it is not surprising that the *tragédie-lyrique* would be judged at first not on its own terms but on those established by the classical critics for the plays of Racine and Corneille and their contemporaries. This is why much of the operatic criticism of the period seems naïve to the modern reader; the finest literary critics, notably St.-Evremond and Boileau,[55] find fault with opera for being sung, and with the libretto for being tailored to a musical setting.[56]

Lecerf's Comparaison:
Classical Doctrine as Musical Criticism

Lecerf's criticism, like that of St.-Evremond and Boileau, is based on classicism in literature, but unlike those writers, he sees a particular type of opera (the *tragédie-lyrique* of Lully) as fulfilling the requirements of classical doctrine. Though his standards are arbitrary and his judgment biased, his careful construction of a set of standards and his subsequent evaluation of different bodies of music according to those standards give his work a modern critical outlook. The *Comparaison* represents Lecerf's indebtedness to the classical tradition and his application of that tradition to the music of the seventeenth century.[57]

Lecerf had received a broad humanistic education under the Jesuits. All of his major works except for the *Comparaison* had been in the field of ancient literature; he used Greek and Latin easily and had read all of the important classical critics, including Aristotle, Plutarch, Plato, Longinus, Horace, Cicero, and Quintilian. His knowledge of the French seventeenth-century classical critics was no less profound, and references to such names as Boileau, Bouhours, La Mesnardière, Balzac, and Dacier[58] run copiously through the *Comparaison*.

If Raguenet's *Parallèle* was modeled on the ideas of Charles Perrault's *Parallèle des anciens et des modernes*, one might see Lecerf's *Comparaison* as inspired by Bouhours' *La manière de bien penser*. As a student at the Jesuit school in Rouen, Lecerf had undoubtedly come into contact with the critical theories of Bouhours, for Bouhours had taught there from c.1660–1668, some years before Lecerf's attendance.[59] In 1698 Lecerf wrote a letter in verse to Bouhours celebrating the convalescence of the critic, and this letter, though never published, helped to establish Lecerf's reputation more than any other work before the *Comparaison*. When Bouhours died in 1702, Lecerf composed an epitaph:

> Here lies Bouhours. Court and city
> Come one by one to pay homage
> To the tomb of a great author
> Who brought refinement to both.[60]

In the *Comparaison*, Lecerf refers both to Bouhours' *Entretiens d'Ariste et d'Eugène* and to his *Manière de bien penser*, and in one dialogue speaks of Bouhours as a personal friend.[61]

Lecerf was probably moved to write the *Comparaison* not only in response to Raguenet's *Parallèle*, but also in response to the quarrel that had arisen over Bouhours' *Manière de bien penser* when the Italian Marquis of Orsi had published his *Considerazione sopra un famoso libro fran-zese, intitulato: La manière de bien penser dans les ouvrages de l'esprit* (Bologna, 1703). This book caused a certain furor among the followers of Bouhours in France, for not only did Lecerf publish the *Comparaison* in the following year, but the Jesuit editors of the *Memoires de Trévoux* rose to defend Bouhours in a series of articles published in 1705.[62]

The *Manière de bien penser* represents the only extended compar-ison of French and Italian literature from the viewpoint of late seven-teenth-century classicism. The treatise consists of detailed examinations of specific passages in literature which are judged on their conformity to the ideals of classical doctrine: reason, good taste, moderation, simplicity, clarity, and imitation of the ancients. Though few authors, ancient or modern, are exempt from Bouhours' criticism, it is the Italian poet Tasso whose works are analyzed the most thoroughly as examples of Italian bad taste.

Lecerf's work is more comprehensive than Bouhours', but its method is similar: Italian works are measured against classical standards and invariably found lacking. Just as Bouhours takes the works of Tasso, an especially popular author but notorious violator of the rules, Lecerf chooses for special analysis the works of Giovanni Bononcini, the Italian "dieu des cantates."[63]

Lecerf, then, in responding to the rather innocuous *Parallèle* of Raguenet, was responsible for the transformation of the literary quarrel over French and Italian literature into a developed system of musical criticism. Lecerf himself explains his objective:

> It is not only in music that they [the Italians] consider themselves the first in the world. . . . It is also in their poetry, where reigns the same presumption, the same affectation, the same temerity. Poor nature is banished from it in the same way. . . . For a long time people of taste, and the *honnêtes gens* of France, have declared themselves of this sentiment. But luckily for the musicians of Italy, they have not been thoroughly compared to the poets, and because they became known here much later than the poets, there has not been time to see how the ones resemble the others, and how much the character of the poetry and that of the music conform to each other. . . .[64]

Lecerf equally deplores Italy's poetry and music as examples of bad taste, in contrast to that country's sculpture, painting, and architecture, all of which he considers a fulfillment of the classical ideal, "for the same nature and beautiful simplicity that they love, search for, and seek out in architecture, sculpture, and painting, they hate, flee and mistrust in po-etry and music."[65]

Lecerf's debt to Boileau is summed up in the quotation with which he illustrates his emphasis on classical values in music; he sees his own treatise as a defense of the classical French tradition against the modern, extravagant art of the Italians, just as Boileau had fought for a classical French style against the Moderns in literature:

> All of those who love as you do antiquity, and who do not prefer "the glitter of Tasso to all the gold of Virgil," will be likewise obligated to renounce the Italian masters in favor of Lully.[66]

Lecerf's transfer of literary doctrine to musical aesthetics is based on two premises: that the purpose of music is primarily an expression of the text to which it is set, and that all the arts can be successfully subjected to the same modes of criticism. The first postulate is crucial to an understanding of Lecerf, for his entire theory of opera is based on the supremacy of text, on a view of opera as "musical tragedy" rather than as a primarily musical production:

> . . . the first beauty, the true beauty, the unique beauty of an air, is to be fashioned to the words; on which [principle] a person of *bon esprit* said very justly that one excellent mark of the quality of an air is that no words fit it except those for which it was composed.[67]

An opera follows essentially the rules of poetry and the theater, and can thus be judged accordingly:

> . . . I freely agree with Mr. de Saint Evremond, that the stubbornness and ignorance of musicians (I mean a shameful ignorance of the plot, the proprieties of the theater, the rules of poetry and grammar, to which our composers are subject) are responsible for a number of idiocies in opera. One could say that in general for the constitution of a piece, the poet should be absolute master. . . .[68]

As for the second premise, that all the arts are subject to the same modes of criticism, Lecerf states explicitly that his theory of good taste can be applied to painting, poetry, and eloquence by virtue of their common nature: "I take for a good sign," he says, "that what can be said of any one is in part true of the others."[69] Lecerf's belief in this common nature of the arts enables him to transfer to music the theories of the French classical critics, the most influential of which are an understanding of all good art as an imitation of nature and an imitation of the ancients, and a rationalistic interpretation of musical and poetic art as an affective moving of the passions.

Lecerf combines the Horatian line "*ut pictura poesis*" with Aristotle's theory of imitation by defining imitation as painting: "All genres of poetry are only, according to him [Aristotle], different *imitations*, or different paintings."[70] Music, then, is an imitation of poetry, or an imitation of nature once removed. Lecerf sees music as reinforcing the visual image created by poetry, rendering the image so vivid that it is literally brought to life for the listener:

> What, now, does the beauty of operatic music consist of? In rendering the poetry of the opera a painting which really speaks. That is, to retouch it, to add the final colors. Now how can music repaint poetry, how can they serve each other if they are not combined with an extreme justice, if they are not joined in a most perfect accord?[71]

By repainting, Lecerf means a perfect fitting of the general affection of the music to that of the text, not the illustration of specific words or phrases. "Word-painting" may be allowed in a few conventional circumstances, on words such as "fly," "descend," "thunder," all of which have traditionally received musical embellishment. The Italians, however, overemphasize this shortsighted view of imitation: "They forget, they weaken the general expression of the verset and the idea, to amuse themselves on the particular expression of the word."[72]

Finally, Lecerf emphasizes the universality of beauty imitated from nature, opposing this beauty to bizarre and shocking effects for their own sake: "Beauties taken from the breast of nature, the true expressions, are felt by all men, while false beauties do not share this privilege."[73] Because true beauty is universal, Lecerf prefers a repetition of proven formulas to variety for its own sake, which he accuses Raguenet of admiring in Italian music.

Aristotle's theory of the purpose of artistic imitation is quoted by Lecerf as the words of "a great man": "Music is useful for three things: to instruct, to purge the passions, and to provide agreeable recreation worthy of an *honnête homme*."[74] Lecerf's idea of imitation, while recognizing the importance of catharsis, emphasizes the pleasure derived from imitation more as an end in itself. Stressing the moral and aesthetic aims of art, Lecerf quotes André Dacier's preface to his translation of Aristotle's *Poetics*: "What is the good and the beautiful? That which pleases Nature."[75]

Though Lecerf is not particularly concerned with the purgation of the passions, he does consider the most important function of imitation to be the portrayal of human emotion. As such, the primary goal of music is to communicate the passions, to touch the emotions of the audience, "since one only sings for the same reason one speaks, because one has sentiments to express."[76] Thus Lecerf, like the literary critics, emphasizes the passions as the most important aspect of nature (human nature) to be imitated, but de-emphasizes the Aristotelian concept of catharsis.[77]

The imitation of the ancients is as closely linked to the imitation of nature in Lecerf as in his literary models: for Lecerf the universality and eternality of nature impose the same ideal standards on both ancient and modern musical works. Lecerf, using the old argument that antiquity knew of no instruments with over ten strings, believes that the simplicity of ancient monophony was responsible for the marvelous effects recounted by the poets. He uses this belief as proof that the more closely music follows nature (that is, the more closely it follows the text which represents an imitation of nature), the more closely it follows the ancient affective ideal:

> A melody which is simple, natural and which flows from its source without labor, will pierce to the bottom [of the heart] much more easily. . . . Antiquity, that admirable and ingenious antiquity, knew nothing of instruments with over ten strings which could have played in five parts, and because of that they carried their arts to such a high point of liveliness and perfection.[78]

Because Lecerf characterizes ancient music as the epitome of simplicity and affectiveness, he sees any music which succeeds in combining word and tone in a simple, affective manner as fulfilling the ancient ideal. To Lecerf, the composer who imitated the ancients the most perfectly is Lully who, working in the milieu of French classicism, was more easily able to apply the ancient ideals to his music:

> If Lully had stayed in Italy and had only composed Italian music, he perhaps would not have brought it to the point of perfection to which he has led ours, to the extent that he would not have been guided by some idea of the admirable simplicity of the music of the ancients (simplicity which he has known better how to imitate than anyone for 1600 years, which I consider the source and character of his merit).[79]

It is inevitable, then, that Lecerf would equate the quarrels of Ancient and Moderns with those of French and Italian music, Lullists and anti-Lullists:

> . . . it is precisely the quarrel of Ancients and Moderns, renewed under different names. On one side the natural and simple: on the other the affected and brilliant. Here the true, embellished with justice, there the false, masked by a thousand refinements, and charged with the excesses of a monstrous science. For a long time I have held to this conformity of Lully to the ancients: and the heroes of Italian music to the moderns: which has not failed to augment and reawaken the interest which I had already taken in the glory of our music.[80]

Lecerf's greatest contribution to the quarrel of Ancients and Moderns in music is his refutation of the treatise of Claude Perrault on the music of the ancients, which had attempted to show that because the ancients had not known counterpoint, their music was necessarily inferior to modern music. Lecerf's critique of Perrault again links the quarrel of Ancients and Moderns with that of French and Italian music, for he claims that while Lully has recaptured, through the simplicity of his music and his successful combination of word and tone, the affective powers of the music of antiquity, the purely sensual effects of Italian music represent the antithesis of the ancient ideal. Although Perrault had said nothing of French and Italian music, Lecerf claims that "the reproaches of M. Perrault against the music of antiquity" are in reality "praise for the music of Italy."[81] The refutation of Perrault leads directly into the "Traité du bon goût dans la musique"; for by defending the principles governing the music of antiquity, Lecerf thinks to preclude objections to his own classical standards.

In the final analysis, Lecerf sees French music as primarily expressive, appealing to the intellect (and through the intellect to the heart), Italian music as primarily sensuous, appealing strictly to the ear. Though Lecerf does admit the pleasure of the senses into his theory, he places more emphasis upon the intellect; quoting Cicero, he considers the first aim of music, like oratory, is to "move" the affections, and the second to "delight" the ear.[82] Lecerf's insistence on textual expressiveness rather than on sensual appeal places him squarely on the side of reason in the age-old dispute between reason and sense. Expressiveness and naturalness (the absence of artificial ornamentation) come first and second, and harmony—the contentment of the ear—only third:

> . . . without the natural and expressive, music is only a trifle, a child's game, unworthy of occupying *honnêtes hommes*. . . . The ear is, for music, the door of the heart. To open this door, flattering the ear is thus the third care of the musician, but only the third . . . the less powerful the affection, the less quickly will it pierce the heart, and the more it is permitted to amuse the ear.[83]

These, then, are the underlying principles of Lecerf's critique of Italian and of modern music: imitation of nature and the ancients, the absolute rule of reason and of moderation and simplicity. It is his application of these principles, however, presented in his "Traité du bon goût en musique," that represents Lecerf's most original contribution. Taste, for Lecerf, is the absolute standard, the ultimate tool for discerning beauty and truth in music as in the other arts. As shown above, *bon goût* represents the critical function of pure reason as it is applied systematically to objects in the external world. With Lecerf and through the remainder of the century, good taste becomes practically synonymous with criticism itself.[84]

For Lecerf, as for the French classical critics, good taste represents the individual's capacity for judging works of art. This capacity depends fundamentally on instinctive feeling (Bouhours' "instinct of right reason"), but this instinct must be purified and clarified by an absolute adherence to the rules of art promulgated in ancient times and passed down through the centuries. For the first time in musical thought, the search for beauty becomes a *raison d'être* of criticism; thus, the two aspects of *bon goût* for Lecerf consist of 1) distinguishing what the beauties of music are, and 2) evaluating musical works according to the degree of beauty they possess. Lecerf's preface indicates how his criticism of Italian music fits into a new perspective:

> I had often thought that, although we have in our language sufficient treatises on music, we have no treatise that enters into a discussion of the *beauty* of our music. There are only treatises concerned with mechanics and craftsmanship, if I may say so; treatises which teach the rules in a dry manner, and none of which teaches us how to feel the esteem we ought to have for compositions which follow these rules. Not one leads gentlemen to judge as a whole the worth of a symphony or an air. I believed that there would be some merit and some glory in being the first to write a treatise of this nature.[85]

Lecerf goes on to comment that such a goal is easily achieved by refuting Raguenet's *Parallèle*, which is a perfect compendium of bad taste.

Lecerf's defintion of good taste therefore amounts to a definition of criticism, which in its essentials is simple: the judgment of works of art according to the beauty which they possess and, for the attainment of this end, a dependence on inward feeling guided by a strict adherence to the rules. These rules, aside from the minor precepts of the counterpoint treatises, consist of four major stipulations based on the principles enumerated above: that music should be natural, expressive, harmonious, and within the bounds of moderation.

To aid the amateur in becoming a person of good taste, Lecerf sets out a syllabus of areas to be mastered. First, the ear must be developed, for the person of good taste—or, in modern terms, the critic—must know, for example, when a band of violins is playing out of tune. Aside from this innate dependence on the ear, however, the remainder of Lecerf's advice concerns "knowing music in a rational manner" ("*sçavoir raisonnablement la Musique*"). Before any of the more esoteric aspects of the aesthetics of music can be undertaken, this involves a complete mastery of the basic craft of composition, which must be learned under the tutelage of a music master.

Next, the student must practice judging all the music he hears, forming an opinion not only as to whether it is good or bad, but to what degree it is either. Most concertgoers, says Lecerf, judge a piece by the amount of applause it receives or the fame of the composer. The true critic, on the other hand, asks whether it moves the heart as well as flatters the ear, whether it finds favor with his interior feelings besides following the rules. Lecerf gives an example from Lully's *Phaeton*, Act II, scene 3, the air "Que l'incertitude est un rigoreux tourment." This air certainly pleases the ear and follows the rules of being natural, simple, and harmonious. But examination proves it not to be expressive, for the text and music do not coincide: the heroine sings a song of lament, and yet the setting is gay; the air is therefore defective (see Example 6).

In contrast to this "reasoned taste" ("*goût de raisonnement*"), Lecerf offers another, simpler means of judgment, a "taste based on comparison" ("*goût de comparaison*"), by means of which the listener may have a touchstone of good taste fixed firmly in his mind. For example, "Bois épais," the famous air from Lully's *Amadis*, may be used as an infallible standard for sad airs (see Example 7). For certain results, the two types of taste based on reason and on comparison may be used to complement each other; such is the basis for the criticism of Lecerf's *Comparaison* itself.

Additional suggestions for developing good taste include knowing something about the composer of a piece, cultivating the company of professional musicians, and taking note of the reception of the piece by other people and other periods. This last suggestion, though not to be used exclusively, is important, for universal opinion outweighs individual opinion. In this sense Lecerf is quite democratic: "We should not flatter ourselves that our good sense is worth more than the good sense of the people."[86]

Lecerf's discussion of the opera audience documents a new attitude prevalent in the early eighteenth century. He divides the audience into two groups: the *sçavants* and the people (*le peuple*). The latter can be further subdivided into the *honnêtes hommes*—people of quality who frequent the opera though without necessarily being aware of its rules— and the populace, "shop boys, porters, cabaret servants, and cooks, who listen to *chansons* on the Pont Neuf and never go to the opera."[87] The *sçavants* tend to follow the rules blindly, the people to follow their individual sentiment, and a third classification, the *connoisseurs* (drawn from both classes), to follow sentiment and feelings, but with some knowledge of the rules.

Lecerf trusts first the judgment of the educated public, the *honnêtes hommes*, with whom the *connoisseurs* usually agree. He trusts least that of the *sçavants*, for their absorption in the rules of the craft, the *science*, makes them shortsighted as to the work's true aesthetic worth. The universality of reason and nature serves as a foundation for Lecerf's democratic view of taste: "Nature, which surpasses everything, speaks better, or rather speaks more loudly, by means of a thousand tongues than ten."[88]

Example 6.   Lully, "Que l'incertitude est un rigoureux tourment," from *Phaeton,* Act II, scene 3
Reprinted with the permission of Broude Brothers Ltd.

Example 7.　　Lully, "Bois épais," from *Amadis*, Act II,
scene 4
(Courtesy of *Revue musicale*, Editions Richard Masse, Paris)

som _ bre, Tu ne peux trop ca _ cher mon mal heu _ reux a _ mour Je sens un dés _ es _

_ poir dont l'horreur est ex _ trê _ me; Je ne dois plus voir ce que j'ai _ me

Je ne veux plus souf _ frir le jour Je sens un dés _ es _ poir dont l'horreur est ex _ trê _ me;

Je ne dois plus voir ce que j'ai _ me Je ne veux plus souf _ frir le jour.

The existence of this public of *honnêtes hommes* explains not only the opera audience of Lecerf's time, but also the audience to whom his treatise itself is directed. The count and countess of the dialogues serve as typical examples of the class: educated people, appreciative of good music and theater, widely read, but unversed in the technicalities of music. It is this amateur public whose tastes are to be shaped, and who actually have more potential for being good critics than the professional musicians themselves.

Lecerf sees himself, of course, as the critic *par excellence*. Neither he nor his spokesman in the dialogues, the chevalier, is a professional musician, but both presumably represent Lecerf's ideal critic. The chevalier is referred to as a critic in the first dialogue;[89] Lecerf says of himself in the disquisition on sacred music, "I speak as a critic, not as a preacher."[90] The essay on sacred music, and especially the final "Eclaircissement sur Bononcini," represents concrete examples of criticism such as Lecerf has advocated in the "Traité du bon goût." The chapter on Bononcini, for example, includes an analysis of the cantata *Arde il mio petto amante*,[91] which Lecerf chooses as one of the shortest and best of Bononcini's works ("for my own interests oblige me to choose one of the best," he says, "for fear of never finishing").[92] After pointing out the incongruities in the text, all typical of Italian poetry, Lecerf catalogues, measure by measure, the solecisms found in the music of the piece. These include 1) the mannerism of ending a phrase with a short note value followed by a rest, obscuring the word of text ending the phrase; 2) dissonances, including a diminished third in one place, and in another, the progression from a perfect fourth to a major seventh to a ninth, then back to a sixth and a fourth; 3) the ridiculous use of word-painting, as in a passage which rises and falls through two octaves to depict the rising and falling of lovers' eyes; and 4) the arbitrary use of melismas and vocalisms which have nothing to do with the sense of the text.

The cantate *Arde il mio petto amante* is not available for this study, but exerpts from two other cantatas by Bononcini, *Idolo mio tu sei* and *La Violetta* (Examples 8a and 8b), will show certain features criticized by Lecerf, especially dissonance treatment and the florid, instrumental character of the vocal line. Though these examples hardly seem extreme to twentieth-century listeners, Lecerf's comments may be better understood in the context of his touchstone of good taste, the air "Bois épais" (Example 7).

Although Lecerf speaks occasionally of the *goût français* and the *goût italien*, he is no advocate of national styles as such. At one point he apologizes for the overgeneralization of equating the Italian taste with *mauvais goût*, French taste with *bon goût*, for there are many Italians

Example 8a.　　Giovanni Bononcini, "Datti pace," from *Idolo*
mio tu sei
(Courtesy of Edizione Curci, Milan)

E. 9763 C.

Example 8b.　　Bononcini, "É bella e vezzosa la rosa," from
La Violetta
(Courtesy of Edizione Curci, Milan)

with good taste and many Frenchmen with bad taste. *Bon goût* for Lecerf always consists of an adherence to reason and nature; it is universal and unchanging, and any deviation automatically signals *mauvais goût*. Because so many Italians have departed from the dictates of reason and nature, they have gained a reputation for bad taste, just as the Germans have for wine and the Spaniards for women. (This does not mean, Lecerf explains dryly, that all Germans drink and all Spaniards have mistresses.)

In summary, Lecerf considers good taste the ability to judge works of music and to appreciate those which are good. The chevalier, Lecerf's symbol of good taste, judges music by standards of seventeenth-century French classicism and interprets his judgment for an amateur audience of *honnêtes hommes*, thus fulfilling the requirements of musical criticism as defined at the beginning of this chapter. However, not only does he evaluate and interpret music, he also presents a manual of good taste for teaching others the discernment required of the critic.

V

"Les goûts-réunis"

The quarrel of Lecerf and Raguenet encompassed many of the problems that were to occupy scholars and critics in the Age of Criticism. On the one hand, the controversy over the merits of French and Italian music grew to the proportions of a national pastime, providing an opportunity for passionate debate and occupying the finest minds of the Enlightenment as well as the fashionable *gens du monde*. On the other hand, the aesthetic concerns arising from the dispute mirrored a more general trend in eighteenth-century criticism. At the heart of the quarrel was the urgent question of taste. Were its laws absolute and immutable, or relative and variable from age to age, nation to nation, and even individual to individual? Could works of art flagrantly defy the standards set by the ancients and still have aesthetic value, and if so, could the definition of *bon goût* be expanded to comprehend such works? The task of the eighteenth-century critics was to find a system of thought that could admit a valid "relative" beauty, along with a "relative" taste, into the old fixed scheme of reason and rules.[1]

In his *Philosophie der Aufklärung*,[2] Ernst Cassirer attributes the beginnings of systematic aesthetics to the eighteenth-century application of philosophic principles to the discipline of criticism. He sees the development of a modern aesthetic system as a dialectic which found its synthesis only through the reconciliation of a series of opposing concepts:

> Whether it is the dispute between genius and the rules, the foundation of the sense of beauty in feeling or a certain form of knowledge: in all these syntheses the same fundamental problem recurs. It is as if logic and aesthetics, as if pure knowledge and artistic intuition, had to be tested in terms of one another before either of them could find its own inner standard and understand itself in the light of its own relational complex.[3]

In the eighteenth century, then, we see the culmination and eventual synthesis of the earlier dichotomies of reason and sense, authority and genius, universal and relative taste, objective and subjective theories of artistic value. The old insistence of the classical critics on the superiority of the ancients, and on universal standards and rules derived from them, is challenged and modified by a new subjectivism in the appreciation of art and a greater reliance on individual taste, which is largely determined by the appeal of the artwork to the senses rather than to reason.[4]

Surely one reason that the eighteenth-century disputes over French and Italian music so captured the imaginations of musicians, philosophers, and general public alike was that these different musical styles (in spite of their radical transformations and reciprocal influences) embodied in tangible form the underlying critical and aesthetic questions of the age. French music was seen by its partisans as the ideal embodiment of reason and the rules, the perfect imitation of *belle nature* and of ancient music drama, while Italian music was praised for its sonorous appeal to the senses, its manifestations of creative genius that could be apprehended through feeling rather than through knowledge.[5] If the specific arguments advanced on either side sometimes seem irrelevant to the question of the actual music, it is because of this representational use of music in the wider context. A look at the various philosophical inquiries into the nature of taste shows that, as criticism of the Enlightenment began to admit the value of both sensual and intellectual appeal in the artwork, so did musical thought come to admit the legitimacy of those opposing aspects into musical composition and criticism.[6]

Before Rameau

As we have seen in Chapter I, the leading French journals—the *Memoires de Trévoux* and the *Journal des savants*—participated actively in the debate over French and Italian opera. The journalists, more dispassionate than the contending parties in the quarrel, had offered the first suggestion that the French and Italian styles might be appreciated on their own merits, thus opening the way for the acceptance of varying but legitimate national styles. The exchange between Lecerf and the *"médecin-musicien"* had ended with the *Journal des savant*'s plea for a "dialectical truth" which would grow out of the quarrel,[7] and in comparing the musical quarrel to the literary controversy between Orsi and the followers of Bouhours, had stated:

> The reproaches of French writers can prevent the Italians from becoming too involved in the fire or the ingenuity of their imagination. But the contact with Italian authors can also perhaps contribute to bringing some of that fire and ingenuity to French works. . . .[8]

After the death of Lecerf and the withdrawal of Raguenet from the polemical arena, this conciliatory attitude was continued in a lengthy "Dissertation sur la musique italienne et française par Mr L. T." in the *Mercure de France* of 1713.[9] Though the author himself is inclined toward French music, he attempts a non-partisan description of the musical climate in Paris. The Italian party, he says, characterizes French music as "pale and tasteless, and altogether insipid," while the French partisans describe Italian music as "bizarre, capricious, and opposed to all the rules of art."[10] He emphasizes the existence of a third group, however, composed of those wishing to reconcile the two parties, giving justice to each country's music on its own merits. The author considers himself a member of this group, and evinces a certain broadmindedness in viewing music as simply another cultural difference between France and Italy:

> Does an Italian handle himself like a Frenchman? Their tastes, their habits, their modes, their manners, their pleasures, are not they all different? Why should it not be the same in their songs and playing of instruments? . . . Why should a Frenchman sing and play like an Italian? Each nation has its own practices: why dress up French music in a mask and render it extravagant, whose language is so naïve, and cannot suffer the least violence?[11]

According to the journalist, the best French music is that which incorporates the best qualities of Italian music without its excesses. The use of dissonance, for example, can enhance the expression of text as long as too frequent use does not diminish its effect, as in much Italian music. Monotony, on the other hand, is the corresponding vice of French music, and leaves it open to the criticism of the Italians. The musician of good taste knows what is proper to the distinctive styles, and what each can appropriate from the other without sacrificing its own integrity:

> Finally, from these two different parties there develops a third, more reasonable and less stubborn than the two others: the wise ones, the persons of good taste . . . who give justice to French music in its own right, and to Italian music in its own right, who agree that a perfect genre of music can result from the joining of the learned and ingenious taste of the Italians with the natural and simple good taste of the French. . . .[12]

It should be emphasized, however, that the *Mercure*'s endorsement of the concept of united tastes in this article is not without ambivalence, for an anti-Italian temperament asserts itself throughout and at times conflicts openly with the attempt at reconciliation. While the author theoretically accepts both national tastes, he tends, like many of the earlier literary critics, to associate the term *good* taste more frequently with the restrained simplicity of the French style:

> But if we concede them science and invention, should they not concede to us, with the same justice, the natural good taste which we possess, and the tender and noble execution in which we excel. . . .[13]

The article includes many of the accusations that Lecerf had leveled at Italian music. The journalist extends the analogy in which Lecerf had compared Italian music to a painted courtesan; he characterizes it as "well-painted, full of vivacity," inappropriately expressing tender passions by dancing the gavotte or gigue. French music, on the other hand, is "a beautiful woman, whose simple, natural and unaffected beauty draws at the heart of all of those who see her."[14]

The anonymous author grows more virulent in attacking the influx of cantatas and sonatas, whose excesses he fears will permanently corrupt French music:

> A musician no longer arrives here without one or the other in his pocket. . . . Cantatas are suffocating us here. What has become of good taste? Must it expire under the welter of all these cantatas? What would the Lamberts, the Boessets, the Le Camus, the Baptistes say if they returned to the world to see French song so changed, so degraded and disfigured?[15]

Unlike the critics, musicians saw the question of French and Italian music in a practical light. François Couperin, in the preface to his *Les goûts-réunis* (Paris, 1724),[16] readily admits the general acceptance of Italian instrumental music in France:

> Italian and French taste have shared for some time (in France) the republic of music; as for myself, I have always held in esteem things with merit without regard for author or nation. The first Italian sonatas which appeared in Paris over thirty years ago, and which then encouraged me to compose some, did harm neither to my reputation, nor to the works of Monsieur de Lulli, nor to those of my ancestors who were always more admirable than imitable.[17]

In this preface, Couperin announces his large trio sonata, *L'Apothéose de Corelli*, which represents a tribute to the Italian style, and proposes to undertake a similar piece in the French style as a tribute to Lully. Both works were included at the end of *Les goûts-réunis*, the former subtitled *Grande sonade en trio*, the latter *Concert instrumental*. Both pieces include programmatic titles to depict Corelli and Lully entering Parnassus; thus, though the Italian piece utilizes the Italian instrumental style, its whimsical titles are more in the French tradition. *L'Apothéose de Lully* includes an *Essai en forme d'Ouverture,* in typical French overture style, just after Apollo "persuades Lully and Corelli that the reunion of the French and Italian tastes should achieve perfection in music." This is followed by an Italian trio sonata, entitled "The Peace of Parnassus, made on the expostulations of the French muses, that in speaking their language, one should henceforth say *sonade, cantade,* as often as one says *ballade, sérénade,* etc."

Between the French overture and the Italian trio sonata, there are two airs for two violins, in the first of which "Lully plays the subject, and Corelli accompanies," and in the second, "Corelli takes his turn playing the subject, and Lully accompanies." The first is a very simple diatonic air; the second, though only slightly changed, intensifies the affection somewhat through the use of the minor key and mild dissonances (see Example 9).

The attempts at reconciliation offered in the *Journal des savants* (1706), the *Mercure* (1713), and by Couperin in his *Goûts-réunis,* effected a solution of sorts to the problem raised by Raguenet and Lecerf, and served to bring the controversy over French and Italian music to a temporary conclusion. Although comparisons of French and Italian music had a part in the polemics of the quarrel between *Lullistes* and *Ramistes* in the 1730s and 1740s, the most important discussions of the two styles before the War of the Buffoons at mid-century took place within the more reflective context of treatises on the arts and on good taste, works which taken together may be seen as forming the beginnings of the new aesthetics resulting from the interaction of philosophy and criticism. Unlike Lecerf's work, which had begun with the question of French and Italian music, gradually expanding to include discussions of taste and criticism, most of these treatises begin with the more general definition of beauty and taste in all the arts, and usually include ancillary chapters applying these definitions to music.

In general, the treatises are based on the premises of classical rationalism, but incorporate the new doctrine of sensibility to varying degrees. At one end of the spectrum we find theorists who, like Lecerf, regard music as an imitative art inseparable from language, an art to which the criteria of excellence in literature and drama can be transferred because of the primary importance of the expression of text. At the other end we find theorists who, drawing on the mechanistic rationalism of Descartes and the philosophy of sense perception developed by the British philosophers Locke and Hobbes,[18] emphasize the physiology of the passions as well as more scientific, geometrical criteria for beauty. Most systems fall somewhere between the two and attempt reconciliations of the extremes in various ways.

Example 9.   François Couperin, *L'Apothéose de Lully,* "Air
léger; Second Air pour deux violons"
(Courtesy of Editions de l'Oiseau Lyre, Monaco)

Air léger

POUR DEUX VIOLONS.

Lulli
jouant le Sujet;

et Corelli
l'acompagnant.

Second Air.

Corelli
jouant le Sujet
à son tour,

que Lulli
acompagne.

*On joue ces 2 Airs deux fois
chacun alternativement.*

Jean-Pierre de Crousaz (1663–1750), the Swiss philosopher whose *Traité de beau* appeared in Amsterdam in 1715,[19] was one of the first enthusiastic champions of sensibility and relativity of taste in music; the requirements for beauty which result from his theory are derived from scientific sources—chiefly physics and geometry—rather than from literary classicism. Crousaz gives a new direction to the distinction between universal and relative taste by attributing the first to geometric qualities: unity, variety, order, proportion, and regularity; the second to the physical senses and feelings which vary according to the individual's capacity. Moreover, he draws a sharp distinction between beauty of ideas and beauty of sentiment, the first related to universal taste and the second to relative, or individual, taste. Both are valid, though an object which appeals both to the ideas (such as a perfect circle or a mathematical formula) and to the senses (such as a taste or a sound) may be said to possess a double beauty.

For Crousaz, good taste depends on an equal partnership of reason and feeling: "Good taste makes us judge by sentiment what reason has approved, after having had the time to judge on the basis of correct ideas."[20] All of this applies to the apprehension of beauty in music,[21] but Crousaz emphasizes especially the relativity of musical beauty. He attributes this to the differences in "humor" among human beings (music which pleases one causes inquietude in another, for example), and the differences in the manner in which musical sounds interact with the physical senses.

The *Réflexions critiques* of the abbé Dubos (Paris, 1719) has been recognized as one of the most cogent attempts at a synthesis of the classical doctrine of imitation and the new doctrine of sensibility.[22] Dubos sees sentiment, or sensation, as an immediate sensual perception akin to seeing or tasting, and assigns it a place more important than reason in the judgment of a work of art:

> Sentiment is a far better guide to whether a work touches us, and makes the impression it is supposed to make, than all the dissertations composed by critics to explain its merits and calculate its perfections and faults. The means of discussion and analysis which these gentlemen use is indeed good as long as the concern is to find the reasons why a work pleases or does not please; but this way is not as good as that of sentiment when the concern is to answer the question, "Does the work please, or does it not?" It is the same thing. Reason should only intervene in the general judgment we make on a poem or a painting to support a decision of sentiment, and to explain which faults prevent it from being pleasing, and which are the pleasing aspects which make it attractive.[23]

Alfred Lombard interprets Dubos' work not only as a synthesis of reason and sense, but also as a solution to the old quarrel between Ancients and Moderns, which in France had reached its final phases in these years.[24] If sentiment is the true judge of a work, it is no longer necessary to depend upon the precepts of Aristotle to defend ancient works; the proof of their worth is the favorable verdict of sentiment over many centuries. While stressing personal response to the object of art, Dubos deemphasizes the individuality of taste. He attributes bizarre, unorthodox taste to a defect in the mechanism of the body's sensual perception, thus returning "by an indirect route to the universal dogmas of the old [classical] criticism."[25]

Dubos also remains true to the ideal of the imitation of nature, achieved through the expression of the passions. The chapters on music[26] are conservative in this respect: Dubos deplores the interest in agreeable singing and rich harmony at the expense of expressiveness, and finds the number of those conforming to this taste all too great. Always stressing relationships among poetry, painting, and music, Dubos compares music with only richness of harmony and variety of modulation to paintings with nothing more than color, or poetry with nothing more than rhyme. Technical knowledge of composition, like knowledge of versification, should be a handmaid to expression, not (to use Dubos' metaphor) the "mistress of the house." This, of course, is often not the case since it is easier to compose facile poetry and "learned" music than to attain to the truly pathetic in either of these arts.

A large portion of Dubos' chapters on music is devoted to the question of French and Italian taste, and again his views represent the more conservative aspects of his theory. Like Lecerf, Dubos relates his comparison to that of ancient and modern music, finding the same expressiveness in Lully's operas that had been claimed for ancient music. He quotes a passage from Isaac Vossius[27] favoring ancient music because of its expressiveness, but maintains that if Vossius had known the works of Lully, his opinion would have been altered to include that composer in his approbation. The unity of word and tone which places Lully's operas on a level with ancient music is not to be found, however, in Italian music, and if Vossius had compared the Italian "sonatas and cantatas" with the works of Lully, there is no doubt that his preference would have been for the French composer.

The chapter on Italian music[28] uses a passage from the Italian writer Giovanni Vincenzo Gravina to summarize the case against Italian music. This passage, taken from Gravina's *Della tragedia* (Naples, 1715), foreshadows the later critiques of modern Italian opera by Benedetto Marcello and Francesco Algarotti.[29] Gravina voices the familiar complaint that modern dramatic music no longer produces the same effects as that of the ancients. Wheras vocal music ought to reproduce the "natural language of the passions," instead it tries to imitate canaries. Gravina blames the corruption of music upon the previous corruption of literature:

> But our poetry having been corrupted by the excess of ornaments and figures, the corruption has spread from there to our music. It is the fate of all the arts, which have a common origin and object, that contagion passes from one to the other. Our music is therefore so filled with trifles that it is difficult to recognize in it any trace of natural expression.[30]

The remainder of Dubos' chapter attempts to prove that the renaissance of music after the "barbarism" of the Middle Ages was due not to the Italians, as others had maintained, but to the musicians of the Low Countries. Here we see the intersection of new historical modes of thought with the question of French and Italian music, and we recall the use of historical documentation in Lecerf to prove the superiority of ancient music to modern, thereby proving French music superior to Italian.

The first French history of music, the *Histoire de la musique et de ses effets* by Bonnet-Bourdelot,[31] had indeed appeared only four years before Dubos' work. It is intimately associated with the quarrels over French and Italian music, for its second edition contains not only the history proper, but also a reprint of the "Dissertation" which had first appeared in the *Mercure* in 1713, as well as a full reprint of Lecerf's *Comparaison*.[32] Bonnet himself acknowledges the superiority of French music in his dedication to the Duc d'Orléans:

> Music is a heroine, who, after having run her course for four thousand years, in all the courts of the world, comes to give an account of her conquests to her Protector, the most enlightened Prince in Europe.
>
> The favorable asylum you have given her, Monseigneur, will forever be a monument to the esteem and taste you have showed her and will mark the time during which French Music has equalled, nay, possibly surpassed, that of other nations, due to the great Progress she has made since the establishment of *l'Académie Royale de Musique* in this flourishing kingdom. . . .[33]

The inclusion of the *Comparaison* in Bonnet-Bourdelot's *Histoire* marks the beginning of the disassociation of Lecerf's name from his authorship of the work. As a part of the larger historical treatise, the *Comparaison* appeared more academic than polemical, and except for a biographical notice written by Lecerf's brother in the *Mercure* of 1726,[34] the original quarrel as well as its protagonists were almost entirely forgotten.

The *Parallèle* and the *Comparaison*, however, remained influential well into the eighteenth century. In 1732 an *Essai sur le bon goust en musique* by Nicolas Ragot de Grandval was published in Paris. Examination reveals this work to be a pirated version of the "Traité du bon goût en musique" from Lecerf's *Comparaison*. Grandval, a church organist and composer of theatrical *divertissements*,[35] deserves credit for making of Lecerf's long, discursive dialogue a concise *précis*, retaining and clarifying the main ideas while eliminating the repetitive passages as well as the *galant* conversations of Lecerf's characters.

Lecerf's "Traité du bon goût," following his defense of ancient music, does not itself compare French and Italian music, though it rests on the tacit assumption of the former's superiority. Grandval's work departs from Lecerf's only in this one respect: following the general trend of early eighteenth-century thought, it calls for an acceptance of both national styles. In the early part of the treatise Grandval makes a pointed reference to his esteem for the Italians:

> It is necessary to do justice to everyone. Let us say that among the musicians of Italy, there are those infinitely appealing, who know how to join to *science* (which they possess in general to a much higher degree than ourselves) beautiful and natural melody. . . . Which I confess openly in order to make it known that I, far from attacking their good music, embrace the beautiful wherever it may be found, and know nothing more estimable than the good Italian composers.[36]

And in closing, Grandval declares himself not only on the side of modern and Italian music, but also, unlike Lecerf, on that of instrumental music:

> . . . nourish yourselves on good things, that is to say, perform only that music recognized as good by general consent, as is that of Lully, of our good Moderns, and the choice airs of several composers of Italy, of which there is a large number of estimable ones, especially symphonies.[37]

Lullistes and Ramistes

Only a year after the publication of Grandval's treatise, the first performance of J. P. Rameau's *Hippolyte et Aricie* (1733) shattered the temporary calm of the musical world and sparked the second *querelle* of the century, that between the conservative followers of Lully and the progressive partisans of Rameau. Paul-Marie Masson[38] assesses this revival of hostilities as a direct continuation of the quarrel between Raguenet and Lecerf, for Rameau's style was viewed by the conservatives as a blatant capitulation to Italian bad taste. In a more general sense, it represented another clash between the advocates of simplicity and expressiveness in music and those of complexity and sonority.[39]

A typical Lullist's position may be seen in the humorous allegorical piece submitted to the *Mercure* in May 1734,[40] the "Lettre de M *** à Mlle *** sur l'origine de la musique." According to this account, music was invented by the child of Eros and Psyche, whose "tender, pure, true, strong, constant and faithful" love lent its character to the music:

> . . . all the music of the ballet was characterized in such a way that, with the eyes closed, one could guess what the dancers were doing and almost follow the different figures of the ballet, so much did the same expression reign in the music and the dance; it seemed that both sprang from the same nature; and without one's being aware of it, the dance reflected the most delicate nuances of the sweet passions expressed by the sounds.[41]

Venus, however, was obliged to appease anti-Eros and his wife Cithère by building them a theater and commissioning music for it:

> Everyone worked in hopes of composing music, everyone boasted his work and the pain it caused him, even the geometers became involved, they praised the immense calculations they made to find means of employing in the violin airs all the possible combinations of *re* and *mi* with the other notes; it is true that this air had no melody, and in this constrained music so painful to compose, nothing flowed naturally, no genius animated it, they fled nature and sentiment. . . . Sadness replaced tenderness, the singular partook of the baroque, fury of [mere] babbling. . . ."[42]

An important point is made in the closing portion of this allegory. No longer can the quarrel be confined to the simplistic opposition of two national styles; discernment must be more sophisticated, it must be guided by taste:

> . . . do not believe that the two musics came exclusively from one country: the two musics have spread in all countries, your heart and your taste will tell you which is their origin.[43]

Another amusing document dating from the later years of the quarrel (1748) is a chapter from Denis Diderot's *roman à clef, Les bijoux indiscrèts*.[44] In this novel, Louis XV and the personages of his court are represented as the sultan and inhabitants of the exotic land of Banza, where opera is enjoyed. At the moment of the novel two composers occupy the operatic stage: Utmiutsol (Lully) and Uremifasolasiututut (Rameau):

> Of all the spectacles of Banza, only opera persisted. Utmiutsol and Uremifasolasiututut, celebrated musicians, one of whom was beginning to age while the other was just born, occupied alternatively the lyric scene. These two original composers each

had his partisans: the ignorant and the bearded ones supported Utmiutsol; the youth and the virtuosos were for Uremifasolasiututut; and the persons of taste, young as well as old, made a case for both.

> Uremifasolasiututut, said the latter, is excellent when he is good, but he nods from time to time and who does not? Utmiutsol is more sustained and even: he is full of beauties; however he possesses none which are not found, and even more strikingly, in his rival, in whom one finds traits which are his alone and not to be found except in his works. The old Utmiutsol is simple, natural, unified—too much so at times— and that is his fault. The young Uremifasolasiututut is singular, brilliant, "composed," learned—too learned at times—but that is perhaps the fault of the listener. . . . Nature leads Utmiutsol in melody's paths, study and experience have shown Uremifasolasiututut the sources of harmony. Who can declaim, and who will ever recite like the ancient? Who gives us light *ariettes*, voluptuous airs and character symphonies like the modern?[45]

It was amidst the controversy between Lullists and Ramists that treatises on good taste and beauty began to proliferate, and in these we find the underlying aesthetic implications of the squabbles over the new music and the old. The first treatise to annouce itself as a study of taste was François Cartaud de la Vilate's *Essai historique et philosophique sur le goût* (Amsterdam, 1736). The plan of the work is novel, showing a new comprehension of the division between the historical and systematic aspects of taste. The first part, on the history of taste, describes chronologically the types of artistic creation that appealed to the Greeks, the Romans, and other civilizations up to the present. In discussing contemporary Italian taste, Cartaud takes an opportunity to denounce its exaggerated *concetti*, stating:

> I have never been able to understand why men of a character so enamored of commerce, and with such profound judgment in affairs of state, would have an imagination so unruly and incapable of containment.[46]

The systematic portion of the discussion begins with the always-pressing question, "Is taste arbitrary?" Cartaud, like Crousaz, categorizes beauty into two types, the first of which is universal, depending on a consistency of taste, the second of which may be arbitrary, depending on an inconsistency of taste. Examples of the latter are a Moroccan woman, considered beautiful only in Morocco, or a face considered beautiful only when reflected by firelight.

Cartaud's discussion of taste in relation to music proper is grounded more in the physical/mechanistic aesthetic of Crousaz than in the classical aesthetic of Lecerf. Thus, according to him, our responses to music depend primarily on the mechanism of the brain and the effects of musical proportion on the ear. Although our bodies, however, resemble "little machines," their responses to stimuli can be quite flexible, especially in early development.

Cartaud sees the differences between French and Italian taste in the context of this mechanistic orientation. The early flexibility of physical responses accounts for the fact that the French and the Italians quickly grow accustomed to their own musical styles. If Italian music, then, does not please the French, it is because of their "organs": Italians can enjoy more complicated counterpoint without becoming confused because their ears have been trained to hear all the parts.

All of this relates to the quarrel between Lullists and Ramists because of the rapprochement of the French style and of the Italian and the gradual change in the physical response of the French to a more complex idiom: "Today our brains are beginning to become Italian, and those who never saw [the operas of] M. Lully do not even realize it."[47] Lully's partisans, says Cartaud, accuse harmony of becoming geometric and learned without touching the passions, like poetry written in a fine style but with only algebraic formulas for content. Italian music, too absorbed in its appeal to the educated ear, neglects the heart, and because of its emphasis on harmony and instrumental music, leads music away from the expression of the passions. Cartaud himself favors French music, but admits that ears that have been trained to listen to complicated music might find Lully's works too simple and lacking in variety. He concludes that perfection in the art of music may be obtained only through the reconciliation of Italian compositional technique with French simplicity and naïveté.

One of the most comprehensive and intellectually rigorous treatments of the concept of beauty, Yves-Marie (père) André's *Essai sur le beau*, was published in Paris in 1741.[48] André announces in his first paragraph the furor attending contemporary discussions of the beautiful, and proceeds immediately to the heart of the problem:

> . . . whether the beautiful is something absolute or relative? If there is an essential beauty, independent of all institutions, a fixed beauty, immutable? A beauty which pleases, or has the right to please, in China as well as in France . . . or whether, finally, it is with beauty as with modes and fashions, whose success depends on the caprice of men, on opinion and on taste.[49]

André proposes a solution to the dilemma by introducing a synthesis based on the acceptance of three different types of beauty: 1) an ideal, essential beauty, Platonic, based on order, symmetry and number; 2) a natural beauty based on the physical laws of nature but still independent of men's opinion and taste; and 3) an arbitrary beauty found in human institutions, a beauty consisting of "happy irregularities" founded on genius, taste and sometimes even caprice.

Of all the eighteenth-century theorists, André displays perhaps the most thorough grasp of the aesthetic problem of sense versus reason. He is the first, moreover, to trace this dichotomy to the Greeks, specifically to Pythagoras and Aristoxenus, the former of whom:

> . . . succeeded in pleasing the reason, not a great merit according to the populace; and he did not satisfy the ear, for which his music seemed too simple, too dry, too abstract, which is always a great fault. . . . After more than a century, Aristoxenus tried to remedy this . . . he was then accused of trying to please the ear more than the reason.[50]

Passing briefly over the various attempts to reconcile sense and reason, namely those of Ptolemy, Zarlino, Huyghens, and Sauveur, André finds the most successful synthesis not in theory, but in the *tragédie-lyrique* of Lully. Referring to Rameau as the "new musician," André declines to speak of his achievement in this respect until his works are better established.

André's discussion of the conflict between reason and sense leads directly to his summary of the eighteenth-century versions of that conflict: the quarrels between Ancients and Moderns, French and Italians, Lullists and Ramists. Concerning the first, he says:

> But shall we say nothing of the famous quarrel between the partisans of ancient music and those of the modern? This question does not fit into my scheme; however, if after having read all the authors that I could find on music, I may only be permitted to tell the impression I am left with, I will render it in three words. The ancients are the fathers of music; they have established all the principles, and by the musical taste which their works have imparted to century after century, they have produced in our century children, of whom the majority no longer know their fathers, and of whom others, more ungrateful, refuse to know them.[51]

To André, the quarrels over French and Italian music have succeeded more than those of Ancients and Moderns in placing sense and reason in perspective. Though André admits both sense and reason, he feels that the latter, whose share was equal in the music of Lully, may lose its place altogether in the current rage for Italian music. In the past, Italian opera served as a foil to display the natural beauties of the *tragédie-lyrique*. André fears the present tendency to think of Lully as an "ancient," thereby relegating him to the status of the Greeks and giving the advantage to the more modern composers and the influence of fashion:

For sixty years French music, which was content in its compositions modestly to decorate nature, won out, without contradiction, over the brilliance of Italian music. Lully, Italian in genius and by birth, but French by education and in taste, was everywhere victorious . . . but for several years Lully has begun to become an ancient. That is the fatal moment of the revolution: it suffices to a thousand people to relegate him almost to the status of the Greeks. He is still, however, not so abandoned that he does not have a number of partisans, but how long will they hold out against the torrent of fashion?[52]

André, then, while admitting relativity into his theory of beauty in music, remains conservative in finding the ideal synthesis of sense and reason in the older music of Lully. He speaks out against the empiricists, for whom sentiment is the only judge of harmony, and the ear the only judge of beauty; for whom no universal rules of art exist. André insists, on the other hand, that in spite of individual taste and the existence of valid national schools, universal reason should at least equal the importance of sensual pleasure in the apprehension of artistic beauty, and that chance and irregularity should not be allowed to rage unchecked.[53]

One of the most conservative of all the theorists of beauty and taste is the abbé Pluche, whose *Spectacle de la nature* (Paris, 1746)[54] represents an encyclopedic investigation of the arts and sciences. As the title of the chapter "Des professions instructives" would indicate, Pluche sees the goal of music, as of painting and writing, to be instructive, and considers the idea of sensual pleasure an absolute corruption of music's ideal. Pleasure for pleasure's sake, he writes, is a reversal: "Let us use a clearer term," he adds, "it is a prostitution."[55] Lecerf's belief in the profound unity of music and text remains at the heart of Pluche's aesthetic, and pleasure without expressiveness is to Pluche the second greatest crime after pleasure without instruction. Pluche also follows Lecerf in condemning instrumental music for "speaking to the ear while saying nothing to the soul,"[56] and he claims that the most beautiful instrumental melody must of necessity be cold and dull because it remains expressionless.

All the arts, according to Pluche, are connected by their common aim, which is instruction, by their common method, which is imitation, and finally by their common means of pleasing, which is the understanding and use of taste. Pluche, like Lecerf, equates taste with discretion, moderation, and *bon sens*. Simplicity and the absence of excessive embellishment in the work of art do not assure beauty, but are the prerequisites for its emergence and apprehension.

Pluche's discussion of French and Italian music reflects the change in musical thought effected by the conflict between Lullists and Ramists. Since Rameau and his followers are seen as having assimilated the Italian style into their own works, the former distinctions between French and

Italian music must now be applied to two different styles of French composition. The terms of the argument must be extended, therefore, to define two conflicting aesthetics of music in a more abstract technical manner
than the familiar dichotomy between French and Italian music.

Without naming Lecerf and Raguenet, Pluche admits that the quarrel over French and Italian music has changed since its inception. The
French, although friends of melody, now admit more "fire and harmony"
into their music than in the previous century, while Italian music, though
still more contrapuntal and learned, steadily becomes more "gracious
and charming."[57] Pluche attributes the turn toward compositional complexities and liberties in performance to Rameau and his followers, who
have brought music beyond the point "even to which the Italians had
carried it."[58]

Pluche, while seemingly an advocate of a French-Italian synthesis,
finally reveals himself as a partisan as biased as Lecerf. "Fire and harmony," in his opinion, cannot suffice in the same way as expressive melody to produce beauty of the first order in music. Like Dubos, he compares
beautiful sounds in music to color in painting: neither can support a
lasting pleasure in itself, but must exist as an adjunct to more meaningful
forms of expression.

Since "French" and "Italian" no longer designate opposite musical
styles, Pluche chooses the terms *chantante* and *barroque* for the two
styles in question.[59] Though he proposes an objective investigation of
each, his opening description quickly reveals his preference:

> One finds its melody in the natural sounds of our vocal chords, and in the accents
> of the human voice, which speaks to inform others of what touches us; always
> without grimace, always without effort, almost without art. This we call *la musique
> chantante*. The other attempts to surprise by the boldness of sounds and to pass for
> singing in measuring fast runs and noise: this we call *la musique barroque*.[60]

Pluche extends his metaphor to a mock "transaction" between the
Departments of *Musique barroque* and *Musique chantante*. The rights of
the former include possession of spectacles and public concerts where
meaningless sonatas are played, and the use of esoteric languages or ridiculous nonsense words and baby-talk. The rights of the latter include
possession of all sober, ecclesiastical music which shuns the absurdities
of the theater, the predominance of melody over harmony, and entry into
public taste by means of expressive text.

Pluche includes a revealing passage on performance practice, showing that the differences between "singing" and "barroque" music were
well understood and hotly disputed not only by the public, but also by

performers of his day. The violinist Guignon,[61] who represents the *baroque* style of the virtuoso school, wastes his talents by seeking only to amuse and surprise. Baptiste Anet,[62] on the other hand, represents the *chantante* style of the school favoring imitation of the human voice, which pleases through "sweet and varied emotions." Pluche quotes Anet's criticism of the virtuoso style, saying, "It is the painful search for baroque pearls at the bottom of the sea, while diamonds are to be found on the surface of the earth."[63] Finally, the composer and artist Mondonville[64] excels in both tastes, and both parties place him at their head; Pluche reproaches him for encouraging this division, which threatens to become a civil war.

In the same year as Pluche's essay, another conservative theorist of taste, Bollioud de Mermet, published a treatise on the subject of good taste in music, *De la corruption du goust dans la musique françois* (Lyon, 1746). Probably influenced by Anne Lefebvre Dacier's *Des causes de la corruption du goût* (Paris, 1705) as well as by Lecerf's *Comparaison*, Bollioud applies the classical standards of reason, imitation, and expressiveness to the music of his time. Though he admits that music has improved over the past two centuries, and that modern music has improved over ancient, he complains that since the time of Lully French taste has degenerated: "The constitution of our music has changed so much that one might say we had ceased being French, and had been transplanted to another region!"[65]

Bollioud chides the composers of his country for seeking the bizarre, singular, surprising, and astonishing at the expense of the rules and a true expression of the text. He further criticizes French performers for ignoring the intentions of the composer: singers attempt to imitate the brilliant passagework of instrumentalists, and instrumentalists, who should imitate the natural sounds of the human voice, strive only for virtuoso effects.

The invasion of Italian music is blamed for these faults, but according to Bollioud, Italian taste is not necessarily bad. Corruption lies in the attempt of Frenchmen to incorporate the Italian style into their own music, producing a "bizarre and evil mixture of the French and Italian taste." French composers flatter themselves that they imitate the Italian manner well, but they are in no position to judge. The Italians are wiser, understanding better the gulf that separates their music from that of the French; an Italian composer who tried to incorporate the French style into his own music would become a laughingstock in Italy.

According to Bollioud, there is one central cause for this tendency of French composers to throw away their own genius so foolishly: lack of good taste. Answering the charge that the dominant taste of a country and a historical period changes, Bollioud still insists along with the seventeenth-century classicists that "there is a certain truth in the arts as elsewhere, which is of all eras and of all nations. Reason and nature, which never change, have established laws, against which variations and *bizarreries* introduced by artists cannot prevail."[66] Only this is true taste: "*C'est le Goût. C'est le vrai Goût.*"

One year after the discussions of Pluche and Bollioud, André Batteux, professor of rhetoric at the *Collège royal* of Navarre, published his *Les beaux arts réduits à un même principe* (Paris, 1747). Batteux's work, like that of Pluche and Bollioud, grows out of the seventeenth-century classical tradition of expressiveness and imitation; only the emphasis is different, showing the eighteenth-century trend towards expanded discussions of taste and an understanding of all the arts within the context of *bon goût*.

As the title indicates, the conservative thesis of Batteux's book is the common principle at the basis of all the arts, which is imitation of *belle nature*;[67] sharing this principle, the arts are incomplete in themselves and must interact with one another if the demands of taste are to be met. Music, poetry, and dance are seen as the primary arts, forming the foundations of theatrical productions, with architecture, painting, and sculpture in the supporting role of setting the scene. All music must possess what Batteux calls "significance," an appeal to the intellect, and this can be achieved only through the combination of words and music. Along with Pluche and Lecerf, Batteux believes that instrumental music can never be fully satisfying because of its failure in this respect:

> If music has any significance in the symphony, where it has only a half-life, a portion of its potential, how much more would it have in song, where it becomes the tableau of the human heart?[68]

Batteux opposes theorists such as Crousaz, who find a certain beauty in the proportions of the tones, or the geometry of the consonances; he compares such beauty to that of a prism, which reflects colors without representing an object, or to a chromatic harpsichord piece, whose passage work and colorful harmonies "perhaps amuse the eyes but certainly tire the spirit."[69]

Batteux's central section on taste, along with the discussion of Cartaud and Bollioud, represents one of the most extensive treatments in the early part of the century. His position on the argument over the existence of a universal good taste as opposed to different relative tastes is stated flatly in his opening sentence, "There is a good taste."[70] It is to the arts what intelligence is to the sciences: a means of discerning the good and the beautiful, as in science intelligence is a means of discerning the true.

Taste never changes, and it regulates all the arts through its immutable laws, the first of which is the imitation of *belle nature*. Antiquity serves as a model for modern artists just as nature did for ancient artists, and because the moderns lose touch with nature in imitating only copies, art has degenerated.

Time and again, Batteux returns to his central thesis: there is one good taste, that which leads us to *belle nature*, and any other taste is necessarily bad. Once this has been sufficiently emphasized, however, Batteux aligns himself with André in finding a place within his scheme for the concept of individual tastes, which he calls *goûts en particulières*.[71] Tastes can be different, then, while still true to nature and thus good:

> However, one sees different tastes in men and nations which have the reputation of being enlightened and cultivated. Will we be so bold as to prefer our own to the others, and to condemn theirs? That would be temerity, if not outright injustice: because particular tastes can be different, even opposed, without ceasing to be good in themselves. The reason is found on one hand, in the richness of nature, and on the other, in the reaches of the heart and the human spirit.[72]

The richness of nature and the infinite possibilities of using its materials are compared to the many different perspectives from which an artist may depict his model: each face will be different, and yet the model remains the same.

Batteux's comparison of French and Italian music is seen in this context. Both are imitations of *belle nature*, although from a different perspective; both are manifestations of the universal *bon goût*, though their particular tastes are opposed:

> French music and Italian music both have their own characters. One is not good music, the other bad. They are two sisters, or rather the two faces of the same model.[73]

Out of the original quarrel, then, between Lecerf and Raguenet, and its continuation in the Lully-Rameau controversy, two important critical trends occurred. The first was a broadening of the definition of *bon goût* in music: a new willingness to include the appeal to both sense and reason within the realm of taste, and a move toward the acceptance of French and Italian music as valid national idioms. The second, a corollary to the first, was a growing awareness of the concept of style, which may be seen in the attempt to render stylistic descriptions and definitions, such as Pluche's *musique chantante* and *musique barroque*. These developments formed the foundations on which more modern critical techniques, especially those introduced by the Encyclopedists, could be based.

The War of the Buffoons

The middle of the century saw the rise of the Encyclopedists and the transformation of the continuing controversy over French and Italian music into the *guerre des bouffons*. Again, it was neither the venomous pamphlets traded by the more belligerent members of the two parties nor the morsels of wit published in the journals, but rather the penetrating critical minds of the Encyclopedists, particularly Diderot, d'Alembert, Rousseau, and Grimm, that coaxed new insights from the old quarrel.

At mid-century, however, none of these critics had become the ardent champions of Italian music for which later ages would know them. Jean-Jacques Rousseau's letter to Friedrich Melchior Grimm,[74] in fact, written in 1750, could almost be taken for the work of a Lecerf or a Pluche. Beginning with the quality of the libretti, he sees those of Quinault as far superior to those of Metastasio, not only because of their regularity and nobility, but also their more successful imitation of nature and their suitability for operatic conventions. Italian opera libretti, on the other hand, are "a fabric of completely trivial conversations of fourteen or fifteen hundred lines, divided into three acts and sung through four mortal hours; that is the taste of the Italians with regard to the poem."[75] As for the music, the Italians have brought its sheer sonority to the height of perfection, knowing better than any other composers how to compose brilliantly for voices and instruments. Moreover, the Italian style fits other languages better than the French style, which is so intimately tied to the French language. However, using the old classical criteria of expressiveness and appeal to the passions, Rousseau finds Italian music devoid of worth:

> Italian music pleases me without touching me. French music pleases me because it touches me. The *fredons*, the *passages*, the *traits*, the *roulements* of the first make the vocal organ sound brilliant and charm the ears, but the seductive sounds of the second go straight to the heart. If music is only made to please, let us give the palm to Italy, but if it should also move, let us keep it for our own music, and especially when it is a question of opera which is supposed to excite the passions and to touch the spectator.[76]

Rousseau ends his letter with the standard criticisms that Italian opera orchestras, composed only of strings, lack the variety and beauty of the French, and that Italian opera choruses, employing only the principal singers, "are hardly worth the name."[77]

Another precursor to the actual *guerre des bouffons* was Grimm's "Lettre sur *Omphale*" (1752), a pamphlet attacking Destouches' opera of that name.[78] Though Grimm claims to judge French music on its own merits, he cannot help showing his preference for Italian music, both for its superior forms of recitative and aria and for the sheer pleasure it gives to "everyone with ears." Most important for the present discussion is a new element which Grimm brings to the controversy over French and Italian music: a direct attack on French music, not for its failure to provide the same kind of pleasure as Italian music, but for its failure on its own grounds, those of good taste, fidelity to nature, and expressiveness. The French advocates, says Grimm:

> . . . speak of taste, of the natural, and of expression which are found in the music of this opera, and it is precisely these things which I wish to attack. In my opinion, this music is from one end to the other in bad taste and full of contradictions, lugubrious, without any expressiveness, and always inappropriate to its subject, which itself is the worst fault of all.[79]

The actual *guerre des bouffons*, of course, did not officially begin until after the performance of Giovanni Battista Pergolesi's *opera buffa*, *La serva padrona* (1733), on August 1, 1752.[80] While Grimm's "Lettre sur *Omphale*" served only as a precursor of the war, his later *Petit prophète de Boehmischbroda* (Paris, 1753)[81] is considered one of the major pieces of the quarrel of the *bouffons*. In it he satirizes French music and performance practice at the *Opéra*, and in the mock-Biblical tone of the prophets, he warns the French not to call "baroque" that which is harmonious, or "simple" that which is dull. If the French do not mend their ways, they will be doomed to their own boring music, never learning to appreciate the genius of the Italians.

Grimm's pamphlet was answered by a writer of the pro-French forces, Mathieu François Mairobert de Pidansat, whose *Réponse du coin du roi au coin de la reine* (Paris, 1753) claims briefly that Italian music is too "light and coquettish," whereas only French music can adequately portray the passions in a serious manner.[82] Pidansat also wrote a parody of the *Petit prophète*, called *Les prophéties du grand prophète Monet* (Paris, 1753).

Both of these attacks were skilfully countered by the Encyclopedist and able critic Denis Diderot.[83] His *Arrêt-rendu à l'amphithéâtre de l'opéra* (Paris, 1753)[84] refutes Pidansat's *Réponse* point by point, scornfully calling the author "the young lawyer" and caustically chiding him for "responding" when no one had spoken to him. Much more important for the history of musical criticism, however, is Diderot's *Au petit prophète de*

Boehmischbroda et au grand prophète Monet (Paris, 1753).[85] Of the
hundreds of pamphlets and articles written in the *guerre des bouffons*,
this is one of the few to rise above the level of wit and venom and to
display an objective critical attitude.

Addressing both Grimm and Pidansat (the "petit" and "grand"
prophets), Diderot opens by stating:

> I have read, gentlemen, your little works, and the only thing they would have taught
> me, if I had not known it already, was that you have a great deal of spirit and an
> excess of wickedness. . . . But after allowing you to act like *beaux esprits* and inspired
> prophets as much as you please, could one invite you to descend from the sublimity
> of the *bon mot* and to lower yourselves to the level of common sense?[86]

Diderot goes on to offer a method of comparative criticism that, if heeded,
would transfer the quarrel of the *bouffons* to a higher level. He challenges
the protagonists of each side to take the famous monologue from Lully's
Armide and to set against it a similar scene from Terradellas' *Nitocris*.[87]
Both operas are tragedies, and both scenes place the heroine in a similar
dramatic situation; both employ beautiful music worthy of serious criticism:

> The opera *Armide* is the *chef-d'oeuvre* of Lully, and the monologue is the *chef-
> d'oeuvre* of this opera. Defenders of French music will be, I hope, most satisfied
> with my choice; however, either I understand poorly the enthusiasts of Italian music,
> or they will have taken a great step forward if they show us that the scenes from
> *Armide* are in comparison with those from *Nitocris* only a languishing psalmody, a
> melody without fire, without soul, force, or genius; that the musician of France owes
> everything to his poet, and that to the contrary the poet of Italy owes everything to
> his musician.[88]

Diderot pleads with the Italians and the French alike to compare
their music, measure by measure and note by note. He warns the French
not to hide behind their language, saying that *Armide* is superior to anything that could be composed to a French text: "It is not a question of
the libretti, but of the music, not a comparison of Quinault and Metastasio, but of Lully and Terradellas." If the music itself becomes the focus
of the quarrel, Diderot argues, then reason will replace personalities,
common sense will replace epigrams, and enlightenment will replace
"prophesies."

Diderot's admonition went unheeded by most of the later pamphlet-
eers, who continued to attack each other on grounds coincidental to the
central question of musical style. At least one writer, however, attempted
to face squarely the challenge posed by Diderot; this was Jean-Jacques
Rousseau, in his *Lettre sur la musique française* (Paris, 1753).[89] By 1753,
Rousseau's opinion has changed radically from his earlier letter to Grimm,

and has become as biased against French music as formerly against Italian. His work deserves credit, however, for its close analysis of a musical work according to an explicit set of standards.

These standards, which are set forth by Rousseau in the first part of his essay, are 1) flexibility of language, 2) boldness of modulation, 3) exactness of rhythm and tempo, and 4) unity of melody. This last requirement forbids complicated counterpoint and harmonic texture, and stipulates that the musical ensemble must present only one melody to the ear, and thus one idea to the mind. In all of these aspects Italian music is found superior to French.

Rousseau shirks the actual comparison of the scene from *Armide* and that from *Nitocris*, but he gives a line-by-line analysis of Armide's monologue, attempting to convince the reader that Lully's music lacks "fire, soul, force and genius." He combats Rameau's praise of this scene's form and harmony by insisting that such a perfect textbook example is inappropriate for a scene that ought to depict such violently contrasting emotions. There is not the slightest inflection of the harmony to depict Armide's agitation, and the alternation between tonic and dominant is altogether trivial. The bass line, instead of supporting the melody, attempts to rival it, and the ornaments are in poor taste.

Rousseau's detailed analysis attempts to show how each line fails to meet adequately the exigencies of the text, thus challenging what had become a cliché—the status of the monologue as one of the most expressive passages in opera. Lully, he says, falls into the trap of depicting single words like *charme* and *sommeil* at the expense of the text.[90] The worst fault, however, is that Lully depicts lines of violent contrast (such as "Qu'il éprouve toute ma rage/Quel trouble me saisit? Qui me fait hésiter?") in the same manner, often employing the same harmony. In summary, Rousseau states:

> If it is regarded as song, one finds no measure, no character, no melody; if recitative, one finds nothing natural or expressive. . . . In a word, if the music of this scene were executed without joining to it the words, without crying or gesticulating, it would not be possible to deduce anything of the situation which [the music] wants to express, and all of it would seem only a monotonous succession of sounds. . . . But, without the gesticulation and the acting of the actress, I am persuaded that no one would be able to bear the recitative, and that such a music has great need of the help of the eyes to be bearable to the ears.[91]

Whereas Lecerf's *Comparaison* had been pirated for use at the time of the controversy between Lullists and Ramists, Raguenet's *Parallèle* reappeared in the same year as Rousseau's *Lettre*, thus during the midst of the crisis surrounding the *bouffons*. The treatise, however, called *La paix de l'opéra, ou parallèle impartial de la musique française et de la musique italienne* (Paris, 1753), was in no way attributed to Raguenet. Its transformation by an anonymous editor resembled in several ways Grandval's treatment of the *Comparaison*, for it had been brought up to date to suit the more recent aspects of the quarrel over French and Italian music. Though Raguenet's name was absent, however, the editor remained modestly content to transmit the treatise with only slight alterations, confining his own comments pertaining to the present controversy to the footnotes and to a few paragraphs at the close of the work. His *avertissement* provides an interesting insight into a mid-century writer's conception of the earlier quarrel, and reveals the oblivion into which its participants had fallen:

> The work to be presented to the public is only a portion of a little book which appeared in 1702 under the title, *Parallele des Italiens & des Francois, en ce qui regarde la Musique et les Opera*. The work is excellent on the whole: but the style is so diffuse and so far from correct, that it has been necessary to condense and to rectify many things. It also seemed necessary to add several remarks.
>
> If this *Parallele*, such as it is given, seems written with more solidity than appeal, one must recall that it was originally written in 1702, and is not a current brochure. The author writes naturally, without enthusiasm: he never assumes a dogmatic tone, he offends no one, he delves into the matter, he judges wisely. This distinguishes his work from all the modern pamphlets which have appeared on the same subject.[92]

The second paragraph here applies more to the anonymous editor than to Raguenet, for his comments do represent a quite objective, unbiased appraisal. Like Grandval, he emphasizes the conciliatory portions of his treatise, and plays down Raguenet's opposition to the French style. Though he agrees with many of Raguenet's criticisms of French opera, his earnest desire is not to sacrifice the noble heritage of Lully to the modern Italian taste, but to restore the true French style through a correction of its deficiencies:

> The libretti of these operas are very good, the recitative is admirable, there are even excellent bits of orchestral music. Why deny ourselves such a rich fund? Why renounce a heritage that one could recapture, and even amplify at small cost? Why especially, why let fall into oblivion all the admirable poems which would necessarily have the same fate as the music? . . . All the inconveniences could be remedied by the project of which I speak, the repertory of opera could be enriched, the attention and curiosity of the public could be reawakened, and finally our ancient music could be saved and its imminent destruction avoided.[93]

The last of the important pro-Italian essays was *De la liberté de la musique* (Paris, 1759),[94] written by Jean d'Alembert a number of years after the end of the quarrel of the *bouffons*. Written from a distance in time, d'Alembert's essay represents a less inflammatory discussion of the opposed styles as well as a lucid history of the *guerre des bouffons*. Interestingly, d'Alembert appears to be the only writer to refer by name to either of the participants in the first controversy over French and Italian music. His brief reference to Raguenet shows that although the ideas and terms of the original quarrel had left their mark at mid-century, the details of its history had been forgotten. D'Alembert, indeed, seems never to have heard of Lecerf or of any response to Raguenet's *Parallèle*, but his assessment of the *Parallèle* is more perceptive than that of its anonymous editor:

> At the beginning of this century, the abbé Raguenet, a writer with a lively imagination, brought out a little work in which our music was almost as maltreated as in the letter of Rousseau. This work excited no wars, no hate during the time at which it appeared; French music then reigned peacefully on our drowsy organs: Raguenet was regarded as seditious but isolated, a plotter without accomplices, from whom there was no reason to fear revolution.[95]

After surveying the history of the quarrel, d'Alembert proposes a plan to render French music superior to Italian by applying characteristic traits of Italian music to the French language. Though his proposal reveals the naïve optimism of the musical amateur, his recognition of the need for a comparative technical analysis of the two styles is sound: "This proposition demands that we enter into certain details on the character of the two musics. . . ."[96] It is this analysis, rather than the author's ultimate aim, that gives the treatise worth; in describing the respective compositional practices of the French and Italians in their recitatives, airs, and orchestral pieces, d'Alembert not only concludes the *guerre des bouffons*, but also, along with Rousseau and Diderot, makes a further contribution to stylistic awareness and technical description.

C. H. Blainville's *L'esprit de l'art musical, ou reflexions sur la musique et ses différentes parties* (Geneva, 1754), though written during one of the *guerre*'s most violent years, was written at a distance from the scene of combat, and thus also represents a more reflective appraisal of the war over French and Italian music. In the tradition of the eighteenth-century critics of taste, Blainville summarizes the various aspects of the century's quarrels in the more erudite context of an analysis of good taste and of musical style. For Blainville, the essential distinction between the French and Italians is a linguistic one: the French language is suave and tranquil, based on reason and good taste, but with a tendency toward monotony, whereas the Italian language is more impetuous, tending toward variety and astonishment. The French language is naturally the more expressive because its clarity and transparency focus the listener's attention on its content rather than its sound.

Blainville's use of the terms *cantabile* and *sonabile* to describe the two styles recalls Pluche's distinction between *musique chantante* and *musique baroque*, but avoids the derogatory implication of the latter while pointing up the Italian emphasis on instrumental music. Like Lecerf and the *Mercure*'s anonymous writer of 1713, Blainville calls French music an elegant lady in contrast to Italian music, a seductive coquette. Granting that the Italians have more fire and enthusiasm, he prefers the natural and expressive style of the French, "for singing only for the voice is the same as speaking only for the sound."[97] The true art of music is found in its expressiveness; otherwise sounds only flatter the ear without entering the heart.

According to Blainville, music is essentially no different from language; it is, in fact, the language of the gods. The greatest talent of the French lies in their discovery of an expressive musical style appropriate to, and inseparable from, their language. Italian opera has a wider vogue in Europe because its music can be set to any language, but the idea of using French music for any language other than its own is absurd.

Blainville's theory of taste grows out of this conservative emphasis on expressiveness, as well as a corresponding rejection of sensation as an exclusive criterion for musical judgment. Essentially a classicist, he understands true beauty as an absolute universal standard but, like Batteux and André, he admits the possibility of variations within its general boundaries. It is good to know, he says, the tone of the century and the taste of the public, but one must always remain faithful to the truly beautiful, while allowing the details of ornament enough variety to satisfy varying tastes.

Blainville deplores the present national tendency to judge by sensation, and to look only for amusement rather than for true aesthetic pleasure. Sensation is the "motor," the unthinking, instinctive aspect of taste, and while it helps us to distinguish mediocre, good and sublime music, it will fail us when put to the test of changing musical fashions. Only a solid intellectual knowledge of music can penetrate beneath changing styles and discover whether a work possesses the eternal qualities of the truly beautiful; otherwise the critic is faced with the necessity either of changing his own taste to fit the fashion or of deploring the "bad taste of the century."

It is this new tolerance of different styles, all faithful in their own way to the more flexible standards of *bon goût*, that accompanies the historical sense of style that also develops in the eighteenth century. Rather than seeing good taste as the exclusive property of the ancients,

Blainville, following Dubos, traces the dawn of good taste to the supplanting of the *goût gothique*, or the contrapuntal church style. In the more recent past, he finds taste changing from the style of Lully to that of Rameau to that of the *bouffons*, but discovers some elements of *bon goût* in all these styles.

Finally, the concept of style itself becomes a conscious part of the discussion of French and Italian music with Blainville. He begins by categorizing styles as to function: the tragedy is heroic, the ballet *galant*, the *chanson* familiar. He further speaks of genres of music deriving from the general character (synonymous with the language) of a nation; this is associated with "*style*, which consists of the character, the turn of the melody, the manner of adding the bass and the other parts. The Italians are as different from us in this genre as they are in character and in language.[98]

Though Blainville implies at times that Italian music, which opposes the good taste of French music, must exhibit the bad taste of the Italians, in the end he defines taste as the instrument for reconciling the two "opposite beauties." Unfortunately, however, Italians can find only monotony in French music, and the French only folly in Italian. The treatise ends with a plea for the appreciation of different merits in music and an end to the foolishness of appreciating only the music of one's own country.

In Chapter IV we defined criticism as the evaluation and explanation of art to an audience, often an amateur one. The critic was defined as a judge who explains to his audience what he considers good and why; most criticism of value, it was seen, lies somewhere between the two extremes of recounting personal impressions and imposing rigid, artificial standards. In early eighteenth-century France, then, musical criticism was forged out of the opposition of these two means of determining quality. "Objective" preference for the style of the "ancients" met and intermingled with "subjective" preference for the modern Italian style; the outcome, partially realized by Blainville and the Encyclopedists at midcentury and more fully developed slightly later by German critics, was a more mature critical mode, based on rational, comparative analysis and tempered with the description of personal response and appreciation.

VI

National Styles and Good Taste in Music in Britain and Germany

Britain

British criticism of the early eighteenth century continued the French trends of a slightly earlier period. The quarrel between Ancients and Moderns, which had been set out in John Dryden's *Essay of Dramatic Poesy* (1668),[1] reached its zenith with the publication in 1704 of Jonathan Swift's satire, *The Battle of the Books*.[2] As in France, the quarrel included not only literature, but also music: Sir William Temple, a leader of the Ancients, included a denunciation of modern music in his important *Essay upon the Ancient and Modern Learning* (1690):

> What are become of the Charms of Musick, by which Men and Beasts, Fishes, Fowls, and Serpents were so frequently Enchanted, and their very Natures changed; By which the Passions of men were raised to the greatest heighth and violence, and then as suddenly appeased, so as they might be justly said to be turned into Lyons or Lambs, into Wolves or into Harts, by the Power and Charms of this admirable Art? 'Tis agreed by the Learned that the Science of Musick, so admired of the Ancients, is wholly lost in the World, and that what we have now is made up out of certain Notes that fell into the fancy or observation of a poor *Fryar* in chanting his Mattins. So as those Two Divine Excellencies of Musick and Poetry are grown in a manner to be little more, but the one Fidling, and the other Rhyming; and are indeed very worthy of the ignorance of the Fryar and the barbarousness of the *Goths* that introduced them among us.[3]

Temple's essay was answered by a lengthier treatment of the question in Alexander Malcolm's *A Treatise of Music: Speculative, Practical and Historical* (Edinburgh, 1721).[4] Malcolm, who seems to have studied with diligence the French quarrel, calls Temple's argument "the poorest Thing ever was said," and, citing Claude Perrault, defends modern music with the same points that the Frenchman had made fifty years earlier. He shows that the ancient *symphonia* was only unison singing at the octave, that the ancients could not have known true counterpoint, and that the modern opera of his own country and of Italy is as capable of moving the passions as was ancient music. Historians are perfectly capable of exaggerating the supposed effects of the music of antiquity, he says, but those listeners with sensitive ears cannot mistake the "noble Effects" of modern music:

> Yet perhaps it will be replied, That this proceeds from a bad Taste, and something natural, in applauding the best Thing we know of any Kind. But let any Body produce a better, and we shall heartily applaud it. They bid us bring back the ancient Musicians, and then they'll effectively shew us the Difference; and we bid them learn to understand the modern Musick, and believe their own Senses: In short we think we have better Reason to determine in our own Favours, from the Effects we actually feel, than any Body can have from a Thing they have no Experience of, and can pretend to know no other Way than by Report.[5]

Malcolm's musical modernism may be seen as part of a larger revolt against the classical aesthetic, for in the end he questions the old necessity of expressiveness as exclusive criterion for musical worth. Citing examples of painting and architecture which give pleasure purely through design and proportion, he insists that music may give pleasure and "recreate the Mind" without exciting any particular passion at all, and declares that the moderns have introduced a new art no longer based on the old exigencies of expressiveness.

Until later in the century, however, the Ancients continued to wield more power in Britain than the opposing Moderns. Like the French classical critics, the British attacked Italian literature and music; in fact, the decline in popularity of Italian literature during the first two decades of the century has been attributed to the war waged upon it by the critics.[6] Joseph Addison, one of the most respected arbiters of taste at this time, was one of the most vehement in his critique of the Italians; the following quotation, taken from an article in the *Spectator*, refers specifically to the excesses of Italian opera libretti:

> The truth of it is, the finest writers among the modern Italians express themselves in such a florid form of words and such tedious circumlocutions as are used by none but pedants in our own country: and at the same time fill their writings with such poor imaginations and conceits, as our youths are ashamed of before they have been two years at the university. . . . I must agree with Monsieur Boileau, that one verse in *Virgil* is worth all the *clincant* or Tinsel of Tasso.[7]

In speaking of what he calls "mixed wit," or conceits, Addison says, "The *Italians*, even in their Epic Poetry, are full of it. . . . Monsieur *Boileau*, who formed himself upon the ancient Poets, has every where rejected it with scorn.''[8]

John Dennis, in his *Essay on the Opera's after the Italian Manner* (1706),[9] brings together the arguments for reason over sense, ancient taste over modern, and British (or French) taste over Italian. He blames an excess of luxury for the degeneration of manners and morals in modern Italy, and believes that ''the reigning Luxury'' of Italy is ''that soft and effeminate Music which abounds in the *Italian Opera*.'' Such music has not had the same influence in France because that country's military-mindedness has increased its people's resistance to music that is ''meltingly moving.''

Dennis equates the Italian opera with the ''bewitching Pleasure of the Sense,'' British drama (portions of which may be sung, as in ancient times) with the ''severe Delight of Reason,'' and believes that, because men are too indolent to educate themselves to the more difficult form, opera threatens to drive true drama from the stage:

> Musick may be made profitable as well as delightful, if it is subordinate to some nobler Art, and subservient to Reason; but if it presumes not only to degenerate from its antient Severity, from its sacred Solemnity, but to set up for it self, and to grow independent, as it does in our late Operas, it becomes a mere sensual Delight, utterly incapable of informing the Understanding, or reforming the Will; and for that very reason utterly unfit to be made a publick Diversion; and then the more charming it grows, it becomes the more pernicious.[10]

Dennis defines British drama, like ancient drama, as reasonable, artful, beneficial, and natural; modern Italian musical tragedy as ridiculous, absurd, pernicious, and monstrous. While opera in Italy is at least a ''beautiful, harmonious'' monster, in Britain, the temperament of whose people is so unsuited to it, it becomes ''an ugly, howling one.'' Just as the British would not grow olive and orange trees, so should they obey the dictates of their ears, voices, language, and climate in the matter of music.

Dennis, like Boileau and St.-Evremond, sees drama as a species endangered by the opera's new, more facile appeal to the animal nature in man. His work thus parallels the early stages of operatic criticism in France, in which opera was criticized by the same criteria as drama. With Dennis and later critics, the opposition of Italian opera to British drama continues in Britain, both because of this failure of the critics to distinguish between the two genres and because Britain had no strong national opera of her own to oppose to the Italian.

There were also in Britain advocates of Italian opera. One of these was the anonymous translator and annotator of Raguenet's *Parallèle*, who appended a rather lengthy "Critical Discourse on Opera's and Musick in England" to the work.[11] This appendix begins with a defense of modern music, a defense based largely on the existence of harmony in modern times. The author attributes the invention of opera to Italy, from whence he maintains it spread gradually into Germany, France, and finally Britain.

In considering the requirements for a British opera, the author includes little of note that would distinguish it from the Italian. Opera, in the first place, must be sung in Italian, "a Language the most proper for Musick of any other in Europe." Other recommendations include those aspects of Italian opera that had come in for criticism by the conservatives:

> 'Tis not enough if the Air be lively and diverting, unless there be something beautiful in the instrumental Part also. There must be a sort of Contest between the Voice, and the Instrument, and both must contend for the superiority. The Airs ought to be studied without being stiff, melancholy without being heavy, and lively without being trivial: There ought to be something new and uncommon, sweet and entertaining in every part.[12]

Finally, recognizing the difference between pleasure and edification, and between spontaneity and expressiveness, the author declares himself a strong defender of the former attributes:

> And I look on it as an undoubted Maxim in Musick (the Business of which is to regale the Ear, as it is that of Painting to regale the Eye) that whatever is Good ought to please, and whatever pleases ought to be esteem'd as Good.[13]

This annotator did not have the last word in the matter, for an anonymous commentator later added his own marginal comments to the copy of the work now in the Cambridge University Library.[14] This later writer takes issue not only with Raguenet's original ideas, but also with the pro-Italian annotations of the translator. He comments rather devastatingly on both authors' lack of musical knowledge in such phrases as "All this is French tattle," and "This is the finest piece of Raillery I ever read."[15]

This annotator lavishes his most extensive marginalia on the "Critical Discourse on Opera's and Musick in England." He refutes its author's claim that modern music had surpassed the ancient, and contests the assertion that the Italians invented opera with the comment, "If the Antient tragedys were all sung as is very likely and the contrary hard to bee proved what becomes of this assertion [?]"[16] Like Lecerf, he favors the older music of his own country to the influx of the modern Italian style; of Purcell, whom the translator had mentioned in passing, the annotator writes, "I will only add to this that I have seen much Italian musick. And in all that wch came or could come to Mr. Purcells sight I never saw anything but what I could have matchd with something of his as good att least.''[17]

At the end of the work, this annotator sums up his views on British opera and on the writer of the "Critical Discourse"; noting that the title page had proposed a means for the improvement of British operas, he expresses his irritation that the author "has been Labouring all along pro viribus to prove that wee must have an Italian opera (wch wee knew before) and that wee cant have an English one (wch I dont know yet). . . . I was never so tird in all my life."[18]

The British journals played a major role in the condemnation of Italian opera. As early as the fourth issue of the *Tatler*, which ridiculed opera for affording "the shallow Satisfaction of the Eyes and Ears only,"[19] the critics had revealed their conservative penchant for music as well as for literature. Addison's letter in the *Spectator* of March 8, 1711, continues the conservative tendency to judge opera according to the critical standards of drama, although his contempt for opera leads him to take it less seriously:

> An Opera may be allowed to be extravagantly lavish in its Decorations, as its only Design is to gratify the Senses, and keep up an indolent Attention in the Audience. Common Sense however requires, that there should be nothing in the Scenes and Machines which may appear Childish and Absurd. How would the Wits of King *Charles*'s Time have laughed to have seen *Nicolini*[20] exposed to a Tempest in Robes of Ermin, and sailing in an open Boat upon a Sea of Paste-Board?[21]

In Britain the quarrels between Ancients and Moderns and the ancillary opposition of universal and relative taste eventually came to an end with compromises and syntheses similar to those in France. The philosopher David Hume, in his essay "Of the Standard of Taste" (1741),[22] presents a solution to the problem of French and Italian music, without confronting that problem directly. He declares the universality of the principles of taste, while admitting that in most men the "organs of internal sensation" are not highly enough developed to produce a feeling corresponding to those principles. Notwithstanding necessary efforts to fix a standard of taste, however, Hume maintains that two sources of variation still remain to produce a difference in degrees of critical approbation or blame: the different humors of particular men, and the peculiar manners and opinions of a certain age or country. One man may prefer simplicity, another ornament, and men generally tend to prefer artistic characteristics familiar to their own country and historical period; these preferences Hume calls "innocent and unavoidable." As for "the celebrated controversy concerning ancient and modern learning," Hume insists that changes in manners and customs should not obscure the eternal validity of classic works of literature and art:

> The poet's *monument more durable than brass*, must fall to the ground like common brick or clay, were men to make no allowance for the continual revolutions of manners and customs, and would admit of nothing but what was suitable to the prevailing fashion. Must we throw aside the pictures of our ancestors, because of their ruffs and fardingales?[23]

Another successful synthesis of universal and relative taste in Britain may be found in Alexander Gerard's *An Essay of Taste* (Edinburgh, 1759),[24] which includes a series of chapters concerning a standard of taste. Like Hume, Gerard admits that differences of taste are unavoidable, and that, in music, some prefer simplicity, others variety; likewise, every age and country has something unique which distinguishes its taste. Gerard, however, defines and contrasts more clearly than previous critics the differences between taste based on sensation and taste based on discernment. The first, which depends on the external organs and the feelings of the individual, apprehends an absolute standard only intuitively, but the second—through objective analysis of the intuition—establishes such a standard upon firm principles and rules:

> Every man whom we acknowledge to possess any degree of taste, not only approves or disapproves, but specifies what it precisely is that pleases or displeases him, what is the nature of the pleasure or the disgust which it excites, and what the manner in which it excites them. The very operation of taste, when in any measure improved, implies so much of judgment, reflection, and analysis, as plainly intimates how serviceable they may be in defining, vindicating, or correcting its sensations.[25]

Thus one naturally has personal tastes based on sensation, but one may seek to refine and improve these tastes through the use of analysis and judgment. However, if one is destitute of taste altogether, "general principles and rules, however just, will not supply the want of it."[26]

In a chapter on music, "Of the Sense or Taste of Harmony," Gerard defines the sense of harmony as "that which enables us to perceive a kind of beauty in sound." Immediate pleasure arises from the sensation of the present sound, a memory of foregoing sounds, and an anticipation of succeeding sounds. An absolute standard in music, however, must be found in the proper balance of variety, uniformity, and proportion. Like Malcolm, Gerard considers these principles important enough to impart very high pleasure even in the absence of the expression of the passions, but, like the classicists, he finds the chief virtue of music to be its expressiveness.

In the realm of the strictly musical treatises of the period, we also see the attempt to assess the relative importance of expressiveness on one hand and of sonority on the other. Charles Avison, in his *Essay on Musical Expression* (London, 1752),[27] advocates a careful balance of melody, harmony and expression. He admires the melodic invention of the airs of Hasse, Porpora, and especially Bononcini and Pergolesi, while maintaining that:

> . . . the Critic of Taste is almost tempted to blame his own Severity in censuring Composition in which he finds Charms so powerful and commanding. However, for the Sake of Truth, it must be added, that this Taste, even in its most pardonable Degree, ought to be discouraged, because it seems naturally to lend to the ruin of a noble Art.[28]

Avison blames other composers, notably Palestrina, Tallis, Allegri, Carissimi, Stradella, and Steffani, for exploiting harmony (counterpoint) at the expense of melody and expression. He advocates instead "an unaffected Strain of Nature and Simplicity," and though his aesthetic reminds us of Lecerf and the French classicists, he surprises us by finding his ideal not in the music of Lully, but in that of two Italian composers, Benedetto Marcello in vocal music, and Francesco Geminiani in instrumental music.

Thus, as the eighteenth century reaches its midpoint in Britain, the questions of taste remain the same, but without the precise applications to national style that had obtained in the earlier quarrels. The British theorists, perhaps not so chauvinistic as the French, began to praise Italian music even when their theories rested on the conservative tenets of French classicism. A somewhat later example of such a case is the treatise by James Beattie, *Essays on Poetry and Music* (London, 1776). Beattie, though breaking away from the old view of music as a purely imitative art, follows Avison in his advocacy of expression as the "chief excellence" of music, and declares that "natural sensibility is not taste, though it be necessary to it." Likewise, faithful to the classical aesthetic, he rails against music which only "tickles the ear" rather than making a "powerful address" to the heart. But his lengthy discourse on national styles in music, while paying tribute to the music of his own native Scotland, recognizes Italian music as the finest of the era.

"It is an amiable prejudice," Beattie comments, "that people generally entertain in favour of their national music"; he attributes this prejudice not only to nostalgia and patriotism, but also to national temperament. In a description of the gloomy countryside and melancholy personality of the Scots that foreshadows the nineteenth-century romantic movement, Beattie explains Scottish music—especially its haunting folk tunes—as a direct result of "clouds, precipices, and torrents . . . of corpses, funeral processions, and other objects of terror."[29]

Similarly, Beattie ascribes the Italian tonal sensitivity to environmental causes:

> Whether it be owing to the climate, or to the influence of the other arts; whether it be derived from their Gothic ancestors, or from their more remote forefathers of ancient Rome; whether it be the effect of weakness or of soundness in the vocal and auditory organs of the people, this national niceness of ear must be considered as one cause of the melody both of their speech and of their music.[30]

In a historical sketch, Beattie traces the present artistic orientation of the Italians to Pope Leo X's love of art and luxury, and posits the works of Raphael and Palestrina as standards of taste for future generations. Since that time, he lists Scarlatti, Corelli, Geminiani, Martini, and Marcello as upholders of the standard, and concludes with the familiar argument that the abundance of vowels and liquid sounds in the Italian language renders it superior not only for musical setting, but also for poetry itself.

Finally, brief mention should be made of Charles Burney's comments on French and Italian music, made in his journal during a tour of those countries (1770).[31] Speaking more from a practical, rather than a philosophical, viewpoint, Burney criticizes performance practice more than composition, but in both he finds the Italians far superior to the French:

> I crawled to the theatre and was more disgusted than ever at French music after the dainties my ears had long been feasted with in Italy. Eugenie a pretty comedie preceded Sylvain an opera of Gretry—there were many pretty passages in the music but so ill sung, so false the expression—such screaming, forcing and trilling as quite turned me sick. I tried to observe on the road by what degrees the French arrive at this extreme depravity in their musical expression—and it does not come on all at once.[32]

During this same stay in Paris, Burney speaks of a visit with Jean-Jacques Rousseau. The content of their conversation, according to the journal, was largely praise for the music of Italy. Both awarded highest honors to the Venetians, especially Galuppi and Sacchini, though they considered as close competitors certain composers of Rome and Naples.

Thus with the later eighteenth-century critics in England as with Rousseau and Grimm in France, we see Italian music become established as an ideal for clarity, simplicity, and expressiveness, while French music takes on the old epithets that Lecerf and others had used for the Italians at the beginning of the century: ill sung, false expression, screaming, forcing, trilling. With this reversal it may be said that a new age, the Classic Era, has begun.

Germany: Transmission of the Quarrels over French and Italian Music

In Britain, as in France, musical criticism in the early eighteenth century was largely confined to more general treatises and periodicals. The first country to produce a coherent body of musical criticism, in works devoted to that specific purpose, was Germany.[33] Johann Mattheson, influenced by the *Tatler* and the *Spectator*,[34] published the first musical periodical in Germany, the *Critica musica* (Hamburg, 1722–1725), which addressed both amateurs and professional musicians. Johann Scheibe's *Critischer Musikus* (Leipzig, 1737–1740) was, by Scheibe's own account, directed more toward the general public, while Christoph Lorenz Mizler's *Neu-eröffnete musikalische Bibliothek* (Leipzig, 1736–1754) contained scholarly reprints of scientific works on music and acoustics. Friedrich W. Marpurg's *Historisch-kritische Beyträge zur Aufnahme der Musik* (Berlin, 1758–1778) is considered most important for its popularization of Rameau's theory of harmony and the abbé Batteux's theory of aesthetics.[35]

Besides the periodicals, many practical treatises on performance and composition were directed toward the amateur in music. Several of these, such as Johann Joseph Fux's *Gradus ad Parnassum* (Vienna, 1725), Johann David Heinichen's *General-Bass in der Composition* (Dresden, 1728), and Johann Joseph Quantz's *Versuch einer Anweisung die Flöte traversiere zu spielen* (Berlin, 1752), include lengthy guides to the art of judging music and to the acquisition of musical taste; such passages parallel the discussions of taste and criticism in the musical journals.

Thus, in early eighteenth-century Germany, musical criticism came of age. Obviously in Germany, as in Britain, the question of the superiority of French music to Italian could be only an academic one, without the intensity of the French debate. But because of the intrusion of the Italian operatic style into all European countries at this time, German theorists began to voice the same complaints as had the French. Beckman C. Cannon has pointed out the pattern of reaction to the cultural imperialism of any country which is dominant musically in a certain historical period:

> When the dominant or central style was at its climax, or entering its last phase—and by 1713 the Italian baroque was close to the point of its most powerful expansion—musicians living in the peripheral countries often began to voice their dissatisfaction, or even to break into open revolt; and sometimes they spoke what appears to be a

"nationalistic" language. Such expressions had, however, nothing to do with political nationalism, but were indicative of a purely artistic phenomenon related to style. At the end of every stylistic period, a very natural reaction of native forces in the peripheral countries becomes apparent.[36]

Also, because a new form of French musical criticism had arisen out of the debate over French and Italian music, that debate could not help but intrigue the German critics. As the transmission of the French sources shows, the Germans researched the French controversy diligently, and though they saw its results as negligible, they believed that their countrymen could gain something from the quarrel. Many, though not all, agreed with the *Mercure* of 1713 that only a synthesis of the finer aspects of the two different styles could produce a music of true good taste and universal appeal, and their hope was that German music could represent this synthesis which the French and Italian musical styles had failed to produce.

Throughout the first half of the eighteenth century, the writings of Lecerf and Raguenet, as well as the essays of Grandval and the anonymous writer of the *Mercure*, were transmitted more widely in German sources than in French ones. As early as 1713, Mattheson indicated a knowledge of the French quarrel in his discussion of national styles:

> A Frenchman named le Sieur de Vieuville is supposed to have written a response to the abbé Raguenet, which he calls *Comparaison de la musique française & italienne*, but I have not yet been able to find out anything about it.[37]

In his *Critica musica* of 1722–1725, Mattheson included portions of Raguenet's *Parallèle* and what he believed to be Lecerf's *Comparaison*, but was actually the "Dissertation" which had appeared in the *Mercure* in 1713.[38] As he states in his introduction to this presentation, Mattheson's role is not to take sides, but rather to present the two works in as objective a manner as possible. Both writers, says Mattheson, have much to say of worth, but both tend to overstep the line of propriety in their presentations. Mattheson justifies his own comments and corrections by attributing them to his role "not only as a translator but also as a critic . . . ."[39]

Mattheson's source for the "Dissertation" was Bonnet-Bourdelot's *Histoire de la musique*, which in its first edition did not include Lecerf's *Comparaison*. In the introduction, Mattheson confidently explains the likelihood of Lecerf's authorship, but halfway through his translation breaks off in mid-sentence and summarizes in a brief paragraph the conclusion of the work.[40] In a second paragraph he reveals his acquaintance with the new edition of Bonnet-Bourdelot's *Histoire*, mentioning the three volumes which he still does not publicly recognize as the true work of Lecerf, but which have clearly thrown some doubt on his former attribution. He has, he says, acquired a copy of Raguenet's *Defense* and recognizes the censure of that work in the last volume of the *Comparaison*. He concludes by promising his readers summaries of the two works when he has had the opportunity to research the two authors.

Mattheson never accomplished this objective, nor does it seem that he ever discovered the true authorship of the *Comparaison* as it was found in Bonnet-Bourdelot's *Histoire*. His final reference to the "anonymous author of the last three volumes of the *Histoire de la musique*"[41] is found in the fourth part of his *Critica musica* where he refers to an anecdote from the *Comparaison*. Apparently, he never learned that the "Dissertation" from Bonnet-Bourdelot's first volume was not by Lecerf, and this error was transmitted to later research. For example, Johann Walther's *Musicalisches Lexicon* (Leipzig, 1732), citing Mattheson, gives the following entry for Lecerf:

> Vieuville (de la), a Frenchman, wrote a *Dissertation sur le bon gout de la musique française et sur les Opera*, that is, an essay on good taste with regard to Italian and French music and opera; someone in 1712 sent this in the form of a letter to Herr Bonnet . . . where it became the twelfth chapter of his *Histoire de la musique*.[42]

Perhaps the most influential of all the German writers who translated French works on musical aesthetics was Friedrich W. Marpurg, who had lived in France during the period around 1746, and had become friends with a number of leading French aestheticians of his day.[43] In 1749 he transmitted the ideas of Lecerf to the German public by including a translation of Grandval's essay plagiarized from the *Comparaison*, which he calls "Herr Grandvalls Versuch über den guten Geschmack in der Musick," in his *Der critische Musicus an der Spree*.[44] Like Mattheson's translations, it was extensively annotated, Marpurg's comments serving mainly to acquaint his German audience with names and terms already familiar to the French. Marpurg also translated Bollioud de Mermet's *De la corruption du goust dans la musique française* (Lyons, 1746) in the *Critischer Musicus* of 1750,[45] and Noel-Antoine Pluche's essay on music from his *Spectacle de la nature* in the *Historisch-Kritische Beyträge* of the same year.[46] The latter is especially interesting for its translation of Pluche's terms *musique chantante* and *musique baroque* (referring, respectively, to the music of Lully and of Rameau) as *singende* and *schallende musique*. The use of the term *schallende* ("sounding" or "clangorous") points up the contrast between the vocal and instrumental styles, and probably also indicates the lack of currency of the French term *baroque* in Germany at this time.[47]

The first volume of Marpurg's *Kritische Briefe über die Tonkunst* (1760) includes translations of Raguenet's *Parallèle* and the "Dissertation" printed in the *Mercure* of 1713 as well as in Bonnet-Bourdelot's *Histoire*, which Marpurg, like Mattheson, believed to be the work of Lecerf.[48] In a letter which serves as preface to these translations, Marpurg compares the work of Raguenet and Jean-Jacques Rousseau, and although he promises translations of both, declares himself an opponent of their arguments. He actually never published a translation of Rousseau's *Lettre sur la musique française*, although he had published a summary soon after its appearance in 1753.[49] He later included a list of pro-French responses to the letter, to which he added his own comments on the quarrel. In these comments, he sees the war between Rousseau and his opponents as parallel to that between Lecerf and Raguenet at the beginning of the century, and he speculates that it will end no differently:

> Both sides remain sure of their own opinions, after they have exhausted themselves with mutual abuse. One side is not skilled enough in music to give instruction, and the other not secure enough to take it. Perhaps a third nation will put forward its claim, but could a party be found without those who judge with preconceived opinions or who from obstinacy wish to acknowledge only the worst of another nation and never the best? That music always deserves the prize above all others, in which the taste of the country and the period are felicitously united with true purity of harmony in the composition. Without the latter no music is good; to fly in the face of established usage, however, is foolish. But each country has its own music, and always considers it the best.[50]

Germany: Transmission of French Classicism

As important as the transmission of the quarrels of the French over their own music and that of the Italians was the transmission of the underlying premises of that quarrel. French classicism had entered early eighteenth-century German thought through the work of Christian Thomasius (1655–1728), who, as professor at the University of Leipzig, had taught his students to imitate the French not only in philosophy and literature, but also in manners.[51] During this period the advocates of classicism had clashed with writers favoring a more effusive style; at the turn of the century Christian Wernicke, a classicist, had attacked the dramatist Daniel Caspar von Lohenstein for literary "bombast." Heinrich Postel, Reinhard Keiser's librettist, had defended Lohenstein, provoking Wernicke to satirize both writers in his *Heldengedicht Hans Sachs genannt* of 1702.[52]

In the second quarter of the century the banner of French classicism was taken up by Johann Christoph Gottsched, whose *Versuch einer critischen Dichtkunst für die Deutschen* (Leipzig, 1730) attempted a rigorous application of classical standards to German literature. A circle formed around Gottsched at the University of Leipzig, creating the so-called "Leipzig School," which strongly influenced German criticism before the midpoint of the century.[53] In the 1740s, however, Gottsched's theories were somewhat undermined by the challenge of two Swiss critics, Johann Jakob Bodmer and Johann Jakob Breitinger, who championed the freedom of imagination against the restriction of rules.[54] Many of the issues raised in this conflict between German and Swiss schools represent a continuation of late seventeenth-century French thought, and the quarrel itself might be considered a final episode in the larger quarrel between Ancients and Moderns.

In 1751 Gottsched was to translate the abbé Batteux's *Beaux-arts réduits à un même principe*, and his *Critische Dichtkunst* is filled with references to Batteux, Boileau, and other French classicists. The rule of reason and the imitation of nature form a basis for his aesthetic theory; in a chapter on good taste in the first part of the *Critische Dichtkunst* he defines good taste as that "which corresponds to the rules . . . which are firmly established by reason."[55] The second part of that work, which surveys the genres of literature, includes a chapter on opera. Gottsched's ideas concerning this genre are derived from those of Boileau and of St.-Evremond (both of whom he quotes at length), and parallel John Dennis's work in Britain. Gottsched sees the combination of music and drama as unnatural, opposed to the rules of propriety and verisimilitude, and he calls opera "the most absurd work that the human mind has ever invented.[56] Like St.-Evremond, Gottsched, within his general disapproval of opera altogether, particularly disapproves of Italian opera, finding offense in the sensual aria as he had previously found in poetry based on the "wonderful":

> Whatever pleases the eyes and ears is immediately considered good: and one must quiet his reason, when it tries to deny this pleasure through its critical reservations. . . . Thus is effeminacy implanted in the spirits of the people beginning in their youth, and we become like the effeminate Italians before we remember that we are supposed to be masculine Germans.[57]

Finally, complaining of the use of castrati, of trills and artificial liberties, Gottsched equates opera with purely sensual pleasure: "So is opera a work merely for the senses; the mind and heart receive nothing from it. Only the eyes are dazzled: only the ears are . . . stupified: but the reason must be left at home when one goes to the opera."[58]

Gottsched's influence was important for musical as well as literary critics, for those who wished to reform opera as well as those who opposed it altogether found it necessary to cite the *Critische Dichtkunst*, and Gottsched's concepts of form, style, expressiveness and the affections were useful to practical musicians and theorists of music alike. Scheibe, Mizler, and Johann Doles,[59] as well as the Bach sons and nephews, were among those influenced by Gottsched's work,[60] and as late as 1792, J. N. Forkel cites the *Critische Dichtkunst* as a source for "*musikalischen Poesie.*"[61]

Gottsched's most important influence on musical thought was undoubtedly through his disciple Johann Scheibe. Scheibe himself tells us that the *Critische Dichtkunst*, which had changed his whole manner of examining music, also gave him the idea for a journal, the *Critischer Musikus*, which would be based on Gottsched's critical method:

> Because I wanted to demonstrate in this journal to scholars and musicians alike how closely music and poetry are related and that the rules which apply to one apply equally to the other, and because I also wanted to guide them to an imitation of nature and present to them matters which have hardly been explained at all and then only superficially, even though they are necessary for the development of good taste: such an important undertaking could not be executed without the advantages derived from intelligent criticism. Because my aims at times coincided with Herr Gottsched's, and because I wished to some extent to write about music in the same manner which informed his *Critische Dichtkunst* . . . I gave my pages the title, *Der critische Musikus*.[62]

Gottsched, then, represents the rigid rule of classicism in German criticism, and Scheibe to a certain extent bears witness to it in musical thought.[63] An interesting transformation occurs, however, in German musical criticism with the assimilation of the classical doctrine, for instead of coinciding with a conservative critical outlook, the classical doctrine in Germany underlies an advocacy of modern music. Thus, Gottsched's emphasis on simplicity and clarity becomes with Scheibe a preference for the relatively simple homophony of Hasse, Graun, and Telemann in comparison to the florid counterpoint of Bach, which he considers bombastic, old-fashioned, and opposed to the rules of good taste.[64]

*Good Taste and National Styles
in German Musical Aesthetics*

In tracing the German discussions of good taste in relation to the question of musical style, we must return chronologically to earlier musical writings of the eighteenth century, into which the doctrine of sensibility and empiricism in aesthetics—taken from British philosophy as well as from such French writers as the abbé Dubos—was also making strong inroads. While Thomasius and Gottsched were promulgating the doctrine of classical taste based on rules, reason, and a literal imitation of nature, others were recognizing a new kind of taste, one more dependent on the senses and determined to a larger degree by individual opinion. Moreover, in Germany, the term *goût* began to serve, like the term *galant*, as an indication of an ineluctable quality which was exotic, foreign, and *à la mode*: the German rationalists, albeit influenced by French thought, tended to use the German form of the word, *Geschmack*, while the advocates of sensibility more often used the French form *goût*. Johann Mattheson, in the subtitle of his youthful *Neu-eröffnete Orchestre* of 1713, uses the term in connection with the idea of the *galant homme*:

> Universal and fundamental introduction, wherein a *galant homme* may attain a perfect idea of the majesty and dignity of noble music, through which he may form his *goût*, understand the technical terms, and thereby discuss this excellent science with understanding.[65]

Taste, for Mattheson, has lost all vestiges of *bon goût* in the classical sense.[66] Good taste for him implies musical judgment, but a judgment based more on an ability to discern national styles and to recognize their characteristics than to pronounce only one worthy of approval. His use of the word indicates that he considers taste more a result of majority opinion than an ideal standard:

> The Italians, who today seem to take the prize from all other nations, partly through the intrinsic beauty of their works, partly also through their polished, insinuating craft of composition—and who on the whole have general taste on their side—differ in style not only from the French, Germans, and English, but also in certain pieces even among themselves.[67]

The association of *goût* with individual opinion and national style is also applied to performance: as for execution, Mattheson says, much depends upon *goût*, and each nation naturally prefers its own practice.

In all matters of style, Mattheson advocates these national preferences. Though he admits Italian superiority by general consensus, he characterizes the French as preeminent in instrumental music as well as performance practice. He chastises the British, on the other hand, for aping the Italian style, and the Germans for fatuously preferring anything foreign for its own sake. Concluding with the proverb, "*De gustibus non est disputandum*," Mattheson cites the quarrel of Lecerf and Raguenet, apparently as an example of a fruitless dispute over taste.[68]

Fux, in his *Gradus ad Parnassum* of 1725, repeats the maxim, "*De gustibus non est disputandum*," extending the proverb slightly: "My affairs please me, yours please you . . . taste is not to be disputed; no one can be judge in his own affairs.''[69] Fux's general definition of taste, as might be expected in a counterpoint treatise, is more conservative than Mattheson's:

> I will say, then, that a composition is in good taste and earns preference, if it is founded on the rules, contains general and unified ideas, is appropriate, noble, and dignified, expresses everything in a natural order, and is capable of giving pleasure to those with some knowledge of music. . . . The simple is difficult. And on this difficult simplicity is based the excellence, indeed the elegance, of good music.[70]

An important distinction in Fux's discussion, however, reveals a new trend in the early eighteenth century, namely, the growing emphasis on the performer as well as the listener. Thus Fux defines "active" taste as that which guides the performer in interpretation, "passive" taste as that which guides the listener in judgment. And though he advocates a universal good taste based on nature and the rules, he prefaces his discussion of the varying styles (church, *a cappella*, "mixed," and recitative) with an admission that good taste must be adapted to different styles and genres: "Since, however, the differing styles and genres of composition also necessitate a different taste, so it is now our task to treat the differences of style. . . ."[71]

Though Fux never discussed the French and Italian styles as such, an interesting example from his *Concentus musico-instrumentalis* includes a trio sonata with one line (for flute) designated *"aria italiana,"* and the other line (for oboe) designated *aire françoise"* (see Example 10). The two lines seem constructed to be played either together or independently, the French part and continuo following the typically French rhythmic convention of reducing dotted binary notation to ternary rhythms. Fux thus seems to perceive the difference between the styles as primarily notational, for differences in actual musical content are slight.

A fuller discussion of musical taste may be found in Johann David Heinichen's treatise on the thoroughbass in 1728. The connection of *bon goût* with thoroughbass accompaniment is explained by the new preoccupation with taste in performance—Fux's "active" taste. Heinichen, in the most modern manner, considers taste to include the compositional skills through which the senses are moved and the ear flattered. These skills specifically include the use of a dominant *cantabile* melodic line, proper accompaniments, and pleasing modulations.[72]

Heinichen includes a valuable disquisition on national styles, in which his application of the idea of *goût* confirms his association of the term with the more progressive musical practices of his day. The reader may discern, as in Scheibe, a certain coincidence of ideals in the work of Heinichen and the older French classicists, for just as Lecerf, Pluche, and the other champions of French *bon goût* had opposed the simple,

Example 10.   Fux, *Concentus musico-instrumentalis* VII,
"Aria italiana/Aire françoise."
(Courtesy of Akademische Druck- und Verlagsanstalt, Graz)

cantabile style of the French to the "learned," artificial style of the Italians, Heinichen opposes the simple, tasteful styles of France to the intricate counterpoint of Germany:

> One nation [Germany] seeks its greatest art in noisy, intricate musical tiff-taff and pretentious note-mannerisms. The other [France], on the contrary, applies itself to taste, and through this steals the former's universal applause; the paper-artists remain with all their witchcraft in obscurity, and are moreover called barbarians, though they could imitate the other nations blindfolded if they would only apply themselves, like those, to taste and brilliance in music more than to fruitless artificialities.[73]

The direct influence of French musical thought is evident in Heinichen's proposal of a synthesis of opposing tastes; in applying the French call for a *goûts-réunis* to the problem of German music, Heinichen introduces the idea of mixed taste, or the assimilation of French and Italian stylistic traits into German music. Heinichen attributes this theory to a "foreign composer"; his quotation seems to be a paraphrase of certain passages in the "Dissertation" of 1713 which Johann Mattheson had translated in his *Critica musica* (1722) under the name of Lecerf de la Viéville:[74]

> Concerning the usage of his country, a distinguished foreign composer once gave a frank appraisal of the difference in the music of two nations. "Our nation" [France], he said (I translate his words into our own language), "is inclined by nature more towards *dolcezza* (grace, *tendresse*) in music, so much that it must take care not to fall thereby into indolence; most of the *Italians*, on the other hand, are inclined by nature almost too much towards vivacity in music, through which they fall too easily into barbarism: if they would make the effort, however, to rob us of our *tendresse* in music, and mix it with their customary vivacity, a third [style] would emerge, which could do none other than please the whole world." I will pass over the gloss on this subject which I made earlier, and only say this, that this discourse brought to me for the first time the thought that a happy mixture of Italian and French taste would be most striking to the ear, and must surely win out over the tastes of all the other nations of the world.[75]

Heinichen closes this lengthy footnote with a final definition of good taste in music, one that recalls Mattheson's in its recourse to the majority of individual opinions. Asking what German composers must do to assure the presence of good taste in their music, Heinichen answers that music that is in good taste will appeal to many different types of people, no matter what their degree of education, their personal temperament, or their country of origin.

With Johann Scheibe's *Compendium musices* (Leipzig, 1736), the idea of good taste is considerably expanded. Scheibe, citing Heinichen's

General-Bass, retains the older composer's emphasis on *cantabile* melody, but extends taste to include all the qualities of a good composer:

> If a beginner will heed well all that has been set forth in this *Compendium*, then will he finally also acquire taste, and thereby find universal applause. No one, however, will acquire taste until he has comprehended the fundamental rules expounded in the first and other chapters, besides choosing for himself a distinctive style, knowing well the other sorts of styles according to their internal and external characteristics, expressing well the affections and the rest, judging well the time, place, and audience, possessing a knowledge of the different customary instruments, and showing a judicious use of modulation and variation and in all things a dominating cantabile.[76]

Scheibe also attempts a clarification of the distinction between style and taste. In his chapter on style, he cautions the reader not to confuse the term *goût* with the idea of style: the differences between French, German, and Italian music, as well as between personal idioms of individual composers, are stylistic differences, not differences of taste. Style, in other words, governs categories, while taste governs quality; an individual composer's distinctive style must not be confused with *goût*, "for the manner in which each composer presents his thought, no less than his innermost being, is always different from that of another, though both may possess taste."[77]

Scheibe recognizes the individual merits of the three major styles (French, Italian, German), but does not favor a stylistic synthesis; to him, not only is the idea of taste inappropriate for national differences, but the notion of "mixed taste" is wholly opposed to that of style itself, which demands separate categories: "In regarding the music itself, one must take heed, whether working in the French, Italian, or German style, that one should not be mixed with the other, for the clarity of style must be as carefully observed as the expression of the thing itself."[78]

Scheibe's *Compendium musices*, fundamentally a practical handbook, merely adumbrates the theories which figure prominently in his musical journal, *Der critische Musikus*. Scheibe, as we have seen, was strongly influenced by the classical rationalism of Gottsched, which is filtered through his own musical learning to become a deep respect for the art of criticism and a desire to apply it to music, a lasting mistrust of the musical excesses of Italian opera, and a strong desire to see the music of his own country fulfill its latent potential. Scheibe's reverence for the classical ideal of the natural in music causes him to favor the melodic style of the more progressive composers Telemann and Graun, while he frowns upon the complicated counterpoint of Bach; the melodic achievements of the modern composers are natural and reasonable, and the counterpoint of Bach "artificial and tiresome."[79] This theory is elaborated in

Scheibe's discussion of old and new music. After criticizing the artificialities and complexities of music of the past, he extolls the more modern style of his contemporaries:

> If we look, on the other hand, at the symphony in its present state, we certainly will find quite different traits. There a flowing, expressive, and lively melody is followed, which alone has nature for its mother: thus are very different and more pleasant effects acheived. . . . It is through melody, then, that all kinds of affections and passions can be aroused and expressed.[80]

Scheibe's journal, the *Critischer Musikus*, is founded on the ideals of French classicism. Thus, in the opening article (March 5, 1737), Scheibe sets the tone for the entire series. At last, he says, German learning has shaken off the shackles of barbarism and has successfully followed the example of the French in the critical researches into poetry and rhetoric. "Good taste begins to rule, and through it we begin to experience how fortunate those are, who follow reason and nature in a well-proven method of criticism."[81]

Music remains to be investigated with these newly-developed critical tools, but the main stumbling block to such research is the awe in which Italian music is held: "The prejudice on the side of the beauties of Italian music has misled many German composers and musicians. But what else were they to do? Taste was set by those people who had no idea what good taste was. . . ."[82] Calling for the independence of German music, Scheibe pleads with his countrymen to flee the "unnatural and despicable" taken from foreigners, and to establish good taste once and for all in their own country.

Scheibe differs from most other critics in forbidding a stylistic synthesis of French and Italian characteristics. His ideal is rather purity of national style, and he emphatically distinguishes the ideas of style and taste.[83] But the result of what Scheibe proposes is not so different from what other critics call "mixed taste," for to him the touchstone of good taste is a perfect blending of sense and reason. In a footnote to an article by a contributor, Scheibe takes issue with the writer's attribution of good taste to the sole criterion of the senses:

> A mere judgment of the senses without reference to the understanding is by no means good taste. It is true that the impressions of the ears, according to one's feelings, are necessary; but shall we not also perceive the subtle mistakes as well as the finest beauties of a piece? . . . If we combine experience of the senses with the capacity of the understanding, then will we be able to call the resulting judgment good taste.[84]

In his essay on good taste,[85] Scheibe presents a more concise definition of *guter Geschmack* as "an ability of the understanding to judge what the senses experience."[86] He decries the servile imitation of the Italians which has characterized German music and concludes that, among the contemporary generation, German composers have succeeded in achieving the necessary synthesis of sense and reason, whereas the Italians have not:

> This, then, is what I, from past to present, consider necessary regarding good taste in music. My readers can by this time quite easily judge that those composers who oppose the characteristics of good taste are neither regular nor clear-sighted, [but are] miserable bunglers in music. . . . Men who, however, like Hasse, Graun, Telemann, and Handel, write with a healthy imagination and sensibility, in whose works a praiseworthy reason reigns, and who show both rules and spirit in all the notes, such men are these who possess good taste. . . . We are no longer imitators of the Italians; moreover we can justifiably praise ourselves, that the Italians have finally become the imitators of the Germans.[87]

After Scheibe, the general principles of French classicism in music found a proponent in Friedrich W. Marpurg who, like Scheibe, was influenced both by the French classicists and by their German advocate Johann Christoph Gottsched. Marpurg's *Critischer Musicus an der Spree* (Berlin, 1749–1750) was modeled in several respects on Scheibe's *Critischer Musikus*, and just as Scheibe had announced the independence of German music, so Marpurg declares, "Finally Germany approaches the happy period in which it not only should perfect its taste, but even become a model for foreigners."[88] Marpurg's writings are filled with criticisms of Italian music, where, according to him, "the most miserable harmony accompanies the most vulgar melody,"[89] and of performance practice, in which the performer "dies of sweetness."[90] But in his discussions French music hardly comes off better, for Marpurg believes that the preeminence formerly enjoyed by the French now belongs to the Germans.

Marpurg's ideas on national style are clarified in the commentary to his translation of Christian Gottlieb Krause's *Lettre à le Marquis de B. sur la différence de la musique italienne et la musique française* (Berlin, 1748).[91] Krause (1718–1795), a leading German theorist most widely known for his treatise *Von der musikalischen Poesie* (Berlin, 1753),[92] had published this work anonymously in the French language. It is important for its assessment of French and Italian music in terms of the contemporary *style galant*. The Italians, says Krause, prefer to be entertained and diverted than to be genuinely moved by music, and the French, who prefer to be subtly touched, are made uncomfortable by the excesses of Italian opera. Good art, however, must combine the virtues of the French and Italians, besides being always natural, clear, and pleasing. Krause takes the aria "Il mio caro vincitore" from Graun's opera *Cinna* as a good example of the *style galant*, which he equates with "mixed style." This work touches the heart, but also entertains; it exemplifies the simplicity and naturalness of the French style as well as the majesty and strength of the Italian. Thus, Krause declares, the two virtues can be combined, but only where fashion, wittiness, and enthusiasm are not allowed to overshadow simple feelings and agreeable emotions.

Marpurg's strongest disagreement is occasioned by Krause's statement that the Germans have no unique taste in music, that Handel and Telemann incline toward the French taste, Hasse and Graun toward the Italian. Krause had also maintained that the Italian style dominated the French in Germany, but Marpurg insists that the *style galant* as exemplified by Hasse and Graun is German, not Italian, and that Krause is misled by the Italian language of the libretto. On the contrary, Marpurg states, "Our present style has never been known in Italy. The objections which St.-Evremond and the other Frenchmen made to Italian music, even less deserved then than now by the Italians, do not apply to our celebrated taste in music."[93] On the other hand, Marpurg speculates that perhaps any excellent style in music is in reality the result of a synthesis. In this perspective, not only the German but also the French and Italian styles themselves may be considered "mixed styles."

A mid-century summary of national styles in connection with criticism and good taste may be found in Johann Joseph Quantz's *Versuch einer Anweisung die Flöte traversiere zu spielen* (Berlin, 1752). In his chapter on the judgment of music,[94] Quantz gathers together all the aspects of current thought in Germany regarding criticism, and recasts it as a series of formulas that may be used by the amateur in shaping his taste. After opening with a statement of his belief that the only way music can be judged is through good taste, Quantz proceeds to show how this quality is applied to the three objects of criticism: the piece of music, the performer, and the subjective situation of the listener himself. He then gives comprehensive definitions and explanations of the forms and genres of composition, systematized almost to the point of pedantry.

Over half of the chapter is devoted to national styles, indicating Quantz's assessment of the importance of that subject for the criticism of music. France and Italy, Quantz admits, have achieved distinction through the development of their divergent tastes, but have set themselves up as tyrannical arbiters of taste throughout the civilized world. In analyzing the French and Italian tastes (Quantz does not distinguish between taste and style), Quantz makes detailed surveys of the respective vocal and instrumental music, as well as the performance practices, of the two countries. In summarizing his findings, he characterizes the Italians as "unrestrained, sublime, lively, expressive, profound, and majestic in their manner of thinking; they are rather bizarre, free, daring, bold, extravagant, and sometimes negligent in metrics," but at the same time they are "singing, flattering, tender, moving, and rich in invention."[95] The French, on the other hand, are "lively, expressive, natural, pleasing and comprehensible to the public, and more correct in metrics," but they are "neither profound nor venturesome," but rather "limited and slavish, always imitating themselves, stingy in their manner of thinking, and dry in invention."[96]

Conceding that Germany has produced no distinctive taste of its own, Quantz maintains that is possesses the superior virtue of knowing better how to adapt the tastes of other nations. Celebrated German composers such as Froberger, Pachelbel, J. S. Bach, and Telemann, who have either visited France and Italy or studied their musical styles, have contributed to a general improvement of taste in Germany. Though the Italians in the past have called German taste "barbarous," the Germans now have one composer[97] whom the Italians themselves find the most tasteful of all. Quantz foresees the establishment of a universal good taste if only the French and Italians will imitate the German penchant for synthesis as the Germans have imitated their styles of composition:

> . . . if further, the Italians and the French will imitate the Germans in the mixture of tastes, as the Germans have imitated their tastes . . . then might, in time, a general good taste in music be introduced. And this is not so improbable, because neither the Italians nor the French—though I refer more to the amateurs among them than to the professional musicians—are really content with their pure national tastes, but rather for some time have shown more pleasure in certain foreign compositions than in those which are indigenous to their own countries.[98]

Differences of national style, then, continued to spark lively discussion in Germany at least through the sixth decade of the eighteenth century. The French debates over French and Italian music were dutifully reported to the German readers of musical journals, and a place was quite naturally sought for German music among the national styles. Heinichen's transmission[99] and espousal in 1728 of an earlier French proposal of a "mixed taste," which would incorporate the finest elements of the French and Italian styles, led almost a quarter of a century later to Quantz's declaration of such a synthesis as a *fait accompli*; indeed, such a synthesis characterizes both the pre-classical style of Hasse, Telemann, and Graun and the fully mature classical style of Haydn and Mozart. As in France and Britain, the synthesis of French and Italian styles was symptomatic of a more general aesthetic reconciliation of the opposing criteria of sense and reason in the apprehension of beauty. Such a reconciliation had been proposed by the abbé Dubos in France and David Hume and others in

Britain, but it was the German philosopher Immanuel Kant whose final synthesis of the demands of sensation and individual taste with those of reason and knowledge is considered definitive.[100]

The German writers on national styles and taste differ on details, but all agree on the growing preeminence of the German musical style; the more progressive regard it as a *"vermischte Geschmack,"* while the conservatives—especially Scheibe and Marpurg—defend it against the excesses of Italian music just as Lecerf had defended Lully's style against Italian opera. In a sense, however, the label "conservative" is misleading, for with the German writers influenced by French classical theory, a desire to imitate nature and an abhorrence of the excesses of the Italian (and German) *"barroque"* led to an emphasis in music on simple homophony, clear, undistorted melody, and an avoidance of contrapuntal complexity, thus establishing a link between French classicism and the modern German *style galant*.[101]

This link was forged most forcefully by Gottsched, who transformed the literary criticism of Boileau and the French classicists into German operatic criticism. Scheibe and Marpurg were the direct heirs of this German brand of classicism, but other theorists were also affected by literary classicism itself as well as the quarrels over French and Italian music. Mattheson, Quantz, and C. P. E. Bach call again and again for clarity and simplicity, and Mattheson makes specific reference to the theories of Boileau.[102] Especially for Mattheson, Bach, and the later theorists, however, the classical ideals mingled with the Italian desire for a dominating *cantabile*, as well as the empirical approach of the abbé Dubos and the English theorists. From French classicism, then, came the emphasis on the terms *klar, deutlich, Natur, Simplizität*, while the terms *ausdrückend* (as opposed to *nachahmend*) and *Rührung* bear witness to the theories of the later Enlightenment. Finally, the Germans themselves seem to have contributed the elements of *Zärtlichkeit, sanfte Affekte*, and *Mannigfaltigkeit* along with a conscious tendency toward the breaking of the rules.[103]

Thus, in spite of the protests of Marpurg and Scheibe, the theory of the *vermischte Geschmack* became a reality in the German *style galant*, finally fulfilling the old prophecy "that a perfect genre of music can result from the joining of the learned and ingenious taste of the Italians with the natural and simple good taste of the French."[104] And this synthesis anticipated that of the later Viennese classic composers, whose works represent the ultimate blending of the earlier French, Italian, and German traditions.

Notes

Chapter I

1. Edme Jacques Benoit Rathéry, *L'influence d'Italie sur les lettres françaises du XIIIe siècle au règne de Louis XIV* (Paris, 1853), pp. 52–64 ("Guerres des Français en Italie").

2. Auguste Bailly, *François Ier, restaurateur des lettres et des arts* (Montreal, 1954), pp. 211–31, and Emile Picot, "Les Italiens en France au XVIe siècle," *Bulletin italien de la Faculté des lettres de Bordeaux* 1 (1901):148–54.

3. One of the best of these was Jehan Marot, father of the poet Clement Marot, who described the victory of Louis XII against the Genoans in his *Voyage de Gênes* of 1507; crit. ed. by Giovanna Trisolini (Geneva, 1974). See Trisolini's introduction, pp. 25–35, for a discussion of the work in light of anti-Italian sentiment.

4. Crit. ed. with introduction by Jean Frappier (Paris, 1947).

5. Ibid., pp. 3–6.

6. Ibid., pp. 43–46.

7. On the French reaction to Italian influence in this period, see Lionello Sozzi, "La polémique anti-italienne en France au XVIe siècle," *Estratto dagli Atti della Accademia delle scienze di Torino* 106 (1971–72):99–190.

8. *Divers jeux rustiques* (Paris, 1568), crit. ed. by V. L. Saulnier (Geneva and Lille, 1947), p. 84:

> "Je ne suis point si subtil artizan
> Que de pouvoir d'un parler courtizan
> D'un faulx soupir et d'une larme feincte,
> Monstrer dehors une amitié contraincte,
> Dissimulant mon visage par art,
> Car je ne suis ny Thuscan ny Lombard."

9. Ibid., p. 79:

> "Noz bons ayeulx, qui cest art démenoient,
> Pour en parler Pétrarque n'apprenoient,
> Ains franchement leur Dame entretenoient
> Sans fard ou couverture.
> Mais aussi tost qu'Amour s'est faict sçavant,
> Luy, qui estoit François au paravant,
> Est devenu flatteur et decevant
> Et de thusque nature."

10. Baldassare Castiglione, *Il libro del cortegiano* (Venice, 1528), crit. ed. Vittorio Cian (Florence, 1894), pp. 104–6.

11. Emile Picot, "Les italiens en France," pp. 174–79, gives an extensive list of the Italians surrounding Catherine.

12. Henri Estienne, *Principium monitrix musa* (Basel, 1590), pp. 253–55; Innocent Gentillet, *Discours sur les moyens de bien gouverner. Contre Machiavel florentin* (Paris, 1576), trans. Simon Paterick as *A Discourse upon the means of wel governing. Against Nicolas Machiavel the Florentine* (London, 1602; facs. ed., New York, 1969).

13. Facs. ed. (Geneva, 1972).

14. See, for example, Philausone's greeting of Celtophile (ibid., p. 1): "Bon iour vostre Seigneuserie, Monsieur Celtophile. Puis qu'elle s'allegre tant de m'auoir rencontré, ie iouiray d'une allegresse reciproque de m'estre imbatu en ce lieu," an Italianized version of Celtophile's greeting: "Bon iour, Monsieur Philausone, ie suis fort ioyeux de cette rencontre."

15. Crit. ed. by Léon Feugère (Paris, 1850).

16. Ibid., pp. 15–16. Cf. the proverbial statement of Charles V (1500–1558), Holy Roman Emperor: "Je parle espagnol à Dieu, italien aux femmes, français avec hommes, et allemand à mon cheval."

17. Daniel Heartz, "Les goûts-réunis, or the Worlds of the Madrigal and Chanson Confronted," in *Chanson and Madrigal 1480–1530: Studies in Comparison and Contrast*, ed. James Haar (Cambridge, Mass., 1964), pp. 88–138.

18. As Henry Prunières shows in his *La musique de la chambre de l'Ecurie sous François Ier et Henri II* (Paris, 1912), Italian musicians were prevalent at the French court throughout the reigns of Francis I and Henry II, though Italian singers were less numerous than Italian instrumentalists.

19. Marie Bobillier [Michel Brenet], *Notes sur l'histoire du luth en France* (Turin, 1899; repr. ed., Geneva, 1973), pp. 10–13.

20. André Verchaly, "Les airs italien mis en tablature de luth dans les receuils français du début du XVIIe siècle," *Revue de musicologie* 35 (1953):45–48.

21. Henry Prunières, *L'opéra italien en France avant Lully* (Paris, 1913), pp. xvi–xxv.

22. *Les origines de l'opéra et le Ballet de la reine (1581)* (Paris, 1868), p. 42: ". . . je dois reconnaître que la *Circé* dut son existence en grande partie à l'esprit italien. . . ." On this work, see also Henry Prunières, *Le ballet de cour en France avant Benserade et Lully* (Paris, 1914, pp. 82–88; and Margaret McGowan, *L'art du ballet du cour en France, 1581–1643* (Paris, 1963).

23. Louis Batiffol, *Marie de Medicis and the French Court in the XVIIth Century*, trans. Mary King (London, 1908), pp. 163–69, 220–53, 66–70; Berthold Zeller, in his biography *Henri IV et Marie de Médicis* (Paris, 1877), pp. 82–83, maintains that the course of Henry's reign would probably have been changed entirely if he had been able to diminish the influence of the Italians surrounding Marie.

24. James B. Perkins, *France under Richelieu and Mazarin* (London, 1886; third ed., 1887), pp. 1–30, 61–83, 223–30. On the general political backgrounds of early seventeenth-century France, see also Jean-Baptiste Capefigue's *Richelieu, Mazarin, la Fronde, et le règne de Louis XIV*, 8 vols. (Paris, 1835–36).

25. Rathéry, *L'influence d'Italie*, p. 151. On Italian influence in France during this period, see also F. Neri, "L'italianismo in Francia nel XVIIe siècle," *Letteratura e leggenda* (Turin, 1951); René Pintard, "Influences italiennes en France au XVIIe siècle," *Revue des études italiennes* 1 (1936):194–224; and Philippe van Tieghem, *Les influences étrangères sur la littérature française (1550–1880)* (Paris, 1961).

26. The manners of the Hôtel de Rambouillet and similar salons were based to a large extent on Castiglione's *Il cortegiano* (see note 9 above); Nicolas Faret's influential *L'honnête homme, ou l'art de plaire à la cour* (1632) is largely a translation of Castiglione. See Maurice Magendie's *La politesse mondaine et les théories de l'honneté en France au XVIIe siècle de 1600–1660* (Paris, 1925).

27. René Bray, *La préciosité et les précieux* (Paris, 1948), pp. 101–239. See also Antoine Adam, "Baroque et préciosité," *Revue des sciences humaines* (April–June, 1949): 208–24.

28. On the later application of the stylistic designation "baroque" to this art, see Adam, "Baroque et préciosité"; J. Rousset, *La littérature de l'âge baroque en France* (Paris, 1953); René Welleck, "The Concept of Baroque in Literary Scholarship," *Journal of Aesthetics and Art Criticism* 5 (1946):77–109; and Cecilia Rizza, *Barocco francese e cultura italiana* (Genoa, 1973). Of these Rizza makes the strongest case for the influence of Italy on the French Baroque.

29. Rizza, *Barocca francese*, pp. 69–78 ("Una testimonianza dimenticata sul soggiorno del Marino a Parigi").

30. Ibid., pp. 39–68 and 79–96; also C. W. Cabeen, *L'influence de Marino sur la littérature française de la première moitié du XVIIe siècle* (Grenoble, 1904) and *Marino e i mar-*

inisti, crit. ed. of poetry by Marino and his followers by Giuseppe Guido Ferrero, in *La letteratura italiana: Storia e testi,* vol. 37 (Naples and Milan, n.d.). The classical reaction will be discussed below in Chapter IV.

31. *Menagiana, ou les bons mots et remarques critiques, historiques, morales & d'érudition de Monsieur Menage, receuillies par ses amis* (Paris, 1715; repr. ed., 1729), p. 264: "Les opéras nous viennent d'Italie. Un de leurs premiers Auteurs, c'est Rinoucini. Cet homme étoit un peu fou . . . il se mit en tête que Marie de Médicis l'aimoit. . . . Dans cette ridicule pensée il passa avec elle en France, où la vertu de cette Reine fit bientôt perdre contenance." ("Opera comes to us from Italy. One of its first authors is Rinuccini. This man was a bit mad . . . be became convinced that Marie de Medici loved him. . . . Because of this ridiculous idea he followed her to France, where the queen's virtue soon made him lose face.")

32. Wilhelm Pfannkuch, "Rinuccini," *MGG* 11 (1963), cols. 543–46; Prunières, *L'opéra italien*, pp. xxviii–xxix.

33. Angelo Solerti, "Un viaggio in Francia di Giulio Caccini (1604–1605)," *Rivista musicale italiana* 10 (1903):107–10; on Caccini in France see also Ferdinand Boyer, "Giulio Caccini à la cour d'Henri IV (1604–1605)," *Revue musicale* 7 (1926):241–50, and Prunières, *L'Opéra italien*, pp. xxx–xxxi.

34. The alexandrine structure   immediately comes to mind as a distinguishing feature of French vocal music as late as Lully and even Rameau.

35. James R. Anthony, *French Baroque Music from Beaujoyeulx to Rameau* (New York, 1974; rev. ed., 1978), pp. 345–53; David Maland, *Culture and Society in Seventeenth-Century France* (New York, 1970), pp. 79–80. Guédron did attempt to adapt the Italian recitative style to French music, but his efforts were not well received; see André Verchaly, "Guédron," *MGG* 5 (1956), cols. 1017–22.

36. Examples 1–3 are taken from Théodore Gérold's analysis in *L'art du chant en France au XVIIe siècle* (Strasbourg, 1921; repr. ed., New York, 1973), pp. 86–91 ("Influences étrangères"). On the Italian style see also Hugo Goldschmidt, *Die italienische Gesangsmethode des 17. Jahrhunderts* (Breslau, 1898); and Nigel Fortune, "Italian Seventeenth-Century Singing," *Music and Letters* 35 (1954):211–12 and 214.

37. Tallemant de Réaux, *Historiettes* (first published Paris, 1833); repr. ed. by Antoine Adam, 2 vols. (Paris, 1961), 2:270: ". . . revint à Paris, il y a bien dix-sept ans, où elle se mit à chanter des airs italiens: elle avoit appris à Turin. Elle fit bien de bruit, mais cela ne dura guères; plusieurs trouvent mesme qu'elle chante mal, car c'est tout-à-fait à la maniere d'Italie, et elle grimace horriblement; on diroit qu'elle a des convulsions."

38. Quoted by Verchaly, "Les airs italiens," p. 50: "Leurs accords et musique est fort remplie et ils chantent bien selon leur mode que l'on ne gouste pas du premier abord pour n'y prendre pas beaucoup de plaisir, et la trouve différente de notre usage . . ."

39. Tallemant de Réaux, *Historiettes*, 2:521: ". . . de Niert prit ce que les Italiens avoient de bon dans leur maniere de chanter, et le meslant avec ce que nostre maniere avoit

aussy de bon, il fit cette nouvelle methode de chanter que Lambert pratique aujourd'huy, et à laquelle peut-estre il a adjousté quelque chose. . . ." (Michel Lambert was a well-known composer of the generation preceding Lully.)

40. Edited by Antoine E. Roquet in *Maugars, célèbre joueur de viole, musicien du cardinal Richelieu . . . sa biographie suivie de sa "Response faite à un curieux . . ."* (Paris, 1865: repr. ed., Geneva, 1972). Roquet's introduction is a major source of information on Maugars' biography.

41. Margaret McGowan, in "The Origins of French Opera," *New Oxford History of Music* 5 (London, 1975):187, states that Richelieu sent Maugars to Italy specifically to write the report; Roquet (pp. 1–22) maintains that Maugars' professional haughtiness caused an imbroglio with another of the cardinal's favorites and he was banished. A passage in Tallemant de Réaux's *Historiettes* (2:375) seems to corroborate the latter view. According to this, de Nyert reported to the king a witticism that Maugars had made concerning his taste. This amused the king, but enraged Richelieu, who instructed the abbé de Beaumont to have Maugars banished from France.

42. Roquet, *Maugars*, p. 26: ". . . que leurs compositions de chapelle ont beaucoup plus d'art, de science et de variété que les nostres; mais aussi elles ont plus de license."

43. Ibid.: ". . . aussi ne puis-je approuver l'opinastreté de nos Compositeurs, qui se tiennent trop réligieusement renfermez dans des cathégories pédantesques et qui croirent faire des solécismes contre les règles de l'Art, s'ils faisoient deux quintes de suite, ou s'ils sortoient tant soit peu de leurs modes."

44. Ibid., p. 31: ". . . je suis tombé insensiblement sur la loüange de cet excellent homme. . . ."

45. Ibid., p. 34: ". . . qu'un homme seul peut produire de plus belles inventions que quatre voix ensemble, et qu'elle a des charmes et des licences que la Vocale n'a pas."

46. L. Pannella, "Baroni," *Dizionario biografico degli Italiani* 6 (1964): 456–58.

47. Roquet, *Maugars*, p. 37–38: ". . . j'oubliay ma condition mortelle, et creuz estre desia parmy les anges, jouyssant des contentemens des bienheureux." Not all accounts of Leonora's singing were so flattering, however; Romain Rolland quotes one anonymous contemporary as saying, "One began by thinking that her voice was better suited to the theater, or the church, than to *salons*, and that her Italian method was vocally rather hard" (*Some Musicians of Former Days*, trans. Mary Blaiklock [1915; reprint, Freeport, N.Y., 1968]), p. 74.

48. Ibid., p. 40: ". . . qui a si bien ajusté la méthode Italienne avec la Françoise, qu'il en a reçeu un applaudissement général de tous les honnêtes gens."

49. Ibid., p. 41: ". . . que nous péchons dans le défaut, et les Italiens dans l'excez."

50. Ibid., pp. 41–42: ". . . Compositions, qui eussent leurs belles Varietez, sans avoir toutefois leurs extravagances. . . ."

51. Included in *Correspondance du père Marin Mersenne*, ed. Cornelis de Waard (Paris, 1932–), *passim*. On Doni, see Anna Amalie Abert, "Doni," *MGG* 3 (1954), cols. 673–78.

52. Doni's significance in the quarrels over ancient and modern music will be discussed in Chapter II.

53. Mersenne, *Correspondance* 6 (1960):32: "Car au lieu de faire la melodie variee et artificieuse, ils l'on faicte pour la pluspart simple et triviale, comme l'on voit en la suitte des notes qui s'arrestent souvent sur la mesme corde. Tant s'en faut doncques que voz musiciens soient obbligez à ce stile, que pour moy ils ont le chemin ouvert de la perfectionner beaucoup en le changeant. . . . Et je m'asseure que si voz Princes vouloient faire la despence et que le temps le permist, cela reussiroit assez heureusement."

54. Mersenne, *Correspondance* 5 (1959):2–3: "Pour ce qui est de ce que vous me demandez si la musique Italiene est meilleure que la françoise, c'est une grande controverse, nos François qui vienent ici treuvant la musique italiene desagreable, et les Italiens estimant la nostre ridicule et de nulle consideration. Que si vous en voulez sçavoir mon jugement, je vous dirai que, pour l'artifice, la science et la fermeté de chanter, pour la quantité de musiciens, principalement de chastrez, Rome surpasse autant Paris que Paris fait Vaugirard. Mais pour la delicatesse, et *una certa leggiadria e dilettevole naturalezza* des airs, les François surpassent les Italiens de beaucoup. . . . Le François est plus gentil et agreable, l'Italien plus sçavant et admirable."

55. Mersenne, *Harmonie universelle* (Paris, 1636–37); facs. ed. by François Lesure, 3 vols. (Paris, 1963), 2:356: ". . . auec vne violence si estrange, que l'on iugeroit quasi qu'ils sont touchez des mesmes affections qu'ils representent en chantant; au lieu que nos François se contentent de flatter l'oreille, & qu'ils vsent d'vne douceur perpetuelle dans leurs chants; ce qui en empesche l'energie."

56. Ibid., p. 357: "Mais nos Musiciens sont, ce semble, trop timides pour introduire cette maniere de recit en France, quoy qu'ils en soient aussi capables que les Italiens, si quelques-vns les y poussent, qui vueillent faire la dépence requise en un tel sujet."

57. Quoted by Romain Rolland in "L'Opéra au XVIIe siècle," *Encyclopédie de la musique et dictionnaire du conservatoire*, pt. 1, 3:1346: "La nation italienne n'a aucune aptitude naturelle à la modulation et au chant comparée à la nation française."

58. *Mémoires* 3:206: ". . . bien qu'elle ne soit pas si bruïante, & qu'elle ait plus de douceur; mais il semble que ce ne soient pas des qualités pour la rendre plus mauvaise."

59. Père Ménestrier later described (1681) how Perrin altera la structure of French poetry to render it more suitable for opera. See p. 25 below.

60. Gérold, *L'art du chant*, pp. 101–2.

61. On Mazarin's early training, see Georges Dethan, *The Young Mazarin* (London, 1977), pp. 13–38; Victor Cousin, *La jeunesse de Mazarin* (Paris, 1865), pp. 6–11; and Georges Montgrédien, ed., *Mazarin* (Paris, 1959), pp. 6–51.

62. On Mazarin's patrons, see Dethan, *The Young Mazarin*, pp. 38–67; "Barberini" in *Dizionario biografico degli Italiani* 6 (1964):166–70; and Pio Pecchiai, *I Barberini* (Rome, 1959). On Rome as a center of opera in the seventeenth century, see Paul Kast, "Rom (D. Barock)," *MGG* 11 (1963), cols. 711–39.

63. On Mazarin and Italian opera, see Rolland, *Some Musicians*, pp. 70–71; Robert M. Isherwood, *Music in the Service of the King: France in the Seventeenth Century* (Ithaca, 1973), pp. 116–34; and Lionel de la Laurencie, *Les créateurs de l'opéra français* (Paris, 1921), pp. 132–48.

64. She stayed in Paris for a year in 1644, and left Rome to live in Paris in 1645 (Pannella, "Baroni," p. 457).

65. Isherwood, *Music in the Service of the King*, p. 118.

66. The exact dates of their arrivals are given by Fausto Torrefranca, "Mazarin," *MGG* 8 (1960):1853–54.

67. Per Bjurström, *Giacomo Torelli and Baroque Stage Design* (Stockholm, 1962), pp. 122–26.

68. Claude François Ménestrier, in *Des représentations en musique anciennes et modernes* (Paris, 1681; facs. ed., Geneva, 1972), gives a detailed account of this work, pp. 230–35.

69. Anthony, in *French Baroque Music*, pp. 46–47, gives a brief summary of Italian opera in France before Rossi's *Orfeo*. The most thorough treatment of the subject, which all later accounts continue to follow, is Prunière's *L'opéra italien*, pp. 45–85; see also McGowan, "The Origins of French Opera," pp. 186–97; La Laurencie, *Les créateurs*, pp. 128–49; Charles Truinet and A. E. Roquet [Nuitter et Thoinan], *Les origines de l'opéra français* (Paris, 1886). For a contemporary account of many of these works, see Ménestrier, *Des représentations*, *passim*.

70. Perkins, *France under Richelieu*, pp. 377–446.

71. Discussions of *Orfeo* may be found in Rolland, *Some Musicians*, pp. 83–127; La Laurencie, *Les créateurs*, pp. 136–43; Bjurström, *Giacomo Torelli*, pp. 143–47; Prunières, *L'opéra italien*, pp. 86–150; LaVerne Dalka, "Luigi Rossi's *Orfeo*, Paris, 1647: A Documentary and Analytical Study" (Ph.D. dissertation, Yale, forthcoming); William C. Holmes, "Rossi," *MGG* 11 (1963), cols. 938–42.

72. Joseph Michaud and Jean Poujoulat, eds., *Nouvelle collection des mémoires pour servir à l'histoire de France, depuis le XIIIe siècle jusqu'a la fin du XVIIIe*, 32 vols. in 34 (Paris, 1836–39), 2:6: ". . . qui voyoient bien, par cette dépense excessive et superflue, que les besoins de l'Etat n'étoient pas si pressans, qu'on ne les eût épargnés si l'on eût voulu."

73. *Mémoires de Nicolas Goulas, gentilhomme ordinaire de la chambre du duc d'Orléans*, ed. Charles Constant, 3 vols. (Paris, 1879), 2:212: "Car chacun s'acharna sur l'horrible dépense des machines et des musiciens italiens qui étoient venus de Rome et d'ailleurs à grands frais, parce qu'il les fallut payer pour partir, venir, et s'entretenir en France.

Il y avoit douze ou quinze chastrés et quelques femmes, dont l'une ayant eu réputation de vendre sa beauté en Italie."

74. Isherwood, *Music in the Service of the King*, p. 125; Bjurström, *Giacomo Torelli*, pp. 122–26.

75. C. Moreau, ed., *Choix de Mazarinades*, 2 vols. (Paris, 1853), 2:243: "Ce beau, mais malheureux Orphée/Ou, pour mieux parler, ce Morphée/Puisque tant de monde y dormit." Moreau notes also a line from another poem: "Si vous n'êtes italien/Vous ne verrez pas l'Orphée" ("You will not see Orpheus unless you are Italian")—obviously a *double entendre* on the opera's plot.

76. Ibid., 1:99: "Qui ne scait ce que coustent à la France les comédiens chanteurs, qu'il a fait venir d'Italie, parmi lesquels estoit une infame qu'il auoit desbauchée à Rome, et par l'entremise de laquelle il s'estoit insinué dans les bonnes graces du Cardinal Antonio? Tout cela durant la guerre, dans le temps qu'on mettoit le peuple à la presse pour contribuer à la subsistance des armées; et le sang des pauures estoit employé à faire rire le Cardinal Mazarin . . . faisant connoistre a tout le monde qu'il n'a point d'autre Religion que celle de Machiauel. . . ." (The rumor that Leonora had been Mazarin's mistress in Rome was widespread.)

77. Henry Prunières and Lionel de La Laurencie, "La jeunesse de Lully," *Le Mercure musical* 5 (1909):234–42.

78. André Tessier, "Notice historique: Les premiers ballets de Lully," *Oeuvres complètes de Lully*, ed. Henry Prunières, vol. 3 (Paris, 1931):xiii–xxiii. On Lully's early ballets, see also Marie Christout, *Le ballet de cour de Louis XIV, 1643–1672* (Paris, 1967), pp. 9–66; and Prunières-La Laurencie, "La jeunesse de Lully," pp. 329–53.

79. Prunières, *L'opéra italien*, pp. 194–95.

80. On the ballets between 1653 and 1660, see Christout, *Le ballet de cour*, pp. 67–100.

81. Prunières, *L'opéra italien*, pp. 198–205.

82. Lully, *Oeuvres complètes*, vol. 5, ed. A. Dieudonné (Paris, 1930–39):46–48.

83. The duet is printed in Paul-Marie Masson's "Musique italienne et musique française: la première querelle," *Rivista musicale italiana* 19 (1912):521–25: *M.I.*: "Gentil Musica francese, Il mio canto in che t'offese?" *M.F.*: "En ce que souvent vos chants/Me semblent extravagants." *M.I.*: "Tu sormar altro non sai/Che languenti, che languenti e mesti lai." *M.F.*: "Et crois-tu qu'on aime mieux/Les longs fredons ennuyeux?" *M.I.*: "Io di le canto più forte/Perché amo più di te." *M.F.*: "La manière dont je chante/Exprime mieux ma langueur./Quand ce mal touche le coeur/La voix est moins éclatante."

84. Lully parodied the Italian style in several other works; for a discussion of these, see Norman Demuth, *French Opera* (Sussex, 1963; reprint ed. New York, 1978), pp. 159–61.

85. Opinions vary as to the ultimate influence of Italian opera on late seventeenth-century opera in France. Prunières (*L'opéra italien*) perhaps overestimates the impact of the Italians; Donald J. Grout, on the other hand, in his article "Some Forerunners of the Lully Opera," *Music and Letters* 22 (1941):1–25, sees Italian influence as secondary to that of French tragedy, pastoral, machine play, and—most importantly—ballet.

86. Charles de Bruny, *Examen de ministère de M. Colbert* (Paris, 1774), pp. 62–68.

87. Sources differ as to whether Lully collaborated in these festivites, which included Molière's *comédie-ballet Les Facheux*. Christout (*Le ballet de cour*, p. 183) mentions Lully as a participant, and McGowan ("The Origins of French Opera," p. 183) comments on his excellent performance as a dancer. Prunières (*L'opéra italien*, pp. 269–72) and Bjurström (*Giacomo Torelli*, pp. 180–83) maintain that Lully wisely declined to participate, and Bjurström finds no evidence of his participation in either of the primary sources for the ballet (Loret's *Muze historique* and a letter of La Fontaine to Maucroix). He mentions, however, that because of the haste in which the preparations were made, the ballet interludes did not exactly coincide with the comedy; this would introduce the possibility that preexistent music by Lully may have been used.

88. Prunières, *L'opéra italien*, pp. 269–72.

89. Lully continued, however, to use Italian numbers for special purposes; see, for example, the amusing Italian aria parody sung by "une musicienne italienne" in his *comédie-ballet Le Bourgeois gentilhomme*. Charles Silin, in *Benserade and his Ballets de Cour* (Baltimore, 1940; repr. ed., 1970), p. 197, states that of the six ballets staged between 1661 and 1664, three have Italian elements.

90. Richard Schaal and Eugène Borrel, "Lully," *MGG* 8 (1960), cols. 1299–1300.

91. Grout, "Some Forerunners," p. 14; Anthony, *French Baroque Music*, p. 64; Ménestrier, *Des représentations*, p. 208.

92. "Lettre écrite à Monseigneur l'archevesque de Turin," in *Les oeuvres de poésie de Mr. Perrin* (Paris, 1661), pp. 273–90; reprinted in Arthur Pougin, *Les vrais créateurs de l'opéra français: Perrin et Cambert* (Paris, 1881), pp. 56–68.

93. Ibid. (original edition), p. 286: "La belle et naturelle expression des passions. . . ."

94. Ibid., p. 287: "L'horreur des dames, & la risée des hommes. . . ."

95. A contemporary, Bénigne de Bacilly, manifests a similar attitude in his *L'art de bien chanter* (Paris, 1668), p. 98, in which he attributes any French deficiencies in the composition of Italianate works not to lack of talent, but to the French musical taste, which prefers shorter works to the long theatrical pieces of Italy.

96. For a discussion of anti-Italian criticism in the early seventeenth century, see René Bray, *La formation de la doctrine classique en France* (Paris, 1948), pp. 184–89.

97. On Boileau's anti-Italianism, see Gabriel Maugain, *Boileau et l'Italie* (Paris, 1912). This subject will be discussed in greater detail in Chapter IV.

98. Michael Turnbull, "Ercole and Hercule: les goûts désunis," *The Musical Times* (May 1980):303–7. For comments by a contemporary, see Jean Loret, *La muze historique*, ed. Ch.-L. Livet, vol. 3 (Vichy, 1878):465–92 (on *Ercole*), and 284–90 (on *Xerxes*).

99. Loret, *Muze historique*, p. 465.

100. Anthony, *French Baroque Music*, pp. 66–67.

101. On Lully's musical style, see Joyce Newman, *Jean-Baptiste de Lully and His Tragédies Lyriques* (Ann Arbor, 1979); La Laurencie, *Lully* (Paris, 1911); Anthony, *French Baroque Music*, pp. 39–46, 69–107; Paul-Marie Masson, "French Opera from Lully to Rameau," *New Oxford History of Music* 5 (London, 1975):206–26.

102. Good stylistic analyses of Cavalli and the later Italian composers may be found in Egon Wellesz, "Cavalli und der Stil der venetianischen Oper vom 1640–1660," *Studien zur Musikwissenschaft* 1 (1913):1–103; Prunières, *Cavalli et l'opéra vénitien au XVIIe siècle* (Paris, 1931); and Hermann Kretzschmar, "Die venetianische Oper und die Werke Cavalli's und Cesti's," *Vierteljahrsschrift für Musikwissenschaft* 8 (1892):1–76. Two important recent studies are Ellen Rosand, "Aria in the Early Operas of Cavalli" (Ph.D. dissertation, N.Y.U., 1971), and Jane Glover, *Cavalli* (London, 1978).

103. Grout, "Forerunners," p. 4, makes a strong case for the classical tragedy of Corneille and Racine as a definitive influence on Lully.

104. An excellent stylistic analysis of Lully's recitative is found in Newman, *Jean-Baptiste de Lully and His Tragédies Lyriques*.

105. Jean-Baptiste Dubos, *Réflexions critiques sur la poésie et sur la peinture*, 3 vols. (Paris, 1719; facs. repr. of seventh ed., Geneva, 1967), 3:144.

106. Masson, "French Opera," pp. 221–22.

107. "Sur les opéra à Monsieur le duc de Bouquinquant," *Oeuvres en prose* (Paris and Amsterdam, 1684); new ed. by René Ternois (Paris, 1962–), 3:149–66. On St.-Evremond as literary critic, see Quentin M. Hope, *Saint-Evremond: The Honnête Homme as Critic* (Bloomington, Ind., 1964).

108. Ibid., p. 155: ". . . pour connoître mieux les passions, et aller plus avant dans le coeur de l'homme que les Auteurs."

109. Ibid., p. 156: "Un méchant usage du Chant et de la Parole."

110. Ibid., p. 158: "Il n'y a point de Nation qui fasse voir plus de courage dans les hommes et plus de beauté dans les femmes, plus d'esprit dans l'un et dans l'autre sexe. On ne peut pas avoir toutes choses: où tant de bonnes qualités sont communes, ce n'est pas un si grand mal que le bon goût est si rare."

111. Ibid., p. 160: ". . . pour rendre une musique agréable il faloit des Airs Italiens dans la bouche des Francois."

112. Ibid., p. 163: ". . . comme si nous voulions réparer le faute d'avoir été prévenus dans l'invention, nous pousson jusqu'à l'excès un usage qu'ils avoient introduit. . . . En effet, nous couvrons la terre de Divinités, et les faisons danser par troupes. . . ."

113. *A New Voyage to Italy*, vol. 1 (London, 1699, "done out of French"), pp. 199–201, 242.

114. See note 69 above.

115. Ménestrier, *Des représentations*, p. 206: ". . . et que si l'on meloit un peu des manières de la Musique Italienne à nos façons de chanter on pourroit faire quelque chose qui ne seroit ny l'un ny l'autre, & qui seroit plus agréable."

116. "Lettre à M. de Niert sur l'opéra," *Oeuvres de Jean de La Fontaine*, ed. Jean Frappier, 11 vols. (Paris, 1883–97), 9:154–63.

117. La Fontaine's bitter distaste for Lully's music may be partially explained on the basis of his friendship with the Italophile Nyert, and also as a personal spite as a result of having had a libretto rejected by Lully. He had mounted a more purely personal attack on Lully in his satire *Le Florentin* of 1665, whose title recalls the pamphlets of the previous century against Machiavelli, also called "le Florentin" (see note 11 above). One of the characters condemns Lully: "Non, le diable, ennemi de tous les gens de bien,/Le diable, bien nommé diable, et qui ne vaut rien/Est moins jaloux, moins fol, moins méchant, moins bizzare,/Moins envieux, moins loup, moins vilain, moins avare/Moins scélérat, moins chien, moins traître, moins lutin,/Que n'est, pour nos péchés, ce maudit Florentin" ("No, the devil, enemy of all good people,/The devil, well called devil, and who is worthless/Is less jealous, less crazy, less evil, less bizarre,/Less envious, less a wolf, less a villain, less stingy,/Less criminal, less a dog, less a traitor, less a rogue/Than is, for our sins, this damned Florentine").

118. Obviously a parody of the favorite operatic myth, that of Orpheus, and probably also of Rossi's opera which had begun the furious debate over French and Italian music.

119. *La guerre des anciens et des modernes*, p. 228: "que peu de gens en sortent après une representation de trois heures, sans avoir mal à la tête, & sans y avoir bâillé fort frequemment."

120. Ibid., p. 231: ". . . au lieu que le Musicien devroit suivre les idées du Poéte, qu'il doit n'être employé qu'à augmenter la force de ses expressions, & à animer par des sons appropriées au sujet les grands traits de passion que le Poéte doit jetter dans ces sortes d'ouvrages destinez à être chantez."

121. For a detailed discussion of musical style in the seventeenth century, see Erich Katz, *Die musikalischen Stilbegriffe des 17. Jahrhunderts* (Charlottenburg, 1926).

Chapter II

1. Though critics did not refer to themselves as Ancients and Moderns until the seventeenth century, historians of literary criticism have begun to extend these terms to critics of the sixteenth century.

2. These quarrels are discussed in Bernard Weinberg, *A History of Literary Criticism in the Italian Renaissance*, 2 vols. (Chicago, 1961), 2:819–1105.

3. On the *Poetics*, see Lane Cooper, *The Poetics of Aristotle, Its Meaning and Influence* (New York, 1963); George Saintsbury, *A History of Criticism and Literary Taste in Europe from the Earliest Texts to the Present Day*, 3 vols. (London, 1900–1904; 2nd ed., 1949), 1:29–59; Bernard Bosanquet, *A History of Aesthetic* (London, 1892; second ed., 1904), pp. 55–76; and Weinberg, *History of Literary Criticism*, 1:349–714.

4. *Francisci Robortelli Vtinensis in librum Aristotelis De arte poetica explicationes* (Florence, 1548).

5. Weinberg, *History of Literary Criticism*, 1:808–11; good background information is also given in Joel E. Spingarn, *A History of Literary Criticism in the Renaissance: With Special Reference to the Influence of Italy in the Formation and Development of Modern Classicism* (New York, 1899), and Baxter Hathaway, *The Age of Criticism: The Late Renaissance in Italy* (Ithaca, 1962).

6. Sebastiano Minturno, *Arte poetica* (Venice, 1563; facsimile of 1564 ed., Munich, 1971), pp. 32–33: "Percioche una è la Verità: e quel, che una uolta è uero, conuien che sia sempre, & in ogni età, ne differenza di tempi il cangia. . . . Onde le uarietà de' tempi nata da poi non farà, che nella poesia trattarsi debba più, che una facenda intera, e di giusta grandezza, con la qual tutto l'altro uerisimilmente, e ragioneuolmente conuenga, e sia congiunto."

7. Trans. Paul Eugene Memmo as *The Heroic Frenzies* (Chapel Hill, 1965).

8. As modern musicians who may rival the ancients, Michele cites (p. 4v.) Josquin, Willaert, Lassus, and Marenzio.

9. The only survey of these musical quarrels is the one by Claude Palisca in his "The Beginnings of Baroque Music: Its Roots in Sixteenth-Century Theory and Practice" (Ph.D. dissertation, Harvard, 1953), pp. 87–133; my study is greatly indebted to his work.

10. Jacopo Sadoleto, *De pueris recte instituendis* (Venice, 1533; trans. E. T. Campagnac and K. Forbes as *Sadoleto on Education: A Translation of "De pueris recte instituendis,"* London, 1916), pp. 116–17.

11. A study of Vicentino's theories and musical compositions may be found in Henry Kaufmann's *The Life and Works of Nicola Vicentino, 1511–c.1576* (n. p., 1966); the debate with Lusitano is detailed on pp. 21–32. For the implications of the debate for the quarrel over ancient and modern music, see Palisca, "Beginnings of Baroque Music," pp. 104–23.

12. On the Camerata, see Nino Pirrotta, "Temperaments and Tendencies in the Florentine Camerata," *The Musical Quarterly* 40 (1954):169–89; Horton Lawrence Roe, "The *Camerata da' Bardi* and the Foundations of Music Drama" (Ph.D. dissertation, University of Wisconsin, 1951); and Claude Palisca, "The 'Camerata Fiorentina': A Reappraisal," *Studi musicali* 1 (1972):203–36.

13. On Bardi, see D. P. Walker, "Bardi," *MGG* 1 (1949), cols. 1256–59; also *Enciclopedia dello spettacolo* 1 (1954), cols. 1497–98.

14. Information on Mei's life and works may be found in Claude Palisca's introduction to *Girolamo Mei: Letters on Ancient and Modern Music to Vincenzo Galilei and Giovanni Bardi* (n. p., 1960), pp. 15–40; in Palisca's article "Girolamo Mei: Mentor to the Florentine Camerata," *The Musical Quarterly* 40 (1954):1–20; and in Barbara Hanning's *Of Poetry and Music's Power: Humanism and the Creation of Opera* (Ann Arbor: UMI Research Press, 1980)

15. *Poetics*, trans. Ingram Bywater, in: *The Works of Aristotle*, 11 (Oxford, 1908), 1. 1447a. 14–19: "Epic poetry and Tragedy, as also Comedy, Dithyrambic poetry, and most flute playing and lyre playing, are all, viewed as a whole, modes of imitation." On the importance of this idea for Renaissance music, see Armen Carapetyan, "The Concept of *Imitazione della natura* in the Sixteenth Century," *Journal of Renaissance and Baroque Music* 1 (1946):47–67. For further research on Aristotle and music, see Ulrich Fleischer, "Aristoteles," *MGG* 1 (1949), cols 631–39, and William L. Newman, *The "Politics" of Aristotle*, 4 vols. (Oxford, 1887–1902), 1:348–69.

16. Facs. ed., New York, 1965.

17. Zarlino, *Istitutioni harmoniche*, bk. 4, ch. 32; the passages on imitation are explicated by Carapetyan, "The Concept of *Imitazione*," pp. 54–55, 59–64.

18. *Pietro Vettori commentarii, in primum librum Aristotelis De arte poetarum* (Florence, 1560; facs. ed., Munich, 1967). See also Rosemary Jones, *Francesco Vettori, Florentine Citizen and Medici Servant* (London, 1972).

19. Sixteenth-century theories of catharsis were developed from Aristotle's brief comment in his definition of tragedy, *Poetics* 3.1449b.23–29: "A tragedy, then, is the imitation of an action that is serious . . . with incidents arousing pity and fear, wherewith to accomplish its catharsis of such emotions."

20. Palisca, *Girolamo Mei: Letters*, pp. 44–45.

21. Facs. ed., Brooklyn, 1967, p. 1: ". . . la qual parte da loro intesa, & apprezzata, hanno à poco à poco ridotta nel termine in che ella si ritroua. Ma non pare ad alcuni intelligenti, che l'habbiano resa all'antico suo stato, secondo che si può comprendere da infiniti luoghi dell'antiche historie, de' Poeti, & de' Filosofi; nè che habbiano conseguito di essa la vera, & perfetta notitia; il che può forse hauero ragionato la rozzezza de' tempi, la difficultà del soggetto, & la scarsità de' buoni interpreti. . . "

22. Ibid., pp. 88–89.

23. For a study of this quarrel, see Claude Palisca, :'The Artusi–Monteverdi Controversy," in: *The Monteverdi Companion* (New York, 1968), pp. 133–66; also Hans Redlich, "Artusi," *MGG* 1 (1949), cols. 147–49.

24. Preface to the Fifth Book of Madrigals (1605), in: *Claudio Monteverdi: Lettere, dediche e prefazione*, ed. Domenico de Paoli (Rome, 1973), pp. 391–92: ". . . send'io al servigio

de questa Serenissima Altezza di Mantoa non son patrone di quel tempo che tal'hora mi bisognarebbe: hò nondimeno scritta la risposta per far conoscer ch'io non faccio le mie cose a caso, e tosto che sia rescritta uscirà in luce portando in fronte il nome di SECONDA PRATICA overo PERFETTIONE DELLA MODERNA MUSICA del che forse alcuni s'ammireranno non credendo che vi sia altra pratica, che l'insegnata dal Zerlino; ma siano sicuri, che intorno alle consonanze, e dissonanze vi è anco qu'altra consideratione differente dalla determinata, la qual con quietanza della ragione, e del senso diffende il moderno comporre. . . .''

25. G. C. Monteverdi, gloss on Monteverdi's preface, originally printed at the end of Claudio Monteverdi's *Scherzi musicali* (Venice, 1607); facs. ed. in: *Tutte le opere di Claudio Monteverdi*, ed. Gian Francesco Malipiero (Vienna, 1926–1968), 10:69–72.

26. Scacchi's treatise is discussed by Claude Palisca in "Marco Scacchi's Defense of Modern Music (1649)," in: *Words and Music: the Scholar's View: A Medley of Problems and Solutions Compiled in Honor of A. Tillman Merritt by Sundry Hands*, ed. Laurence Berman (Cambridge, Mass., 1972), pp. 189–209.

27. On the dissemination of Monteverdi's classification of music according to practices and styles, see Erich Katz *Die musikalischen Stilbegriffe des 17. Jahrhunderts*; (Freiburg/Breisgau, 1926); and particularly J. M. Müller-Blattau, *Die Kompositions-Lehre Heinrich Schützens in der Fassung seines Schülers Christoph Bernhard* (Leipzig, 1926; second ed., Kassel, 1963).

28. Claude Palisca, "The Alterati of Florence, Pioneers in the Theory of Dramatic Music," in: *New Looks at Italian Opera: Essays in Honor of Donald J. Grout* (Ithaca, 1968), pp. 9–38.

29. Ibid., p. 17. Doni mentions a letter from Mei to Agostino del Nero as his original inspiration to study the music of antiquity in his *Lyra Barberina* (Florence, 1763), 1:324.

30. Palisca, "The Alterati," pp. 21–29; Hanning, in *Of Poetry and Music's Power*, analyzes in detail Giacomini's importance for musical thought.

31. Palisca, "The Alterati," p. 14.

32. Weinberg, *History of Criticism*, 2:836–47.

33. Ibid., pp. 985–87; Palisca, "The Alterati," pp. 34–35.

34. First published in Giovanni Battista Doni's *Lyra Barberina* (Florence, 1763; facs. ed., Bologna, 1974), 2:233–64.

35. C. Comte and Paul Laumonier, "Ronsard et les musiciens du XVIe siècle," *Revue d'histoire littéraire de la France* 7 (1900):341.

36. *Oeuvres complètes*, ed. Paul Laumonier (Paris, 1914–1917), 7:19–20: "Aussi les diuines fureurs de Musique, de Poesie, & de paincture, ne viennent pas par degrés en perfection comme les autres sçiences, mais par boutées & comme esclairs de feu, qui deça

qui dela apparoissent en diuers pays, puis tout en un coup s'esuanouissent. Et pource, Sire, quand il se manifeste quelque excellent ouurier en cet art, vous le deuez songneusement garder, comme chose d'autant excellente, que rarement elle apparoist. Entre lesquelz se sont depuis six ou sept vingtz ans esleve, Josquin des prez, Hennuyer de nation, & ses disciples Mouton, Vuillard, Richaffort, Janequin, cede en la perfection de cet art, aux anciens, pour estre inspiré de son Apollon Charles Cardinal de Lorraine." (The last sentence is reconstructed with the aid of a note given by Laumonier, 8:117).

37. Ibid., p. 20: "Et de present le plus que diuin Orlande, qui comme une mouche à miel a cueilly toutes les plus belles fleurs des antiens, & outre semble auoir seul desrobé l'harmonie des cieux pour nous en resiouir en la terre surpassant les antiens, & se faisant la seule merueille de notre temps."

38. An excellent study of Baif's ideas on music and poetry, and their indebtedness to earlier Italian and French poets and musicians, is Mathieu Augé-Chiquet's *La vie, les idées et l'oeuvre de Jean-Antoine de Baïf* (Paris, 1909), pp. 302–67 ("Les vers measurés [les principes]").

39. Frances Yates, *The French Academies of the Sixteenth Century*, Studies of the Warburg Institute, vol. 15 (London, 1947; repr. ed., Mendeln, 1965), pp. 36–94.

40. Tyard's musical theories are propounded in his *Solitaire premier, ou, Prose des muses & de la fureur poétique* (Lyons, 1552) and *Solitaire second, ou Discours de la musique* (Lyons, 1552). For biographical information, see S. F. Baridon *Pontus de Tyard* (Milan, 1953); on his musical theories, see Yates, *The French Academies*, pp. 77–87; also *MGG* 13 (1966), cols. 1005–6.

41. The idea of progress as a phenomenon of modern thought has been traced by J. B. Bury in his book *The Idea of Progress* (London, 1920; repr. ed., New York, 1932); Bury's theories have been recently updated and augmented by Robert Nisbet in his *History of the Idea of Progress* (New York, 1980).

42. In: *Scrittori d'Italia* 2 (Bari, 1930):37–240.

43. Hippolyte Rigault, *Histoire de la querelle des anciens et des modernes* (Paris, 1859; repr. ed., New York, 1965), pp. 80–84.

44. René Samuel, "Boisrobert," *La grande encyclopédie* 7:146–47. The evidence that Boisrobert knew Tassoni's work is only circumstantial, but since the book had caused a furor in Italy and had just been translated by another member of the Academy, the conjecture is not untenable.

45. In: *Oeuvres*, ed. Charles Adam and Paul Tannery, 12 vols. (Paris, 1897–1910), 6:1–78. The two standard works on the quarrel of Ancients and Moderns, Rigault's *Histoire de la querelle*, and Hubert Gillot's *La querelle des anciens et des modernes en France* (Paris, 1914), both established the traditional view of Cartesianism as the immediate stimulus for the "revolt" of the Moderns. Antoine Adam has attacked this view in his *Grandeur and Illusion: French Literature and Society, 1600–1715*, (trans. Herbert Tint [London, 1972]) finding a more important cause for Modernism in the sociological fact of the growth of the nation's self-confidence during the reign of Louis XIV. While

modern critical opinion almost without exception views Descartes as a Modern, an older study, still valid in some respects, should also be consulted: Emile Krantz, *Essai sur l'esthétique de Descartes: Rapports de la doctrine Cartésienne avec la littérature classique française* (Paris, 1898).

46. Descartes, *Discours*, p. 18: "Le premier estoit de ne receuoir iamais aucune chose pour vraye, que ie ne la connusse euidemment estre telle: c'est à dire, d'euiter soigneusement la Précipitation, & la Préuention; & de ne comprendre rien de plus en mes iugements, que ce qui se presenteroit si clairement & si distinctement à mon esprit, que ie n'eusse aucune occasion de le mettre en doute."

47. Adam, *Grandeur and Illusion*, p. 143.

48. Seventeenth-century French classicism will be discussed in Chapter IV. Pertinent aspects relevant to the present chapter may be found in Gilbert Highet, *The Classical Tradition* (Oxford, 1949; second ed., New York, 1957), pp. 104–260; and René Bray, *La formation de la doctrine classique en France* (Paris, 1927), pp. 7–48.

49. The best source for Boileau's influence in England is Alexander F. B. Clark's *Boileau and the French Classical Critics in England, 1660–1830* (Paris, 1925).

50. A third Perrault brother, though not a participant in the quarrel between Ancients and Moderns, was an important figure in seventeenth-century France as budget minister to the king; he also translated Alessandro Tassoni's mock epic *La secchia rapita*. The best study of the life and works of the Perrault brothers is André Hallays' *Les Perrault* (Paris, 1926). For a more penetrating study of the issues of their quarrel with Boileau, and its relation to seventeenth-century French thought, see Hans Kortum, *Charles Perrault und Nicolas Boileau: Der Antike-Streit im Zeitalter der klassischen französischen Literatur* (Berlin, 1966); also Emile Deschanel, *Boileau, Charles Perrault*, Le romanticisme des classiques, vol. 4 (Paris, 1886–1891; repr. ed., Geneva, 1970); and *MGG* 10 (1962), cols. 1082–85.

51. Boileau, *Art poétique*, chant 4, lines 1–2, 20–24: "Dans Florence jadis vivait un médecin/Savant hâbleur, dit-on, et célèbre assassin . . . Enfin pour abreger un si plaisant prodige/Notre assassin renonce à son art inhumain/Laissant à Galien la science suspect/De méchant médecin devient bon architecte" ("In Florence there once lived a physician, noted *savant* and celebrated assassin./ . . . Finally, to shorten this pleasant tale/Our assassin renounced his inhuman art/Leaving to Galen this suspect science/From a wicked physician he became a good architect").

52. Perrault recalls this episode in his later work, *Parallèle des anciens et des modernes* (Paris, 1688–1697; facs. ed. Munich, 1964), 3:238–42, where he tells how the Ancients visited Lully for dinner and, each pressing his wine glass against his throat, cried in unison, "Renounce Quinault, or you die." Perrault maintains that he was the only one to support Quinault against the jealousy of the Ancients during those years. This is confirmed by Marc Soriano in his *Dossier Perrault* (Paris, 1972), p. 178, who shows, however, that it was Perrault rather than Quinault who was on the defensive—eager to defend his coveted position of minister to Colbert and Louis, he placed himself under the protection of Quinault and thus Lully, who, he correctly predicted, would retain the king's favor.

53. The *Critique* was published anonymously in 1574, and again the next year in the *Recueil de divers ouvrages . . . de M. Perrault de l'Académie française* (Paris, 1675); the passage above is quoted by André Hallays, *Les Perrault*, pp. 143–44: "Je veux bien avouer si vous le voulez que les auteurs anciens ont plus de génie que ceux de ce temps-ci pour la description des choses de la nature, des sentiments du coeur de l'homme et pour ce qui regarde l'expression. Mais, comme dans les ouvrages de l'esprit, il y à d'autres choses encore à observer, comme la bienséance, l'ordre, l'économie, la distribution et l'arrangement de toutes les parties, ce qui demande une infinité de préceptes qui ne peuvent être trouvés que par une longue suite d'expériences, de réflexions et de remarques, il se pourrait faire que les derniers siècles ont de l'avantage en ces sortes de choses parce qu'ils ont profité du travail et de l'étude de ceux qui les ont précédés. . . ."

54. Published by Coignard in Paris in the same year. According to Charles Perrault's *Mémoires* (first published Paris, 1759; repr. ed., Paris, 1909), pp. 136–37, Boileau groaned throughout the reading and at the end, stood and announced that such a poem disgraced the Academy; in a series of epigrams dating from this occasion, his ire fell not only on Perrault, but also on the Academy for having condoned such an indecency.

55. Quoted by Rigault, *Histoire de la querelle*, p. 150:

"La belle antiquité fût toujours vénérable,
Mais je ne crus jamais qu'elle fût adorable.
Je vois les anciens sans plier les genoux:
Ils sont grands, il est vrai, mais hommes comme nous;
Et l'on peut comparer, sans crainte d'être injuste,
Le siècle de Louis au beau siècle d'Auguste."

56. These journals are discussed in Chapters III and IV.

57. Facs. ed., Munich, 1964; this edition contains an excellent introductory essay by Max Imdahl, "Kunstgeschichtliche Exkurse zu Perraults *Parallèle des anciens et des modernes*."

58. Perrault's comments on music are discussed below, p. 47.

59. Rigault, *Histoire de la querelle*, p. 283.

60. See note 8.

61. See note 42.

62. Tassoni, *Pensieri diversi*, pp. 332–40.

63. Ibid., p. 340: "Nel che poi è stato imitato da don Carlo Gesualdo principe di Venosa, che in questa nostra età ha illustrata anch'egli la musica con nuove mirabili invenzione."

64. Facs. ed., Bologna, 1970.

65. Walker, "Musical Humanism," p. 57.

66. See note 29 above. Doni was also a later member of the *Accademia degli Alterati* (Palisca, "The Alterati," p. 17), and would have known of their earlier discussions of ancient and modern music.

67. See Chapter 1, pp. 10–11; and Anna Amalie Abert, "Doni," *MGG* 3 (1954), cols. 673–78.

68. For Doni's discussions of these two authors, see especially Mersenne, *Correspondance*, vols. 4 and 5, *passim*.

69. A musician who performed for Alexander, inspiring him to wondrous deeds.

70. Mersenne, *Correspondance*, 4:88: "Vous me demandez mon advis sur l'ancienne musique des Grecs, laquelle pour ce que je peu juger, me semble avoir esté en toute excellence. . . . Non pas que je croye estre veritable tout ce qu'on raconte de la force qu'elle avoit et des effects admirables qu'on operoit par icelle. Car en cecy je fay cette distinction que les effects qu'on raconte de la musique de Timothee et d'environ ce temps la, je les estime veritables, mais pour les fort anciens, je ne les crois pas comme ce qu'on dict d'avoir guery la peste etc. Et encores que je croy que les Anciens estoient plus disposez que nous à s'esmouvoir par la musique, pour plusieurs raisons qu'on pourroit alleguer, toutesfois je croy qu'on pourroit faire aujourd'huy presque tout le mesme, si l'on corrigeoit tout plain de defaults qu'on y commet et qu'on renouvellast la maniere ancienne."

71. Mersenne, *Correspondance*, 1:74: ". . . depuis ce temps là, la musique a telement peu changer avec les apetitz, que je croy que si on nous recitoit la meilleure de leur siècle, elle nous sembleroit insuportable aux oreilles. Par exemple ne voy-je pas depuis trente ans telement changer la musique que certain contre-point que l'on met en usage et semble bon maintenant, je l'ay veu blasmer par ceux mesme que s'en sont servis du depuis?"

72. On Parran, see Herbert Schneider, *Die französische Kompositionslehre in der ersten Hälfte des 17. Jahrhunderts* (Tutzing, 1972), pp. 112–36.

73. Antoine Parran, *Traité de la musique theorique et pratique* (Paris, 1639; facs. ed., Geneva, 1972), p. 124: "J'aurois icy sujet de me plaindre justement & raisonnablement si on vouloit escouter ma plainte, du peu d'effet qu'a la Musique de nostre temps; ou pour mieux dire des mauuais effets qu'elle produit le plus souuent, & du peu de bons. Nous sçauons qu'anciennement elle en produisoit de si merueilleux, comme nous lisons de Clitemnestre, laquelle estant laissée par Agamemnon qui alloit au siege de Troye, fut conseruée pudique & immaculée par le chant Dorique d'un Musicien, laissé aupres d'elle à cette fin, contre les importunitez lasciues d'Egiste: mais ayant perdu sa douce & fidelle garde, elle perdit aussi tost le joyau de sa pudicité."

74. This preface was separated from the *Essais de physique* at the time of its publication; it is reprinted from manuscript as an appendix to Gillot, *La querelle*, pp. 576–91.

75. An opera either fictitious or no longer extant, or possibly a mistaken title for Charles D'Assoucy's *Les amours d'Apollon et de Daphné* (1650).

76. Obviously a reference to the *Ballet comique de la reine*, first performed in 1581.

77. Gillot, *La querelle*, p. 578: "C'estoit donc un piteux spectacle dit Paleologue: car il fault que vous scachiez que la mesme difference qui se trouve entre les choses diuines et inimitables que l'Antiquité a fait voir autrefois, et tout ce que nostre siècle est capable de produire, la mesme différence, dis-je, pour ce qui est des Sciences et des Arts se voit entre les Italiens et les François."

78. A reference to Plato's *Republic*, chapter 3. See Benjamin Jowett's translation in: *The Dialogues of Plato*, 5 vols. (New York, 1892), 1:675.

79. Perrault, *Essais de physique*, pp. 320–21: ". . . il y a plus de raison d'attribuer une invention à des gens éclairez, à un siècle poli, scavant, & fécond en merveilles, qu'à un siècle barbare & grossier, tel qu'étoit celui dans lequel on prétend que cette invention a pris naissance."

80. Gillot, *La querelle*, p. 586: "Il me dit qu'ayant quelque conoissance de la musique et que s'estant voulu eclaircir de ce que ce pouuoit estre de celle des anciens a comparaison de la nostre, il luy tomba entre les mains vn liure dans lequel l'auteur pretendoit que la Musique des anciens estoit infiniment plus belle et plus parfaite que la nostre et que si quelqu'vn auoit vn autre sentiment ce n'estoit que parce qu'il ignoroit le fin de cette Musique."

81. Doni's work must have been known in France. Having been dedicated to Mazarin, it would likely have formed a part of the Mazarin library, which was opened to scholars after the cardinal's death in 1661; see Alfred Franklin, *Histoire de la bibliothèque Mazarin et du palais de l'Institut, 1640–1885* (Paris, 1901; repr. ed., Amsterdam, 1969), pp. 127–28. Another Italian author probably known to Perrault was Alessandro Tassoni, whose *La secchia rapita* had been translated by Claude's brother, Pierre Perrault, into French (see above, note 50). This translation included a preface which attacked the theories of Boileau and defended the idea of artistic progress (Hallays, *Les Perrault*, pp. 146–47). It is unlikely that the uproar occasioned by the *Pensieri diversi* earlier in the century would have escaped the brothers Perrault; in any case, Claude Perrault, in writing the *Essais de physique*, may have been led to Tassoni through Doni's mention of that author.

82. Rigault, *Histoire de la querelle*, p. 226.

83. The playwright Pierre Corneille (1606–1684) had been at the center of a controversy surrounding his play *Le Cid* (c.1637), which had been attacked for its violations of the Aristotelian unities of time, place, and action as well as other rules. Torquato Tasso (1544–1595), considered an exponent of Italian modernism, was attacked by Boileau in the *Art poétique*, where he compared the "tinsel" of Tasso with the "gold" of Virgil.

84. François de Callières, *Histoire poétique de la guerre nouvellement déclarée entre des anciens et des modernes* (Amsterdam, 1688), p. 226: "Pensez-vous . . . que la plûpart des hommes qui suivent Lulli avec tant d'empressement se connoissent mieux en Musique que les bêtes qui vous accompagnent & croyex-vous qu'ils ne soient pas plus bêtes qu'elles de porter sans cesse leur argent à son Opera pour y entendre cinquante fois la même chose?"

85. This passage is discussed in Chapter I, pp. 25–26.

86. Callières, *Histoire poétique*, p. 233: "... mais qu'aprez avoir songé meurement à ce que vous aviez fait & aux suites dangereuses d'une pareille entreprise, vous vous retournâtes par ce moyen de'revenir à la lumière; on ne pouvoit pas acquerir plus habilement le reputation de grand Musicien & de bon mari, sans vous charger d'une femme incommode . . ."

87. Ibid., p. 236: "Pour moi . . . j'avoüe franchement que mes Ouvrages ont fait tout le contraire, & que j'ai travaillé utilement à la corruption de mon siècle, mais ils n'en meritent pas moins de gloire, car ils ont en cela suivi les intentions de l'auteur."

88. Sénecé, *Lettre de Clement Marot*, in: *Oeuvres choisies de Sénecé*, ed. Emile Chasles and P. A. Cap (Paris, 1855), p. 298: "... ils jugèrent également à propos d'alonger leurs noms à proportion de l'agrandissement de leur fortune, et se firent appeler, l'un, le seigneur Balthazar de Beaujoyeux, et l'autre, le sieur Jean-Baptiste de Lulli."

89. Cf. Chapter I, pp. 19–20.

90. Sénecé, *Lettre de Clement Marot*, p. 329: "Ainsi l'on vit pour la première fois un jugement équitable rendu par un juge endormi."

91. Bernard le Bovier de Fontenelle, *Oeuvres complètes*, ed. G. B. Depping, 3 vols. (Paris, 1818), 2:364: "... et je maintiens que si Anacréon les avait sues, il les aurait plus chantées que la plupart des siennes."

92. See above, notes 52 and 57.

93. Charles Perrault, *Parallèle*, bk. 4, p. 265: "Si vous en doutez, vous n'avez qu'à lire le traitté que Mr. Perrault de l'Académie des Sciences a composé sur ce sujet, & vous en serez pleinement persuadé. Ce Traitté est à la fin du premier Tome de ses *Essays de Physique*; & a pour Titre: *De la Musique des Anciens*."

94. Ibid., p. 261: "... expressions figurées dont la Poësie s'est servie pour faire entendre qu'il n'y a point d'hommes si farouches ni si stupides qui ne soient émus, & qui ne s'apprivoisent par les charmes de la Musique."

95. The significance of the quarrels between Ancients and Moderns for the discipline of music history is discussed by Warren Dwight Allen, *Philosophies of Music History* (n.p., 1939; repr. ed., New York, 1962), pp. 38–45.

Chapter III

1. Anna Bergerotti was the Italian soprano who had sung the part of *Musique italienne* in Lully's *Ballet de la raillerie* in 1659; see above, p. 16, and McGowan, "The Origins of French Opera," p. 197.

2. Jonckbloet and Land, eds., *Musique et musiciens au XVIIe siècle. Correspondence de C. Huyghens* (Leyden, 1882), *passim*; a letter to de Nyert (M. de Nielles), for example

(pp. 54–55), thanks him for sending works by Rossi and the theorbist Angelo Michele Bartolotti, and expresses regret that he never had the opportunity to meet Bartolotti at the home of Anna Bergerotti.

3. This correspondence is discussed at length by Prunières, *L'opéra italien en France*, pp. 313–20; it is mentioned also by McGowan, "The Origins of French Opera," p. 196, and Anthony, *French Baroque Music*, p. 108. See also Denise Launay, "René Ouvrard," *MGG* 10 (1962), cols 501–2.

4. Parts of this work (Paris, 1734) had already been published under the title *Poeme sur la musique* in 1714, according to the author's preface.

5. Serré de Rieux, *Les dons des enfants de Latone* (Paris, 1734), pp. 112–13: "Cette pressante ardeur que l'exemple [footnote: De la Musique Italienne] fit naître/Forma le goût sçavant que Paris voit s'accroître./Nos chants trop amolis d'une fade langueur,/D'un caractere fort y prennent la vigueur:/Il semble que par lui tout l'Art de l'Italie/Au nôtre s'accommode & se reconcilie./D'un pieux Amateur le zele curieux,/Dans la France attira des Motets précieux,/Qui traçant à nos Chants une route nouvelle,/A nos Auteurs naissans servirent de modèle."

6. Ibid., p. 112.

7. Luigi Rossi (1598–1653), Pier Francesco Cavalli (1602–1676), Maurizio Cazzati (c.1620–1677), Giacomo Carissimi (1605–1674), Giovanni Legrenzi (1626–1690), Giovanni Paolo Colonna (1637–1695), Jacopo Melani (1623–1676), Alessandro Stradella (1642–1682), Giovanni Battista Bassani (1657–1716).

8. Marc-Antoine Charpentier (1636–1704), Michel de Lalande (1657–1726), André Campra (1660–1662), Louis-Nicolas Clerambault (1676–1749), Jean Marie Leclair "l'ainé" (1697–1764), Nicolas Bernier (1664–1734).

9. Michel le Moël, "Un foyer d'Italianisme à la fin du XVIIe siècle," *Recherches sur la musique française classique* 3 (1963):23–28.

10. On Charpentier, see Claude Crussard, *Un musicien français oublié, Marc-Antoine Charpentier* (Paris, 1945); and more recently, H. Wiley Hitchcock, "The Latin Oratorios of Marc-Antoine Charpentier" (Ph.D. dissertation, University of Michigan, 1954); idem., "The Latin Oratorios of Marc-Antoine Charpentier," *The Musical Quarterly* 41 (1955):41–65; and Clarence H. Barber, "Les oratorios de Marc-Antoine Charpentier," *Recherches sur la musique française classique* 3 (1963):90–130.

11. The churchmen Ouvrard and Nicaise had made the Italian tour, as would François Raguenet; see Prunières, *L'opéra italien*, p. 313; Anthony, *French Baroque Music*, p. 108.

12. Anthony, *French Baroque Music*, p. 109.

13. Sébastien de Brossard, *Dictionnaire de musique* (Paris, 1701; facsimile of second ed. [1705], Hilversum, 1965), p. 323: "Jamais on n'a eu plus de goût, ny plus de passion pour la Musique Italienne, que l'on a maintenant en France."

14. Ibid., s.v. "STYLO, veut dire, STILE": ". . . En musique, on le dit de la *maniere* que chaque particulier a de *composer*, ou *d'exécuter*, ou *d'enseigner*, & tout cela est fort différent selon le genie des *Auteurs*, du *Pays* & de la *Nation*; comme aussi selon les *matieres*, les *lieux*, les *temps*, les *sujets*, les *expressions*, &c. Ainsi on dit le *Stile* de *Charissimi*, de *Lully*, de *Lambert*, &c. Le *Stile* des Musiques *gayes* & *enjouées* est bien différent du *Stile* des Musiques *graves* ou *serieuses*; Le *Stile* des Musiques *d'Eglise* est bien différent du *Stile* des Musiques pour le *Théatre* ou la *Chambre*; Le *Stile* des *Compositions Italiennes* est *picquant*, *fleury*, *expressif*; celuy des *Compositions Fran-çoises*, est *naturel*, *coulant*, *tendre*, &c. De-là viennent diverses Epithetes pour distinguer tous ces différens caracteres, comme Stile *Ancien* & *Moderne*; Stile *Italien*, *François*, *Allemand*, &c.

15. Facs. ed., Geneva, 1976. The first edition used the spelling *Paralèle*, but all subsequent editions used the modern spelling *Parallèle*. For a translation see Oliver Strunk, "A Comparison between the French and Italian Music," *The Musical Quarterly* 22 (1946):411–36.

16. The abbé Trublet's *Memoires pour servir à l'histoire de M. de Fontenelle* (Paris, 1761), p. 169: "L'abbé Raguenet eut aussi son coin de folie, puisqu'il finit par se couper la gorge avec un rasoir" ("the abbé Raguenet had his share of madness, for he ended his life by cutting his throat with a razor"). For biographical information on Raguenet, see also Eugène Borrel, "Raguenet," *MGG* 10 (1962), cols. 1870–72. Most scholarly treatments of the quarrel between Raguenet and Lecerf deal almost exclusively with the weightier and more influential treatises of Lecerf; those of Raguenet are discussed briefly, however, in the article by Paul-Marie Masson, "Musique italienne et musique française: la première querelle," *Rivista musicale italiana* 19 (1912):526–30.

17. Cf. above, Chapter 2, p. 38.

18. Raguenet, *Parallèle*, sig. a–ij: "J'Ay lû par ordre de Monseigneur le Chancelier le présent Manuscrit, & j'ay crû qu'il soit capable d'équité."

19. As may be seen in Chapter II (p. 47), Fontenelle had praised modern music in his *Digression sur les anciens et modernes* (Paris, 1688); writing in 1688, however, "modern" for him had meant the style of Lully. According to his biography, (Trublet's *Memoires*, pp. 166–67), Fontenelle never came to like Italian music as French, even when it began to be considered the "modern" style. But, as a good Modern, he believed himself wrong in his preference: "Il sentoit d'une façon, & jugeoit de l'autre . . ." ("He felt one way, and judged another . . .").

20. *Journal des savants*, March, 1702, pp. 186–89. (This journal was also often called the *Journal de Paris*.)

21. *Memoires de Trévoux*, July, 1702, pp. 341–50; repr. ed., Geneva, 1968, 2:386–88. (This journal was also called the *Journal de Trévoux*, though its official title was *Memoires pour l'histoire des sciences et des beaux arts*.)

22. *Comparaison de la musique italienne et de la musique française, où, en examinant en detail les avantages des spectacles, et le mérite des compositeurs des deux nations, on monte quelles sont les vrayes beautez de la musique* (Brussels, 1704; facsimile of the

1706 edition, Geneva, 1972). For a partial translation, see Mary B. Ellison, "The *Comparaison de la musique italienne et de la musique françoise* of Lecerf de la Viéville: An Annotated Translation of the First Four Dialogues" (Ph.D. dissertation, University of Miami, 1973).

23. Dom Philippe Lecerf de la Viéville, "Lettre d'un religieux bénédictin de la congré-gation de Saint-Maur à un de ses amis," *Mercure de France*, April, 1726, pp. 677–90. Much of our knowledge of Lecerf's biography and the quarrel itself derives from this letter written by Lecerf's brother.

24. The letter was never printed and is not extant; an anonymous epitaph to Bouhours is printed in *Memoires de Trévoux*, July, 1702, p. 340, but does not correspond to the few lines quoted by Dom Philippe Lecerf on p. 680.

25. "Lettre d'un religieux," p. 688.

26. Besides in the letter of his brother, biographical information on Lecerf may be found in the following sources: Fétis, *Biographie universelle* 5 (Paris, 1863):243; Henry Pru-nières, "Lecerf de la Viéville et l'esthétique musicale classique au XVIIe siècle," *Bulletin français de la Société internationale de la musique* 4 (1908):623–26; and André Verchaly, "Le Cerf," *MGG* 8 (1960), cols. 425–26.

27. Trublet, *Memoires*, pp. 167–68: "Je ne connois guere d'Ecrits plus vifs, plus amers & plus malins, que ceux que Mr. *de Freneuse* publia à cette occasion. Il n'étoit pourtant qu'Amateur, & non Artiste; mais il étoit amateur jusqu'à la passion. Extrème en tout, il aima l'étude avec la même ardeur, & s'y livra avec le même excès; delà sa mort dans la fleur de son âge. Mr. *de Fontenelle* qui l'avoit vu à Rouen, & depuis à Paris, m'a dit que si quelqu'un, par une vivacité & une sensibilité extrêmes, avoit jamais mérité le nom de fou, de fou complet, de fou par la tête et par le coeur, c'étoit ce Mr. *de Freneuse*."

28. Lecerf, *Comparaison*, sig. â-ij.

29. Ibid., pt. 1, p. 39: "It is the same taste, the same genius, and one cannot describe Italian music in a shorter, more just, more critical manner than to say that it resembles their poetry to perfection" ("C'est le même goût, le même génie, & l'on ne peut peindre la Musique des Italiens d'une maniere plus courte, plus juste, ni plus fâcheuse, qu'en disant qu'elle ressemble en perfection à leur Poësie").

30. *Journal des savants*, August, 1704, pp. 508–9.

31. *Memoires de Trévoux*, November, 1704; repr. ed., Geneva, 1968, 4:568–72.

32. This article appears to have been ignored by scholars attempting to establish authorship for the *Comparaison*. All printings of the *Comparaison* were anonymous, and in 1721 the entire work was incorporated into Pierre Bonnet-Bourdelot's *Histoire de la mu-sique et de ses effets depuis son origine jusqu'à présent* (Paris, 1715; second ed. con-taining the *Comparaison*, Amsterdam, 1721; repr. ed. of the third ed. of 1725, Graz, 1966). It should be noted here that Jacques Bonnet is sometimes cited as the author of the *Histoire*, but his contribution only amounted to finishing the work and publishing

it. His uncle, the abbé Bourdelot, had gathered the materials, and his brother, Pierre Bonnet, had assembled most of them. The latter, to whom the book is properly attributed, is usually called Pierre Bonnet-Bourdelot, for he took the name of his uncle after the abbé's death. See Eugène Borrel, "Pierre Bonnet-Bourdelot," *MGG* 2 (1952), cols. 116–17. Thus the confusion is multiplied, for later writers have attributed the *Comparaison* to Bonnet, Bourdelot, or Bonnet-Bourdelot. See for example Dora Vischer's *Der musikgeschichtliche Traktat des Pierre Bourdelot* (Bern, 1947), which assumes the *Comparaison* and the *Histoire* to be by the same author, in spite of their different outlooks and styles of writing. The whole problem of the authorship and transmission of Lecerf's *Comparaison* has been traced by Robert Wangermée in his article "Lecerf de la Viéville, Bonnet-Bourdelot et l'"Essai sur le bon goust en musique' de Nicolas Grandval," *Revue belge de musicologie* 5 (1951):132–46.

33. Published, like the first edition, by Foppens in Brussels.

34. *Comparaison*, pt. 1, pp. 1–3: "J'avois plusieurs fois fait réflexion, que quoique nous ayons en nôtre langue assez de Traitez de Musique, nous n'en avons point qui entre dans une discussion des beautez de nôtre composition. Ce ne sont que des traitez de méchanique & d'artisan, si je puis parler ainsi: des Traitez qui enseignent séchement les régles, & desquels aucun n'enseignent à sentir le cas qu'on doit faire des Piéces où les régles sont pratiquées: desquels aucun ne conduit les honnêtes gens à juger en gros du prix d'une simphonie & d'un air. Je concevois qu'il y auroit quelque mérite & quelque gloire à donner le premier des Traitez de ce genre-ci."

35. Cf. Chapter II, pp. 42–44; note the similarity of the settings of Lecerf's and Perrault's dialogues.

36. Paris, 1705; facs. ed. (with the *Parallèle*), Geneva, 1976.

37. Raguenet continues to deny, however, that the *Parallèle* had been intended as a provocation; he protests that no Frenchman ever praised French opera more highly than he had in that work, and that the entire treatise had been meant only as a reasoned comparison of the French and Italian styles.

38. *Memoires de Trévoux*, May, 1706, pp. 856–64; repr. ed., Geneva, 1968, 6:227–29.

39. *Journal des savants*, December, 1705, pp. 684–86.

40. Ibid., p. 686: "Après tout, on ne laissera peut-être pas de demeurer persuadé que la Musique Française vaut beaucoup mieux que la Musique Italienne; on pourroit seulement souhaiter que la bonne cause fût en meilleure main."

41. Published again by Foppens, this edition was, like the second, cumulative, including also Parts I and II.

42. *Comparaison*, pt. 3, p. 37.

43. We have seen this tendency to defend composers of the recent past as upholders of the ancient rules already in the Italian Renaissance; Zarlino, for example, had defended

the music of Willaert as the perfect fulfillment of the ideals of the ancient theorists. See Chapter II, p. 30.

44. *Comparaison*, 3:46.

45. *Journal des savants*, April, 1706, pp. 219–22.

46. See notes 39 and 40. The review had actually criticized both Lecerf and Raguenet, but had shown some sympathy to the case for Italian music, "the good cause."

47. *Médecin-musicien*, p. 3: "Qui en servira éternellement de l'étenduë de sa probité & de son génie."

48. Ibid.: "Il nioit fort d'avoir fait son premier extrait, & le rejettoit sur Mr. Pouchard, croyant pouvoir se servir à son gré du nom d'un de ses morts: il s'est vanté noblement de cét ouvrage-ci, parce que tous les Mrs. ses confrères sont en état de parler, s'il le leur attribuoit."

49. Eugène Hatin, *Histoire politique et littéraire de la presse en France*, (Paris, 1859) 2:186–87.

50. *Grand dictionnaire universel du XIXe siècle*, ed. Pierre Larousse, 12 (1874):1527.

51. Hatin, *Histoire politique*, 2:191–92.

52. *Médecin-musicien*, p. 5: "Du reste, je suis à plaindre de n'avoir pas deviné que le disciple de Galien décideroit dans le Journal de Paris des vraïes beautez de la Musique . . ." ("For the rest, I admit to not having guessed that the disciple of Galen should decide, in the *Journal de Paris*, what true beauty in music is . . .").

53. *Journal des savants*, August, 1706, pp. 481–88. Regarding Andry, see p. 482: ". . . il croit pouvoir sans injustice et sans temerité repeter à chaque page le nom de M. Andry, le supposant Auteur de ce 'honteux Extrait' . . ." (". . . he thought himself able without injustice or rashness to repeat on each page the name of M. Andry, supposing him the author of this 'shameful review' . . .").

54. *Journal des savants*, May, 1706, pp. 316–18: "Quant auz questions qui regardent quelques pensées, & quelques expressions des Auteurs Italiens, il faut convenire en general que le même difference qui partage les Conoisseurs en Musique sur le goût Italien, & sur le goût François, se trouve entre le Pere Bouhours et M. Orsi, sur la maniere de penser dans les Ouvrages de l'esprit. Il faut encore convenire qu'il n'y a rien de hardi dans la composition, qu'on ne sauve par l'autorité des exemples, ou par celle des Grammairiens: ce qu'il y a de plus mal'aisé, mais d'essentiel, c'est l'application des exemples ou des preceptes & c'est ce qui dépend du goût sur quoy il est difficile de mettre les hommes d'accord; chacun croit avoir le meilleur. . . . Celuy des François, & celuy des Italians, n'est pas toujours le même. On ne met point en France le Tasse a côte ni de Virgile ni d'Homer. Tout le reste des jugements y ressemblent à celuy-là. En Italie on pense autrement, et les contestations sur ce sujet pourront bien ne pas finir si-tôt. On se fera toujours la guerre: mais cette guerre ne sçauroit être qu'utile aux uns, & aux autres. Les reproches des Ecrivains François pourront empêcher les Italiens de se livrer trop au feu ou à la gentillesse de leur imagination. Mais le com-

merce des Auteurs Italiens contribuera peut-être aussi à mettre du feu & de l'agrément dans les Ouvrages des Français . . ."

Chapter IV

1. Arnaud Machabey, *Traité de la critique musicale* (Paris, 1947), pp. 19–36; Winton Dean, "Criticism," *Grove's Dictionary of Music and Musicians* 2 (1954):521–36; Andrea della Corte, *La critica musicale e i critici* (Turin, 1961), pp. 3–62; Ernest Newman, *A Musical Critic's Holiday* (New York, 1925), pp. 293–330. For an excellent general study of the term "criticism," see René Wellek, "The Term and Concept of Literary Criticism," *Concepts of Criticism* (New Haven, 1963), pp. 21–36.

2. "Concerning Music," ed. William W. Goodwin (and others), in: *Plutarch's Lives and Writings* 6 (Boston, 1909):102–35. Scholars, however, now place the treatise among the spurious works, tracing its contents to Peripatetic sources between 170 and 300 A.D.; see François Lasserre, *Plutarch de la musique* (Lausanne, 1954), p. 104; and "Plutarch," MGG 10 (1962), cols. 362–63.

3. Pseudo-Plutarch, "Concerning Music," p. 130. The quarrel between Pythagoras and his opponent Aristoxenus over whether intervals should be reckoned according to mathematics or according to the ear is discussed in Henry S. Macran, *The Harmonics of Aristoxenus* (Oxford, 1902), pp. 87–97. Claude Palisca, in "The Beginnings of Baroque Music, Its Roots in Sixteenth-Century Theory and Practice" (Ph.D. dissertation, Harvard, 1954), traces the revival of this ancient controversy in the sixteenth century, pp. 1–86.

4. We find only a brief statement in the eleventh century by Johannes Affligimensis (formerly thought to be John Cotton), who says that a knowledge of the rules is indispensable for those who wish to judge the quality of a melody or to compose a new one; see his *Tractatus de musica* (11th century), in: Martin Gerbert, *Scriptores ecclesiastici de musica* (1784; repr. ed., Hildesheim, 1963), p. 233.

5. Joel E. Spingarn, *A History of Literary Criticism in the Renaissance: With Special Reference to the Influence of Italy in the Formation and Development of Modern Classicism* (New York, 1899; repr. ed., 1963), pp. 125–36.

6. An article in the *Mercure galant* (November, 1713), p. 201, blamed the influx of Italian sonatas and cantatas for a corruption of the French taste in music. From this time until at least the mid-point of the eighteenth century, many a contemptuous reference is made to the Italian "sonatas and cantatas."

7. The classic study of French classicism is René Bray's *La formation de la doctrine classique en France* (Paris, 1927; repr. ed., 1966). Other important sources are: Jules Brody, *French Classicism: A Critical Miscellany* (Englewood Cliffs, N.J., 1966); Auguste Bourgoin, *Les maîtres de critique au XVIIe siècle* (Paris, 1889; repr. ed., Geneva, 1970); Antoine Adam, *Histoire de la littérature française au XVII siècle* (Paris, 1962), vols. 4 and 5; Daniel Mornet, *Histoire de la littérature française classique, 1660–1700* (Paris, 1940); and G. H. C. Wright, *French Classicism* (Cambridge, Mass., 1920). Further note should be made of the distinction between the terms "classic" and "neoclassic": the latter is used only by English writers, usually to refer to the continuation

of French classical thought in the works of such authors as Addison and Pope in early eighteenth-century England. Though one occasionally encounters the appellation "neo-classicism," the term "classicism" is more properly used for the French seventeenth-century school.

8. Spingarn, *Literary Criticism in the Renaissance*, pp. 150–55. Spingarn separates the two different Italian traditions in his chapters "The Growth of the Classic Spirit in Italian Criticism" (pp. 78–96), and "Romantic Elements in Italian Criticism" (pp. 97–104). Other writers see this difference as between classicism and baroque: Victor Tapié, *Baroque et classique* (Paris, 1957), pp. 69–162; and Friedrich Schürr, *Barock, Klassizismus und Rokoko in der Französischen Literatur: eine prinzipielle Stilbetrachtung* (Leipzig, 1928), pp. 15–25.

9. The critical doctrine of Malherbe is formulated by Ferdinand Brunot, *La doctrine de Malherbe d'après son commentaire sur Desportes* (Paris, 1891), pp. 105–216.

10. Chapelain's theories are set out in his various prefaces and in *Les sentiments de l'Académie française sur la tragi-comédie du Cid* (1638), in: Armand Gasté, *La querelle du Cid* (Paris, 1898), pp. 355–417.

11. Balzac's important critical works are collected in his *Oeuvres choisies*, ed. Gabriel Raibaud (Paris, 1936).

12. See Castelvetro's *Poetica d'Aristotele vulgarizzata e sposta* (1570; repr. ed., Munich, 1968).

13. The *Art poétique* is contained in *Oeuvres poétiques de Boileau Despréaux* (Paris, 1855), pp. 283–338; for biographical information see Gustave Lanson, *Boileau* (Paris, 1946). For documentation of Boileau's influence on Racine, and thus on French classical tragedy, see Marie Philip Haley, *Racine and the "Art poétique" of Boileau* (New York, 1976); and Louis Racine, *Memoires sur la vie de Jean Racine* (Lausanne, 1747), *passim*.

14. The standard biographical source for Bouhours is George Doncieux, *Le père Bouhours* (Paris, 1886; repr. ed., Geneva, 1970).

15. The older theory of Descartes' influence on French classicism is presented in Emile Krantz, *L'esthétique de Descartes: rapports de la doctrine cartésienne avec la littérature classique française au XVIIe siècle* (Paris, 1898). Gustave Lanson, in his iconoclastic article, "L'influence de la philosophie cartésienne sur la littérature française" (*Revue de métaphysique et de morale* 4 [1896]:517–50), demonstrates that the influence of Descartes on contemporary French classical theorists was slight and that his literary influence in the latter half of the century was confined mostly to the Moderns. General critical opinion in the twentieth century has supported Lanson; see, for example, Bray, *La formation de la doctrine classique*, p. 115; the confusion over differing definitions of the term *raison* has been confronted by R. Michéa, "Les variations de la raison au XVIIe siècle: essai sur la valeur du langage employé en histoire littéraire," in: Brody, *French Classicism*, pp. 94–103.

16. See *The "De arte poetica" of Marco Girolamo Vida*, ed. and trans. Ralph G. Williams (New York, 1976), pp. 84–87, 98–101. For a study of rationalism in sixteenth-century

France, see Henri Busson, *Le rationalisme dans la littérature française de la renaissance (1533–1601)* (Paris, 1957).

17. Discussions of the term and its use in criticism may be found in Bray, *Formation de la doctrine classique*, pp. 114–39; and in Jules Brody, *Boileau and Longinus* (Geneva, 1958), pp. 54–87.

18. To explain the difference between *bon sens* and *bon goût*, one critic states, "Between good sense and good taste there is the difference of cause and effect" ("Entre le bon sens et le bon goût il y a la différence de la cause à son effet"): Jean de la Bruyère, *Caractères* ("Des jugements"), *Oeuvres*, vol. 3, pt. 1 (Paris, 1922), p. 100.

19. Bouhours, *Entretiens d'Ariste et d'Eugene* (1671; repr. ed., Paris, 1962), p. 115.

20. Roger de Rabutin, comte de Bussy, *Correspondance avec sa famille et ses amis (1666–1693)*, ed. Ludovic Lalannec, vol. 4 (Paris, 1858; repr. ed., Westmead/Farnborough, England, 1972), p. 272: "Pour moi, j'avois jugé le bon sens et le jugement la même chose. Madame de Coligny vouloit que le bon sens regardât les pensées et les expressions, et le jugement la conduite. . . . Nous croyons tous que le bon sens, la raison et le bon esprit sont la même chose." Bussy-Rabutin has previously questioned Mme. de Coligny (p. 268) as to the difference between *bonne grâce* and *bon air*, *bon sens* and *jugement*, *raison* and *bon sens*, *bon esprit* and *bon sens*, and other equivocal terms.

21. Boileau, *Art poétique*, p. 287:

> "Evitons ces excès: laissons à l'Italie
> De tous ces faux brillants l'éclatante folie.
> Tout doit tendre au bon sens: mais pour y parvenir
> Le chemin est glissant et pénible à tenir;
> Pour peu qu'on s'en écarte, aussitôt on se noie.
> La raison pour marcher n'a souvent qu'une voie."

22. La Mesnardière, *La poétique* (1640; repr. ed., Geneva, 1972), sig. KK; see pp. 389–90 for further criticism of the Italians.

23. The fourth dialogue of *Entretiens d'Ariste et d'Eugene*, pp. 113–38.

24. Ibid., p. 121: "Mon Dieu! que vous me faites de plaisir, dit Eugene, d'exclure du nombre des beaux esprits ces diseurs eternels de beaux mots & de belles sentences; ces copistes & ces singes de Seneque; ces Mancini, ces Malvezzi, & ces Loredans, qui courent toûjours aprés les brillans & les *vivezze d'ingegno*, comme ils les appellent en leur langue! Car, à vous dire le vray, je ne les puis souffrir; & j'ay bien de la peine à souffrir Seneque luy-mesme, avec ses pointes & ses antitheses perpetuelles."

25. Actually, the authority of the ancients was equated with reason; Chapelain, for example, relies on "the authority of Aristotle, or to put it more clearly, that of reason" (*Sentiments de l'Académie sur le Cid*, p. 370: "une bonne et solide doctrine, fondée sur l'autorité d'Aristote, ou pour mieux dire, sur celle de la raison.").

26. *The Critical Works of Monsieur Rapin*, trans. Basil Kennet (London, 1705; third ed., 1731), 2:144–45.

27. *Poetics*, chapters 1–4. Aristotle sees imitation as the reshaping of a form from nature in a different medium (words in literature, color in painting, harmony and rhythm in music). This different medium gives to each art its own principles of order as well as an ability to improve upon nature in its unrefined state.

28. *La manière de bien penser dans les ouvrages d'esprit* (1687; facs. ed. of the 1715 ed., Brighton, 1971), p. 296: ". . . quelque chose qui n'est point recherché, ni tiré de loin; que la nature du sujet présente, & qui naist pour ainsi dire du sujet mesme. J'entends je ne sçay quelle beauté simple sans fard & sans artifice, telle qu'un Ancien dépeint la vraye eloquence. On diroit qu'une pensée naturelle devroit venir à tout le monde; on l'avoit, ce semble, dans la teste avant que de la lire."

29. As Boileau puts it (*Art poétique, chant* 3, ll. 1–4): "There is no serpent or monster so odious/That, imitated artfully, cannot please the eyes" ("Il n'est point de serpent, ni de monstre odieux/Qui, par l'art imité, ne puisse plaire aux yeux").

30. Robert Finch, in his *The Sixth Sense: Individualism in French Poetry, 1686–1760* (University of Toronto, 1966; repr. ed., 1969), proposes the concept of individualism as a counterweight to classicism, and he traces this concept in the poetry of iconoclasts such as Charles Perrault and Fontenelle. Another work which traces the anti-rational spirit in the seventeenth century is E. B. O. Borgerhoff's *The Freedom of French Classicism* (Princeton, 1950), a study of the unorthodox traits of the classical critics themselves.

31. See, for example, Ariosto, *Orlando furioso* (1532), canto 35, 1. 26; Benvenuto Cellini, *I trattati dell'oreficeria e della scultura* (first published Florence, 1857), p. 41.

32. Balzac, *Lettres choisies* (Paris, 1647), 2:587.

33. *Lettres*, ed. Tamizey de Larroque (Paris, 1883), 1:633: "Le bon goût de l' antiquité." Similarly, La Fontaine speaks in 1661 of the good taste of the ancient comedian Terence ("Lettre à Maucroix sur la representation des *Facheux* à Vaux," *Oeuvres*, ed. Regnier, vol. 9 [Paris, 1892], p. 349.)

34. *Sentiments de l'Académie sur le Cid*, p. 360: "Et certes il n'est pas croyable qu'un plaisir puisse estre contraire au bon sens, si ce n'est le plaisir de quelque goust depravé. . . ."

35. St.-Evremond, "Quelques observations sur le goût et le discernement des François," *Oeuvres en prose*, ed. René Ternois, vol. 3 (Paris, 1966), p. 122: "La raison en est, qu'on juge rarement des hommes par des avantages solides que fasse connoître le bon sens, mais par des manieres dont l'applaudissement finit aussitost que la fantaisie qui les a fait naistre."

36. La Bruyère, *Les caractères* ("Des ouvrages de l'esprit"), *Oeuvres complètes de La Bruyère*, 5 vols. (Paris, 1922), 2:28: "Il y a beaucoup plus de vivacité que de goût

parmi les hommes; ou pour mieux dire, il y a peu d'hommes dont l'esprit soit accompagné d'un goût sûr et d'une critique judicieuse.''

37. Quoted in François de la Rochefoucauld, *Oeuvres* (Paris, 1868), 1:304 (note): ''Vous avez le goût audessous de votre esprit, et M. de la Rochefoucauld aussi, et moi encore, mais pas tant que vous deux.''

38. Ibid.: ''Il y a des personnes qui ont plus d'esprit que de goût, et d'autres qui ont plus de goût que d'esprit. . . .''

39. Ibid., p. 305: ''. . . il y a différence entre le goût qui nous porte vers les choses, et le goût qui nous en fait connoître et discerner les qualités, en s'attachant aux règles. On peut aimer la comédie sans avoir le goût assez fin et assez délicat pour en bien juger, et on peut avoit le goût assez bon pour bien juger de la comédie sans l'aimer.''

40. Ibid., p. 306: ''Dans toutes ces différences de goûts que l'on vient de marquer, il est très-rare, et presque impossible, de rencontrer cette sorte de bon goût qui sait donner le prix à chaque chose, qui en connoît toute la valeur, et qui se porte généralement sur tout. . . .''

41. Bouhours, *Manière*, p. 516: ''. . . le goust n'est autre chose qu'un certain rapport qui se trouve entre l'esprit & les objets qu'on luy présente. . . .''

42. Ibid., p. 517: ''. . . instinct de la droite raison. . . .''

43. Ibid., p. 54: ''Chaque nation a son goust en esprit de mesme qu'en beauté, en habits, & en tout le reste. Comme si la justesse du sens, repartit Eudoxe, n'estoit pas de toutes les langues, & que ce qui est mauvais de soy-mesme, deust passer pour bon en aucun pais parmi les personnes raisonnables.''

44. Abbé de Villiers, *Entretien sur les tragédies de ce temps* (1675), quoted in Bray, *Formation de la doctrine classique*, p. 176: ''. . . il y a dans l'oeuvre d'art ce qui dépend de la raison, et qui ne varie jamais ni nulle part, et ce qui est du ressort du goût et de la coutume, et qui est propre à chaque époque et à chaque nation.''

45. Charles Perrault, *Parallèle*, 3:146–47: ''Je n'ay remarqué aucun défaut, ny dans Homère, ny dans Virgile, que l'on puisse trouver dans les Modernes: Parce que la politesse & le bon goust, qui se sont perfectionnez avec le temps, ont rendu insupportables une infinité de choses que l'on souffroit & que l'on louoit mesme dans les ouvrages des Anciens. Vous ne verrez aucun poeme de ce siècle, ou l'on soit en peine de sçavoir quel en est le sujet, comme dans l'Iliade, & où l'action demeure imparfaite, comme dans l'Eneide.'' This argument led to a resumption of hostilities between Ancients and Moderns in the early eighteenth century, when modern authors sought to modernize Homer, refining his language and the manners of his characters.

46. Cf. Chapter II, p. 42.

47. Plato, *Republic*, trans. B. Jowett, in : *The Dialogues of Plato*, 5 vols. (New York, 1892), 3:662: ''And as for the words, there will surely be no difference between words which are and which are not set to music; both will conform to the same laws, and

these have been already determined by us?—Yes.—And the melody and rhythm will
depend upon the words?—Certainly."

48. *Ars poetica* (19–10 B.C.), lines 361–62: "Ut pictura poesis: erit quae si proprius stes/Te
capiat magis, et quaedam si longius abstes" ("Poems are like pictures: that is that
some look better if you stand close, and others if you stand far away"). On the
significance for this phrase for music, see Margaret McGowan, *L'art du ballet de cour
en France (1581–1643)* (Paris, 1963), pp. 11–15, and Brewster Rogerson, *Ut musica
poesis* (Ph.D., Princeton, 1946).

49. *Poetics*, trans. Ingram Bywater, in: *The Works of Aristotle* 11 (Oxford,
1908):1.1447a.14–19.

50. Bray, *Formation de la doctrine classique*, p. 75. On the passions, see also Anthony
Levi, *French Moralists: The Theory of the Passions, 1585–1649* (Oxford, 1964).

51. Horace, *Ars poetica* lines 343–44: "Omne tulit punctum, qui miscuit utile
dulci,/Lectorem delectando, pariterque monendo" ("He has gained every vote who
has mixed profit with pleasure, at once delighting the reader and instructing him");
see also Cicero, *De oratore* 3:212, where he speaks of *docere*, *delectare*, and *movere*
(to instruct, delight, and move).

52. See Descartes, *Les passions de l'âme*, in: *Oeuvres*, ed. Charles Adam and Paul Tannery, 12 vols. (Paris, 1897–1910), 11:291–497.

53. Jean-Baptiste Dubos, *Réflexions critique sur la poésie et sur la peinture*, 3 vols. (Paris,
1719: facs. of seventh ed., Geneva, 1967), 3:144. See also Peter France, *Racine's
Rhetoric* (Oxford, 1965); and Louis Racine, *Jean Racine*, p. 111.

54. Lecerf de la Viéville tells in the *Comparaison*, 2:204, how Lully modeled his recitative
after the declamation of Champmeslé. See also "Lully's Recitative and Racine's Declamation," Romain Rolland's detailed (though undocumented) account in his *Some
Musicians of Former Days*, pp. 176–209.

55. St.-Evremond, "Sur les opéras," *Oeuvres*, 3:149–64; Boileau, *Satires*, in his *Oeuvres*
pp. 35–190, *passim*.

56. An excellent discussion of the literary opposition to Lully's opera is found in Etienne
Gros, *Philippe Quinault: sa vie et son oeuvre* (Paris, 1926), pp. 715–41.

57. On Lecerf's aesthetic, the best source is Henry Prunière's article, "Lecerf de la
Viéville et l'esthétique musicale classique au XVIIe siècle," *Bulletin français de la
Société internationale de la musique* 4 (1908):619–54. Jules Ecorcheville includes a
chapter on the quarrels between French and Italian music in his *De Lulli à Rameau,
1690–1730: l'esthétique musicale* (Paris, 1906). Unfortunately, Dora Vischer's *Der musikgeschichtliche Traktat des Pierre Bourdelot* (Bern, 1947), confuses the work of Lecerf
with that of Bonnet-Bourdelot and regards his work as historical, rather than critical,
in nature.

58. André Dacier (1651–1722), French classical scholar whose works included editions of Horace and Aristotle's *Poetics*. His wife, Anne Lefebvre, became widely known through her prose translations of the *Iliad* (1699) and the *Odyssey* (1708). It was to this Mme. Dacier that the marquis of Orsi dedicated his attack on Bouhours' *Manière de bien penser* of 1703. One is tempted to attribute the opening letter of Lecerf's *Comparaison*, pt. 2, as addressed to Mme. Dacier, for Lecerf writes "à Mme. D . . ." and speaks flatteringly of the "beautiful preface of Mr. Dacier to the *Poetics* of Aristotle" (2:8); and he tries to persuade her to the side of the Ancients in music.

59. Doncieux, *Le père Bouhours*, pp. 15–19.

60. Quoted by Dom Philippe Lecerf de la Viéville, "Lettre d'un réligieux," *Mercure de France*, April 26, 1726, p. 630:

> "Cy gît Bouhours, que la Cour, que la ville
> Viennent reverer tout à tour
> Le Tombeau d'un Auteur habile,
> Qui polit la Ville & la Cour."

61. *Comparaison*, 2:130.

62. *Memoires de Trévoux*, March, April, May, 1705.

63. *Comparaison*, 3:46 second pagination series). Lecerf's analysis is discussed below, pp. 184–185.

64. Ibid., 1:38–39: "Du reste ce n'est pas seulement en Musique qu'ils se croyent *les premiers hommes du monde*. . . . Il en est ainsi de leur Poesie, ou regnent la même présomption, la même affectation, les mêmes temerités. La pauvre nature en est bannie de même. . . . Il y a déja long-tems que les gens de bon goût, & les honnêtes gens de France, se sont déclarés de ce sentiment. Mais par bonheur pour les Musiciens d'Italie, on ne les a pas encore tout à fait comparés à leurs Poetes, & parce qu'ils ont été connus chés nous beaucoup plus tard que ceux-ci, on n'a pas encore eu le tems de bien voir combien ils tiennent les uns des autres, & combien le caractere de la Poesie & celui de la Musique Italienne sont conformes. . . ."

65. Ibid., 1:54–55: "Car ils aiment, ils cherchent, ils attrapent autant la nature & la belle simplicité, en Architecture, en Sculpture, & en Peinture, qu'ils la haissent, qu'ils la fuyent; qu'ils la méprisent en Poesie & en Musique."

66. Ibid., 1:182–83: "Tous ceux qui aiment comme vous l'antiquité, & qui ne préférent pas *Le clinquant du Tasse à tout l'or de Virgile*, seront de même obligés de renoncer aux Maîtres Italiens pour Lulli."

67. Ibid., 2:221: ". . . la premier beauté, la vraye beauté, la beauté unique d'un air ne soit d'être fait pour les paroles; surquoi une personne de bon esprit, disoit tres-juste, qu'une marque excelente de la bonté d'un air, est que nulles paroles n'y conviennent si bien que celles sur lesquels il aura été fait."

68. Ibid.: "... J'accorderois volontiers à Mr de Saint Evremont, que l'entêtement & l'ignorance des Musiciens, (je dis une ignorance honteuese de la Fable, des bienseances du Théatre, des régles de la Poësie & de la Grammaire, à quoi nos Compositeurs sont sujets.) a mis quantité de sottises dans les Opera. On pourroit dire en gros, que pour la constitution de la Piéce, le Poete doit absolument être le maître. ...."

69. Ibid., 2:282: "... je prens pour un bon signe que ce qu'on dit d'un, soit en partie vrai des autres."

70. Ibid., 1:168: "Tous les genres de Poësie ne sont, selon lui, que différentes *imitations*, de différentes peintures."

71. Ibid., 1:169: "Maintenant quelle est la beauté de la Musique des Opera? C'est d'achever de rendre la Poésie de ces Opera, une peinture vraiment parlante. C'est, pour ainsi dire, de la retoucher, de lui donner les dernieres couleurs. Or comment la Musique *repeindra-t-elle* la Poësie, comment s'entreserviront-elles: à moins qu'on ne les lie avec une extrême justesse, a moins qu'elles ne se mêlent ensemble par l'accord le plus parfait?"

72. Ibid., 3:129: "Ils oublient, ils affoiblissent l'expression générale du Verset & de la pensée, pour s'amuser à cette expression particuliere du mot."

73. Ibid., 1:173: "Beautés tirées du sein de la nature, les expressions bien vrayes se font sentir à tous les hommes, & que les beautés fausses n'ont garde d'avoir ce privilege."

74. Ibid., 2:110: "Un grand homme a dit que la Musique est utile pour trois choses. Pour instruire, pour purgir des passions, & pour donner une recreation agréable & digne d'un honnête homme."

75. Ibid., 2:8: "Qu'est-ce que le bon & le beau? c'est ce qui plaît à la Nature."

76. Ibid., 2:159–60: "Puis qu'on ne chante que par la même raison qu'on parle, parce qu'on à quelques sentimens a exprimer."

77. Though most of Lecerf's references in connection with the passions are to Aristotle and the literary critics, he does mention Descartes once indirectly. Quoting Descartes' counterpoint treatise, *Compendium musicae* (Amsterdam, 1650), Lecerf uses the statement "that the simplest things are usually the most excellent" to substantiate his claim that the simplest music moves the passions the most forcefully (1:79: "que les choses les plus simples sont d'ordinaire les plus excellentes"). Lecerf's only other reference to the philosopher speaks of him slightingly as "having a fair amount of taste for a mathematician" (3:144: "d'assez bon goût pour un Mathematicien"). Lecerf makes no reference either to the *Discours de la méthode* or to the *Passions de l'âme*.

78. Lecerf, *Comparaison*, 1:80: "un chant simple, naturel, & qui en apparence coulera de source & sans travail, en viendra bien mieux à bout. ... L'antiquité, cette admirable & ingenieuse antiquité, n'a point connu d'instrument qui ayent eu plus de dix cordes, & par conséquent qui ayent pû joüer les 5. parties: & avec cela les Musiciens de l'antiquité avoient porté leur Art à un si haut point de vivacité & de perfection."

79. Ibid., 1:157: "Si Lulli eût demeuré en Italie, & qu'il n'eût travaillé qu'en Musique Italienne: peut-être ne l'auroit-il pas amené la nôtre, à moins qu'il n'eût été guidé par quelque idée de l'admirable simplicité de la Musique des anciens (simplicité qu'il a mieux sçu imiter chés nous qu'on n'avoit fait nulle part depuis 1600 ans, ce que je croi la source & le caractere de son mérite)."

80. Ibid., 1:183: ". . . c'est précisément la querelle des anciens & des modernes, renouvellée sous d'autres noms. D'un coté le naturel & la simplicité: de l'autre l'affectation & le brillant. Là le vrai, embelli avec justesse: ici le faux, masqué par mille raffinemens, & chargé des excés d'une science mostrueuse. Il y à long-tems que j'avois pris garde à cette conformité de Lulli, aux anciens: & des Heros de la Musique Italienne, aux modernes: ce qui n'a pas laissé d'augmenter & de réveiller l'interest que je prenois déja à la gloire de nôtre Musique."

81. Ibid., 2:236: "Des reproches que Mr Perraut fait à l'antiquité, & qui seroient de vrayes louanges pour l'Italie. . . ."

82. Ibid., 2:160. Lecerf quotes from *De oratore*: "Il parle de la Musique dans cét admirable passage & explique comme il la veut. 'Natura moveat ac delectet.' Du naturel de l'expression, & puis de la douceur" ("He speaks of music in this admirable passage and explains how he likes it. 'The natural moves and delights.' Naturalness of expression, and then sweetness.")

83. Ibid., 2:161–63: ". . . sans le naturel & l'expression, la Musique est une faidaise, un badinage d'enfant, indigne d'occuper d'honnêtes gens. . . . L'oreille est, pour la Musique, la porte du coeur. S'ouvrir bien cette porte, flatter l'oreille est donc le troisiéme soin du Musicien; mais ce n'est que le troisiéme . . . moins le sentiment est vif, moins on a d'interêt d'arriver promtement au coeur, & plus il est permis de s'amuser a l'oreille."

84. The concept of good taste in music has been treated only superficially, and almost nothing has been written with respect to good taste in Lecerf and the quarrels over French and Italian music. Lionel de la Laurencie's *Le goût musical en France* (Paris, 1905; repr. ed., Geneva, 1970), and Georges Snyders' *Le goût musical en France aux XVIIe et XVIIIe siècles* (Paris, 1968) are, surprisingly, unhelpful; both use the term *goût* only in its broadest sense to mean a general history of the kind of music enjoyed in France during this period; neither makes any attempt to define *bon goût* as it was applied to music.

85. Lecerf, *Comparaison*, 1:a-ij: "J'Avois plusieurs fois fait réflexion, que quoique nous ayons en nôtre langue assez de Traitez de Musique, nous n'en avons point qui entre dans une discussion des beautez de nôtre composition. Ce ne sont que des traitez de mécanique & d'artisan, si je puis parler ainsi: des Traitez qui enseignent séchement les régles, & desquels aucun n'enseigne à sentir le cas qu'on doit faire des Piéces où ces régles sont practiquées: desquels aucun ne conduit les honnêtes gens à juger en gros du prix d'une simphonie & d'un air. Je concevois qu'il y auroit quelque mérite & quelque gloire à donner le premier des Traitez de ce genre-ci."

86. Ibid., 2:317: "Nous ne devons pas nous flatter que nôtre bon sens seul prévaut au bon sens ramassé de tant de gens."

87. Ibid., 2:322: "Garcons de boutique, porteurs de chaise, servantes de cabaret, & cuisinieres, qui écoutent les chansons du Pont-neuf, & ne vont point à l'Opera."

88. Ibid., 2:324: "La nature qui surpasse tout parle mieux, ou plûtôt parle davantage, parle plus haut, par mille bouches, que par dix."

89. Ibid., 1:125. Ironic reference is made to the chevalier's longwindedness (and perhaps Lecerf's): "Monsieur le Chevalier de . . . est un Critique bien long & bien étendu . . ." ("Monsieur le Chevalier is a very long and drawn-out critic . . .").

90. Ibid., 3:67: "Je parle en critique, & point en Prédicateur."

91. Ibid., 3:46–52.

92. Ibid., 3:46: "Car mon propre intérêt m'oblige à choisir une des meillures, de peur de ne point finir."

Chapter V

1. On the concept of taste in eighteenth-century France, and its importance for critical thought, see R. G. Saisseln, *Taste in Eighteenth-Century France* (Syracuse, 1965); Wladyslaw Folkierski, *Entre le classicism et le romanticism, étude sur l'esthétique et les esthéticiens du XVIIIe siècle* (Paris, 1925); Daniel Mornet, *La pensée française au XVIIIe siècle* (Paris, 1926); Heinrich von Stein, *Die Entstehung der neueren Ästhetik* (Stuttgart, 1886).

2. Trans. C. A. Koelln and James P. Pettegrove as *The Philosophy of the Enlightenment* (Princeton, 1951), pp. 275–76.

3. Ibid., pp. 276–77.

4. The idea of individual genius had grown out of the seventeenth-century quarrel between Ancients and Moderns; Robert Finch, in his *The Sixth Sense: Individualism in French Poetry, 1686–1760* (Toronto, 1966; second ed., 1969), p. 4, attributes the first analysis of individualist poetry to Charles Perrault (leader of the Moderns) in his *Le génie* of 1686.

5. The earlier appreciations of Italian music, including the treatise of Raguenet, instinctively appealed to these standards, but without the philosophical-critical system of sentiment and relative taste with which to support their preference.

6. Almost nothing of worth has been written on the subject of good taste in music. The only works which treat the subject at all are: Jules Ecorcheville, *De Lulli à Rameau, 1690–1730: l'esthétique musicale* (Paris, 1906); Georges Snyders, *Le goût musical en France aux XVIIe et XVIIIe siècles* (Paris, 1968); Hugo Goldschmidt, *Die Musikästhetik des 18. Jahrhunderts und ihre Beziehungen zu seinem Kunstschaffen* (Zürich, 1915); Louis Striffling, *Esquisse d'une histoire du goût musical en France au XVIIIe siècle* (Paris, 1912); Rudolf Schäfke, *Geschichte der Musikästhetik in Umrissen* (Tutzing, 1964); and Lionel de la Laurencie, *Le goût musical en France* (Paris, 1905).

7. *Journal des savants*, August, 1706, pp. 481–88. See Chapter III, p. 58.

8. *Journal des savants*, May, 1706, pp. 316–18: "Les reproches des Ecrivains Français pourront empêcher les Italiens de se livrer trop au feu ou à la gentillesse de leur imagination. Mais le commerce des Auteurs Italiens contribuera peut-être aussi à mettre du feu & de l'agrément dans les Ouvrages des Français . . . ."

9. The article also appears as Chapter 13 of the *Histoire de la musique et de ses effets* by Pierre Bonnet-Bourdelot (Paris, 1715; facsimile of second Amsterdam edition, Graz, 1966), pp. 291–317; here it is entitled "Dissertation sur le bon goût de la musique d'Italie, de la musique française et sur les opéra." Jules Ecorcheville (*De Lulli à Rameau*, p. 116) was the first to trace the article's origins to the *Mercure* (Nov. 1713, p. 38), and he speculated that the author may have been a musician named La Tour. Dora Vischer (*Der musikgeschichtliche Traktat des Pierre Bourdelot* [Bern, 1947], p. 67) mistakenly attributes this article, along with Lecerf's *Comparaison*, to Bourdelot; her misattribution has helped to perpetuate the error in later research.

10. "Dissertation," in Bonnet-Bourdelot, 1:293: ". . . l'un Admirateur outré de la Musique Italienne . . . proscrivent absolument la Musique Françoise, comme fade et sans goût, ou tout-à-fait insipide: l'autre parti fidèle au goût de sa Patrie . . . traite la Musique Italienne de bizarre, de capricieuse, & comme revoltée contre les règles de l'Art."

11. Ibid., pp. 299–300: "Un Italien se gouverne-t'il comme un François? Leurs goûts, leurs habits, leurs moeurs, leurs maniéres, leurs plaisirs, ne sont-ils pas tous differens? Pourquoi ne veut-on pas qu'ils le soient aussi dans leurs chants & dans le toucher des Instrumens? . . . Pourquoi veut-on que le François chante & joue comme l'Italien? Chaque Nation a ses usages differens: Pourquoi vouloir habiller la Musique Françoise en masque, & la rendre extravagante? elle dont la Langue est si naïve, & ne peut souffrir la moindre violence. . . . "

12. Ibid., pp. 309–10: "Enfin de ces deux partis differens, il en resulte un troisiéme plus raisonnable & moins entêté que les deux autres, qui est celui des gens sages, & des gens de bon goût . . . mais rendent justice à la Musique Françoise dans son caractére, & à la Musique Italienne dans le sien, conviennent que l'on pourroit faire un genre de Musique parfait, si l'on vouloit joindre le goût savant & ingenieux de l'Italien, au bon goût naturel & simple du François . . . "

13. Ibid., p. 294: "Mais si nous leur cedons la science & l'invention, ne doivent-ils pas nous ceder, avec la même justice, le bon goût naturel dont nous sommes en possession, & l'execution tendre & noble où nous excellons . . . ." See also the quotation above, note 11.

14. Ibid., pp. 294–300: "On peut ici comparer la Musique Françoise à une belle Femme, dont la beauté simple, naturelle, & sans art, attire les coeurs de tous ceux qui la regardent. . . . "

15. Ibid., p. 302: "Un musicien n'arrive plus que l'un ou l'autre en poche . . . enfin les *Cantates* nous étouffent ice. . . . Qu'est donc devenu le bon goût? Faudra-t'il qu'il expire aussi sous le fatras de toutes ces *Cantates*? Que diroient les Lambert, les

Boesset, les Le Camus, & les Batiste, s'ils revenoient au monde, de voir le chant François si changé, si avili & si défiguré?"

16. Reprinted in "Les préfaces de F. Couperin," *Mélanges Couperin* (Paris, 1968), pp. 58–59.

17. Ibid., p. 59: "Le goût Italien et le goût François ont partagé depuis longtems (en France) la République de la Musique; à mon égard, J'ay toûjours estimé les choses qui le meritoient, sans acception d'Auteurs, ny de Nation; et les premiéres Sonades Italiénes qui parurent à Paris il y a plus de trente années, et qui m'encouragerent à en composer ensuite, ne firent aucun tort dans mon esprit, ny aux ouvrages de Monsieur de Lulli, ni à ceux de mes ancêtres, qui seront toûjours plus admirables qu'imitables."

18. See Descartes, *Compendium musicae* (Amsterdam, 1650), trans. Walter Robert as *Compendium of Music*, Musicological Studies and Documents, vol. 3 (Rome, 1961); *Les passions de l'âme* (Paris, 1649), in: *Oeuvres*, ed. Charles Adam and Paul Tannery, 12 vols. (Paris, 1897–1910), 11:291–497. Studies on Descartes and music include André Pirro, *Descartes et la musique* (Paris, 1907); Jan Racek, "L'esthétique musicale de Descartes," *Revue de musicologie* 11 (1930):289–301; Arthur Locke, "Descartes and Seventeenth-Century Music," *The Musical Quarterly* 21 (1935):423–31; and Rudolf Stephan, "Descartes," *MGG* 3 (1954), cols. 209–11. The influence of the British philosophers on musical thought has been less thoroughly researched and is, therefore, less clearly defined; good introductions, however, are found in Clarence de Witt Thorpe, *The Aesthetic Theory of Thomas Hobbes, with Special Reference to his Contribution to the Psychological Approach in English Literary Criticism* (New York, 1940; second ed., 1964), pp. 287–307, and Rosalie Sadowsky, "Jean-Baptiste *Abbé* Dubos: The Influence of Cartesian and Neo-Aristotelian Ideas on Music Theory and Practice" (Ph.D. dissertation, Yale, 1960), pp. 6–26.

19. Facs. ed., Geneva, 1970. Jacqueline de la Harpe, in her *Jean-Pierre Crousaz (1663–1750) et le conflit des idées au siècle des lumières* (Berkeley, 1955), discusses this treatise, pp. 209–13.

20. Crousaz, *Traité de beau*, p. 68: "Le bon goût nous fait d'abord estimer par sentiment ce que la Raison auroit approuvé, après qu'elle se seroit donné le tems de l'examiner assez pour en juger sur de justes idées."

21. Ibid., chapter 11, section 8, pp. 282–302: "Où l'on aplique plus particulierement à la Beauté de la Musique les principes que l'on a établis."

22. See Sadowsky, "Jean-Baptiste *Abbé* Dubos."

23. Dubos, *Réflexions critiques* (sixth ed., 1755), 2:310–11: "Or le sentiment enseigne bien mieux si l'ouvrage touche, & s'il fait sur nous l'impression qu'il doit faire, que toutes les dissertations composées par les Critiques, pour en expliquer le mérite, & pour en calculer les perfections & les défauts. La voie de discussion & d'analyse, dont se servent ces Messieurs, est bonne à la vérité, lorsqu' il s'agit de trouver les causes qui font qu'un ouvrage plaît, ou qu'il ne plaît pas; mais cette voie ne vaut pas celle du sentiment, lorsqu'il s'agit de décider cette question. L'ouvrage plaît-il, ou ne plaît-il pas? L'ouvrage est-il bon ou mauvais en général? C'est la même chose. Le raisonnement ne doit donc intervenir dans le jugement que nous portons sur un poëme ou sur

un tableau en général, que pour rendre raison de la décision du sentiment, & pour expliquer quelles fautes l'empêchent de plaire, & quels sont les agrémens qui le rendent capables d'attacher."

24. Alfred Lombard, *La querelle des anciens et des modernes: l'abbé Dubos* (Neuchâtel, 1908), pp. 30–31.

25. Ibid., p. 30: "Par un circuit aux dogmes universels de l'ancienne critique."

26. Dubos, *Réflexions critiques,* vol. 1, chapters 45–46, pp. 425–57.

27. Isaac Vossius (1618–1689), a Dutch philosopher and theologian, spent the last years of his life at Oxford University, where he published *De poematum cantu et viribus rhythmi* in 1673. This work, which examines rhythm and meter in poetry and music, finds their most effective use in the music of the ancients; for his comparison of ancient and modern music, see particularly the Appendix, p. 317. (Vossius also makes some comments on French and Italian music, pp. 122–25.)

28. *Réflexions critiques*, vol. 1, chap. 46: "Quelques réflexions sur la Musique des Italiens. Que les Italiens n'ont cultivé cet Art qu'après les François & les Flamands."

29. Marcello, *Il teatro alla mode* (Venice, 1722), trans. R. G. Pauly in *The Musical Quarterly* 34 (1948):371–403, and 35 (1949):85–105; Algarotti, *Saggio sopra l'opera in musica* (n.p., 1755). Interestingly, Italian opera theorists did not discuss the quarrels over French and Italian music, presumably because Italian music itself was not influenced by French music in the powerful way that French was influenced by Italian, and French music was not imported into Italy as Italian music had been imported into France.

30. Quoted by Dubos, *Réflexions critiques*, 1:447–48: "Mais notre poësie ayant été corrompue par l'excès des ornaments & des figures, la corruption a passé de-là dans notre musique. C'est la destinée de tous les Arts, qui ont une origine & un objet commun, que l'infection passe d'un Art à l'autre. Notre musique est donc aujourd'hui si chargée de colifichets, qu'à peine y reconnoît-on quelque trace de l'expression naturelle." The original passage may be found in Gravina, *Scritti critici e teorici*, ed. Amedeo Quondam (Rome, 1973), pp. 555–56.

31. See Chapter III, note 32, for bibliographical information on Bonnet-Bourdelot.

32. This edition (Amsterdam, 1725) comprised four volumes, the latter three of which constituted the *Comparaison*. The "Dissertation" was included in vol. 1, pp. 291–317.

33. This dedication is not included in the editions of the *Histoire de la musique* cited above. It is quoted without reference by Dwight Allen, *Philosophies of Music History* (New York, 1939; repr. ed., 1962), p. 160.

34. Dom Philippe Lecerf de la Viéville's "Lettre d'un religieux bénédictin de la congrégation de Saint-Maur à un de ses amis," *Mercure de France*, April, 1726, pp. 677–90.

35. Robert Wangermée, "Lecerf de la Viéville, Bonnet-Bourdelot et l'"Essai sur le bon goust en musique' de Nicolas Grandval," *Revue Belge de musicologie* 5 (1951):132.

36. Grandval, *Essai sur le bon goust*, pp. 25–27: "Il faut pourtant rendre justice à tout le monde. Disons que parmi les Musiciens d'Italie, il s'en trouve d'infiniment aimables, & qui sçavent joindre à la science (qu'ils possedent en general à un plus haut degré que nous) le beau Chant et le naturel. . . . Ce que je confesse hautement pour faire connaître que, bien loin de mépriser leur bonne Musique, je cours après le beau, de quelque part qu'il vienne, & ne sçais rien de plus estimable que les bons Compositeurs d'Italie. . . ."

37. Ibid., p. 65: ". . . nourissez-vous de bonnes choses, c'est à dire, à n'executer que de la Musique reconnuë bonne d'un consentement general, comme de celle de Lully, de celle de nos bons Modernes, et des Airs choisis de plusieurs Compositeurs d'Italie, dont il en est grand nombre d'estimables, & principalement des symphonies."

38. Masson, "Lullistes et Ramistes, 1733–1752," *Année musicale* 1 (1911):187–213.

39. Masson states ("Lullistes et Ramistes," p. 211): "When Rameau is reproached for his excess of *science*, his complicated harmony, his difficult and bizarre melodies, his mistrust of poetry or even his Italianism, all of these reproaches may be reduced to one: too much music" ("Qu'on reproche à Rameau son excès de science, son harmonie trop compliquée, ses chants bizarres et difficiles, son mépris de la poésie ou même son italianisme, tous ces reproches se réduisent au fond à un seul: trop de musique").

40. Pp. 863–70; facs. ed., Geneva, 1969, pp. 235–37.

41. Ibid., p. 866: ". . . toute la Musique de Ballet étoit caractérisée, les yeux fermez, on pouvoit deviner quels étoient les Danseurs et se raprésenter à peu près les différentes figures du Ballet tant la même expression regnoit et dans le Chant et dans la Danse; il sembloit que la nature seule eut produit l'une et l'autre; et sans que l'on s'en apperçut, on ressentoit les plus delicates nüances des douces passions exprimées par les Sons."

42. Ibid., pp. 868–69: ". . . tous travaillent à l'envi à composer de la Musique, chacun vantoit son travail et la peine qu'il s'étoit donnée. Les Geométres même s'en mêlerent, ils loüoient les calculs immenses qu'ils avoient fait pour trouver moyen de parcourir dans les Airs de violon toutes les differentes combinaisons d'un *ré* ou d'un *mi*, avec les autres Notes; il est vrai que cet Air n'avoit point de chant, et dans cette Musique contrainte et si pénible à composer, rien ne couloit de source, nul génie ne les animoit, ils fuioient la nature et le sentiment. . . . De la tristesse au lieu de tendresse, le singulier étoit du barocque, la fureur du tintamare. . . ."

43. Ibid., p. 869: ". . . ne croyez pas qu'une nation s'en soit approprié l'une à l'exclusion de l'autre; les deux musiques se sont répandües dans toutes les nations, vôtre coeur et vôtre goût vous feront démêler quelle est leur origine."

44. Ed. J. Assézat (Paris, 1908), Chapter 13, pp. 57–61.

45. Ibid., pp. 57–59: "De tous les spectacles de Banza, il n'y avait que l'Opéra qui se soutînt. Utmiutsol et Uremifasolasiututut, musiciens célèbres, dont l'un commençait à vieillir et l'autre ne faisait que de naître, occupaient alternativement la scène lyrique. Ces deux auteurs originaux avaient chacun leurs partisans: les ignorants et les barbons

tenaient tous pour Utmiutsol; la jeunesse et les virtuoses étaient pour Uremifasolasiututut; et les gens de goût, tant jeunes que barbons, faisaient grand cas de tous les
deux.

Uremifasolasiututut, disaient ces derniers, est excellent lorsqu'il est bon; mais il dort
de temps en temps et à qui cela n'arrive-t-il pas? Utmiutsol est plus soutenu, plus
égal: il est rempli de beautés; cependant il n'en a point dont on ne trouve des exemples,
et même plus frappants, dans son rival, en qui l'on remarque des traits qui lui sont
propres et qu'on ne rencontre que dans ses ouvrages. Le vieux Utmiutsol est simple,
naturel, uni, trop uni quelquefois, et c'est sa fault. Le jeune Uremifasolasiututut est
singulier, brillant, composé, savant, trop savant quelquefois: mais c'est peut-être la
faute de son auditeur. . . . La nature conduisait Utmiutsol dans les voies de la mélodie;
l'étude et l'expérience ont découvert à Uremifasolasiututut les sources de l'harmonie.
Qui sut déclamer, et qui récitera jamais comme l'ancien? qui nous fera des ariettes
légères, des airs voluptueux et des symphonies de caractère comme le moderne?''

46. François Cartaud de la Vilate, *Essai historique et philosophique sur de goût* (Amster-
    dam, 1736; facs. ed., Geneva, 1970), p. 179: "Je n'ai jamais pû bien comprendre que
    des hommes d'un caractere si envelopé dans le commerce, & d'un jugement si profond
    sans les affaires d'état, eussent une imagination si bondissante, & si peu capable de
    se contenir.''

47. Ibid., p. 292: "Aujourd'hui nos cerveaux commencent à devenir Italiens, & ceux qui
    n'ont point vû M. Lulli, ne s'en apperçoivent point.''

48. Reprinted in: *Oeuvres philosophiques de Père André*, ed. Victor Cousin (Paris, 1843),
    pp. 1–190. Cousin surveys André's life and works in his introduction.

49. Ibid., pp. 1–2: ". . . si le beau est quelque chose d'absolu ou de relatif? s'il y a un
    beau essentiel, et indépendant de toute institution? un beau fixe, et immuablement tel?
    un beau qui plaît, ou qui à droit de plaire à la Chine, comme en France . . . ou, enfin,
    s'il en est de la beauté comme des modes et des parures, dont le succès dépend du
    caprice des hommes, de l'opinion et du goût?'' In this work, taste is always used in
    its relative sense, and no reference is made to *bon goût* or to taste in its critical
    function. In the "Discours sur le goût,'' however, published later in vol. 3 of André's
    collected works (Paris, 1747; facs. ed., Geneva, 1971), pp. 384–408, he discusses *bon
    goût* in the classical sense of *bon sens*, dependent on the rules and on reason. To
    support this view he quotes Boileau's passage, "Evitons ces excès. Laissons à l'Italie/De
    tous ces faux brillans l'éclatante folie,'' and denounces the marinistic style based on
    ornament and excess.

50. Andre, *Essai sur le beau*, pp. 73–74: ". . . il réussit à plaire à la raison, ce qui n'est
    pas un grand mérite auprès du peuple; et il ne contenta pas l'oreille, à qui sa musique
    parut trop simple, trop sèche, trop abstraite; ce qui est toujours un grand défaut.
    . . . Après un peu plus d'un siècle, Aristoxène chercha le moyen d'y remédier . . . et
    on l'accusa bientôt d'avoir cherché à plaire à l'oreille aux dépens de la raison.''

51. Ibid., p. 74–75: "Mais ne dirons-nous rien de la fameuse querelle entre les partisans
    de l'ancienne musique et ceux de la moderne? Cette question n'entre pas dans mon
    dessein; cependant, si après avoir lu tous les auteurs que j'ai pu trouver sur la musique,
    depuis Aristoxène jusqu'à M. Rameau, il m'était seulement permis de dire l'impression

qui m'en est restée, je la rendrais en trois mots. Les anciens sont les pères de la musique; ils en ont établi tous les principes, et par le goût musical que leurs ouvrages ont répandu de siècle en siècle, ils ont produit dans le nôtre des enfants, dont il m'a paru que la plupart ne connaissent pas leurs pères, et que d'autres, encore plus ingrats, refusent de les reconnaître.''

52. Ibid., p. 75: "Il y a soixante ans que la musique française, qui se contente, dans ses compositions, de parer modestement la nature, l'emportait, sans contradiction, sur tous les brillants de la musique italienne. Lulli, quoique Italien de génie et de naissance, mais Français d'éducation et de goût, l'avait rendue partout victorieuse . . . mais depuis quelques années Lulli commence à devenir ancien. Voilà le moment fatal de la révolution: cela suffit à mille gens pour le reléguer presqu'au rang des musiciens grecs. Il n'est pourtant pas si abandonné qu'il n'ait encore nombre de partisans; mais combien de temps tiendront-ils contre le torrent de la mode?''

53. Three witty epigrams "Pour et contre M. Rameau" are included in André's collected works, vol. 4 (Paris, 1747; facs. ed., Geneva, 1971), pp. 371–72. The first:

"Contre la modern musique,	Against modern music
Voici ma dernière réplique.	Here is my last reply.
Oui, si le difficile est beau,	Yes, if the difficult is beautiful,
C'est un grand homme que Rameau;	A great man is Rameau.
Mais si le beau par avanture,	But if by chance the beautiful
N'était que la simple nature,	Is nothing but simple nature,
Dont l'art doit-être le tableau,	Which art should only paint,
Le petit homme que Rameau.''	Then an insignificant man is Rameau.

And in response:

"Avec le censeur de Rameau	With the critic of Rameau
Je tombe d'accord, que le beau	I agree that the beautiful
N'est en effet que la simple nature,	Is in effect only simple nature,
Dont l'art doit-être le tableau.	Which art should paint.
Mais s'il croyoit par avanture,	But if he believe by chance,
Que ce n'est point un art difficile et nouveau	That it does not take a difficult, new art
D'exceller dans cette peinture,	To excell in this painting
Je tiens, que le bon sens murmure	I insist that *bon sens* murmurs
Contre le censeur de Rameau.''	Against this critic of Rameau.

And finally, another response:

"Le difficile n'est point beau;	The difficult is not beautiful;
Mais quolqu'en dise enfin la paresse indocile	But whatever the hostile laziness
Des censeurs dégoutés de l'Amphion nouveau,	Of the disgusted censors says of the new Amphion [Rameau]
Le beau fut toujours difficile.''	The beautiful is always difficult.

54. The complete work was published in Paris over a period of eighteen years, 1732–1750, the section on music (vol. 7, "Professions instructives," p. 96–142) appearing in 1746.

Ecorcheville (*De Lulli à Rameau*, p. 117), dating this section from 1732, saw Pluche's discussion of French and Italian music as an aftermath of the quarrel between Lecerf and Raguenet, whereas it should properly be considered a response to that between Lullists and Ramists (see Masson, "Lullistes et Ramistes," p. 196, note 1).

55. Pluche, *Spectacle*: "Présenter le plaisir pour le plaisir même, c'est un renversement: servons-nous d'un terme plus clair, c'est une prostitution."

56. Ibid., p. 112: ". . . parler à l'oreille sans rien dire à l'esprit." See Lecerf, as quoted above, Chapter IV, note 83: "The ear is, for music, the door of the heart. To open this door, flattering the ear is the third care of the musician, but only the third . . . the less powerful the affection, the less quickly will it pierce the heart, and the more it is permitted to amuse the ear" (*Comparaison*, 2:161–63).

57. Ibid., p. 98: "Les François, quoiqu'amis du chant, mettent depuis long-temps plus de feu & d'harmonie dans leur composition, qu'on ne faisoit au siècle passé. La musique Italienne quoique figurée & savante, devient de jour en jour plus gracieuse & plus charmante."

58. Ibid., p. 99: "M. Rameau, après avoir fait une étude profonde de l'harmonie & des moyens de la perfectionner, a porté cette partie de la musique à une hardiesse de composition, & à une liberté d'exécution, où les Italiens mêmes ne paroissent pas l'avoir amenée."

59. Pluche may have gotten the term *barroque* from the article in the *Mercure* of 1734; see above, p. 207, note 208.

60. Ibid., pp. 228–29: "L'une prend son chant dans les sons naturels de notre gosier, & dans les accens de la voix humaine, qui parle pour occuper les autres de ce qui nous touche; toujours sans grimace; toujours sans efforts; presque sans art. Nous la nommerons *la musique Chantante*. L'autre veut surprendre par la hardiesse des sons & passer pour chanter en mesurant des vitesses & du bruit: nous la nommerons *la musique Barroque*." For a brief discussion of these terms, see Claude Palisca, *Baroque Music* (Englewood Cliffs, N.J., 1968), p. 2.

61. Jean-Pierre Guignon (1702–1774), violinist and composer known especially for his performance of Italian works. See *MGG* 5 (1956), cols. 1081–84.

62. Violinist and composer, 1661–1775. See *MGG* 15 (Supplement, 1973), cols. 216–17.

63. Pluche, *Spectacle*, p. 103: "C'est, selon lui, aller arracher péniblement quelques perles baroques au fond de la mer; pendant qu'on peut trouver des diamans à la surface des terres."

64. French composer and violinist, 1711–72. See Boris Schwartz, "Mondonville," *MGG* 9 (1961), cols. 454–56.

65. Bollioud de Mermet, *De la corruption du goût*, p. 14: ". . . on a changé si considérablement la constitution de notre Musique, qu'on diroit qu'à cet égard nous avons cessé d'être François, ou que nous avons été transportés dans une autre région!"

66. Ibid., pp. 45–46: "Je dis qui'il y a un certain vrai dans les Arts comme ailleurs, qui est de tous les temps, de tous les païs. La raison, la nature qui ne changent point, ont établi des loix, contre lesquelles les variations & les bizarreries qu'introduisent les Artistes, ne sçauroient prévaloir."

67. *Belle nature* had for the classical critics of the seventeenth century come to stand for the ideal object of imitation in all the arts. Denis Diderot, in his *Recherches philosophiques sur l'origine et la nature du beau* of 1751 (*Oeuvres complètes*, ed. J. Assézat, 10 [Paris, 1876]:5–42) complains that Batteux has summarized all his principles of beauty in art as the imitation of *belle nature*, but without giving a definition for it (p. 17). Diderot offers his own: "If you want to paint a flower, and it does not matter which you paint, choose the most beautiful of all the flowers . . . if you want to paint any object from nature, and it does not matter to you which one, choose the most beautiful" ("Si vous avez à peindre une fleur, et qu'il vous soit d'ailleurs indifférent laquelle peindre, prenez la plus *belle* d'entre les fleurs . . . si vous avez à peindre un objet de la nature, et qu'il vous soit indifférent lequel choisir, prenez le plus *beau*").

68. Batteux, *Les beaux-arts*, p. 284: "La Musique étant significative dans la symphonie, où elle n'a *qu'une demi-vie, que la moitié de son être*, que fera-t'elle dans le chant, où elle devient le tableau du coeur humain?"

69. Ibid., p. 286: "Pour amuser peut-être les yeux, & ennuyer sûrement l'esprit."

70. Ibid., p. 55: "Il est un bon Goût."

71. Ibid., p. 108.

72. Ibid: "Cependant on voit des Goûts différens dans les hommes & dans les Nations qui ont la réputation d'être éclairées & polies. Serons-nous assez hardis, pour préférer celui que nous avons à celui des autres, & pour les condamner? Ce seroit une témérité, & même une injustice; parce que les Goûts en particulier peuvent être différens, ou meme opposés, sans cesser d'etre bons en soi. La raison en est, d'un côté, dans la richesse de la Nature: & de l'autre, dans les bornes du coeur & de l'esprit humain."

73. Ibid., p. 110: "La Musique Françoise & l'Italienne ont chacune leur caractere. L'une n'est pas la bonne Musique: l'autre, la mauvaise. Ce sont deux soeurs, ou plutôt deux faces du même objet."

74. The letter is reprinted in Albert Jansen, *Jean-Jacques Rousseau als Musiker* (Berlin, 1884), pp. 455–63. On Rousseau and music, see also A. Pougin, *Jean-Jacques Rousseau musicien* (Paris, 1901) and J. Tiersot, *Jean-Jacques Rousseau* (Paris, 1912). On Grimm, see Charlez, *Grimm et la musique de son temps* (Caen, 1872).

75. Rousseau, letter to Grimm (Jansen, p. 459): ". . . un tissu de conversations tout à fait trivial de quatorze à quinze cent vers, divisées en trois actes et chantées pendant quatre mortelles heures: voilà par rapport au poème le goût des opéra italiens."

76. Ibid., p. 461: "La musique italienne me plait souverainement, mais elle ne me touche point. La francaise ne me plait que parcequ'elle me touche. Les fredons, les passages, les traits, les roulements de la première font briller l'organe et charment l'oreille, mais

les sons séduisants de la seconde vont droit au coeur. Si la musique est faite pour plaire seulement, donnons la palme à l'Italie, mais si elle doit encore émouvoir, tenons en à la notre, et surtout quand il est question de l'opéra où l'on se propose d'exciter les passions et d'y toucher le spectateur."

77. Ibid., p. 463: ". . . car le peu de choeurs qu'il y a dans ses opéra chantés seulement par les principaux acteurs, ne sont pas dignes de porter le nom."

78. *Correspondance littéraire, philosophique et critique par Grimm, Diderot, Raynal, Meister, etc.*, ed. Maurcie Tourneux, 16 (1882):287–309. See also Paul-Marie Masson, "La 'Lettre sur *Omphale*' (1752)," *Revue de musicologie* 27 (1945):1–19.

79. "Lettre sur *Omphale*," p. 290: "Ils me parleront du goût, du naturel et de l'expression qui sont dans le chant de cet opéra, et c'est précisément sur ces choses-là que je veux l'attaquer. Selon moi, ce chant est d'un bout à l'autre de mauvais goût et rempli de contre-sens, triste, sans aucune expression, et toujours au-dessous de son sujet, ce qui est le pire de tous les vices."

80. On the War of the *bouffons*, see Louisette Richebourg, *Contribution à l'histoire de la querelle des bouffons* (Paris, 1937). On the role of the *philosophes*, see Alfred Richard Oliver, *The Encyclopedists as Critics of Music* (New York, 1947); Adolphe Jullien, *La musique et les philosophes au XVIIIe siècle* (Paris, 1873); and Eugen Hirschberg, *Die Enzyklopädisten und die französische Oper im XVIII. Jahrhundert* (Leipzig, 1903).

81. *Correspondance littéraire* 16:313–36.

82. Oliver, *The Encyclopedists as Critics of Music*, p. 91.

83. On Diderot see Daniel Mornet, *Diderot, l'homme et l'oeuvre* (Paris, 1941); R. L. Evans, "Diderot et la musique" (Ph.D., Birmingham, 1932); and the sources listed in note 79 on the Encyclopedists and music.

84. *Oeuvres complètes*, ed. Assézat, 12 (1876):143–51.

85. Ibid., pp. 152–70.

86. Ibid., p. 152: "J'ai lu, messieurs, tous vos petis écrits, et la seule chose qu'ils m'auraient apprise, si je l'avais ignorée, c'est que vous avez beaucoup d'esprit et beaucoup plus de méchanceté. . . . Mais après avoir laissé faire les *beaux esprits* et les *inspirés* tant qu'il vous a plu, pourrait-on vous inviter à descendre de la sublimité du bon mot et à vous abaisser jusqu'au niveau du sens commun."

87. Terradellas (1713–1751) was actually Spanish, though he had found employment in Naples as early as 1732. See *Grove's Dictionary of Music and Musicians* 8 (1966):396–97, and *MGG* 13 (1966):243–45; neither source, however, lists the opera *Nitocris*. The scene from *Armide* is included in *Chefs-d'oeuvre classiques de l'opéra français* (Paris, n.d .), pp. 136–43.

88. Ibid., p. 154: "L'opéra d'*Armide* est le chef-d'oeuvre de Lulli, et le monologue d'Armide est le chef-d'oeuvre de cet opéra. Les défenseurs de la musique française seront, je

l'espère, très-satisfaits de mon choix; cependant, ou j'ai mal compris les enthousiastes de la musique italienne, ou ils auront fait un pas en arrière s'ils ne nous démontrent que les scènes d'*Armide* ne sont en comparaison de celles de *Nitocris* qu'une psalmodie languissante, qu'une mélodie sans feu, sans âme, sans force et sans génie; que le musicien de la France doit tout à son poëte, qu'au contraire le poëte de l'Italie doit tout à son musicien."

89. *Oeuvres complètes* 13 (Paris, 1821):229–85.

90. Lecerf, defending Lully, had charged the Italians with the same fault.

91. Rousseau, "Lettre sur la musique française," pp. 283–84: ". . . si on l'envisage comme du chant, on n'y trouve ni mesure, ni caractère, ni mélodie; si l'on veut que ce soit du récitatif, on n'y trouve ni naturel, ni expression. . . . En un mot, si l'on s'avisoit d'exécuter la musique de cette scène sans y joindre les paroles, sans crier ni gesticuler, il ne seroit pas possible d'y rien démêler d'analogue à la situation qu'elle veut peindre et au sentiment qu'elle veut exprimer, et tout cela ne paroîtroit qu'une ennuyeuse suite de sons. . . . Mais, sans les bras et le jeu de l'actrice, je suis persuadé que personne n'en pourroit souffrir le récitatif, et qu'une pareille musique a grand besoin du secours des yeux pour être supportable aux oreilles."

92. *La paix de l'opera*, "avertissement": "L'Écrit que l'on présente au Public n'est que l'extrait d'un petit Ouvrage qui parut en 1702, sous ce titre: *Parallele des Italiens et des Francois, en ce qui regarde la Musique et les Opéra*. L'Ouvrage est excellent pour le fond: mais le stile est si diffus & si peu correct, qu'il a été nécéssaire d'élaguer & de rectifier beaucoup de choses. Il a même fallu ajoûter quelques remarques.
   Si ce Parallele, tel qu'on le donne, paroît écrit avec plus de solidité que d'agrément, il faut se rappeller que c'est originairement un Ouvrage de l'année 1702, & non un brochure de jour. L'Auteur écrit naturellement, et sans enthousiasme: il ne prend point un ton dogmatique, ou railleur: il n'offense personne: il approfondit la matiére: il juge sainement. C'est ce qui distingue son Ouvrage de toutes les brochures modernes qui ont paru sur le même sujet."

93. *La Paix de l'opéra*, p. 39: "Le canevas de ces Opéra est très-bon, le Récitatif est admirable, il y a même d'excellens morceaux de symphonie. Pourquoi se priver d'un si riche fond? Pourquoi renoncer à un héritage qu'on pourrait recueiller, & même amplifier à peu de frais? Pourquoi surtout, pourquoi laisser tomber dans l'oubli tant de Poëmes admirables qui auront nécessairement la même destinée que la Musique? . . . On remédieroit à tous ces inconveniéns par le projet dont j'ai parlé, on enrichiroit le fond le l'Opéra, on réveilleroit l'attention & la curiosité du Public, enfin l'on préserveroit notre ancienne Musique de la chute prochaine dont elle est menacée."

94. *Oeuvres complètes* (Paris, 1805):337–441. D'Alembert, one of the most astute of the Encyclopedists, took a great interest in music; see the sources listed in note 79 as well as *MGG* 1 (1949–1951), cols. 310–11.

95. D'Alembert, *De la liberté de la musique*, pp. 345–46: "Au commencement de ce siècle, l'abbé Raguenet, écrivain d'une imagination vive, mit au jour un petit ouvrage où notre musique étoit presque aussi maltraitée que dans la lettre de Rousseau. Cet écrit n'excita ni guerres, ni haine dans le temps où il parut; la musique française règnoit alors

paisiblement sur nos organes *assoupis*; on regarda l'abbé Raguenet comme un *séditieux isolé*, un *conjuré sans complices*, dont on n'avoit point de révolution à craindre."

96. Ibid., p. 364: "Cette proposition demande que nous entrions dans quelques détails sur le caractère des deux musiques. . . ."

97. Blainville, *L'esprit de l'art musical*, p. 118: "Car ne chanter que pour la voix, c'est ne parler qu'à l'ouie. . . ."

98. Ibid.: "Style qui consiste dans le caractere, le tour de chant, & dans la maniere d'ajouter la Basse, & les autres parties. Les Italiens sont aussi différents de nous en ce genre, qu'ils le sont de caractere & de langage."

Chapter VI

1. In: *Criticism: The Major Texts*, ed. Walter Jackson Bate (New York, 1952), pp. 129–60. For a discussion of the quarrel in England, see R. F. Jones, *Ancients and Moderns: A Study in the Rise of the Scientific Movement in seventeenth-century England* (Washington University, St. Louis, 1961).

2. In: *The Prose Works of Jonathan Swift*, ed. Temple Scott, 1 (London, 1897; repr. ed., 1907):155–87.

3. Sir William Temple, *Essay upon the Ancient and Modern Learning* (1690), in: *Critical Essays of the Seventeenth Century*, ed. Joel Elias Spingarn (Oxford, 1909), p. 56.

4. Repr. ed., New York, 1970. Malcolm (1687–?), was known chiefly for his books on mathematics; see *Grove's Dictionary of Music and Musicians* 5 (1954):528–29, and Karl Darenberg, *Studien zur englischen Musikästhetik des 18. Jahrhunderts* (Hamburg, 1960), p. 19.

5. Malcolm, *A Treatise of Music*, pp. 589–90.

6. Alexander F. B. Clark, *Boileau and the French Classical Critics in England* (Paris, 1925), p. 358.

7. *The Spectator*, ed. Donald F. Bond, 5 vols. (Oxford, 1965), 1:26.

8. Ibid., p. 384.

9. *Critical Works of John Dennis*, ed. Edward Miles Hooker, 1 (Baltimore, 1939; repr. ed., 1964):382–93.

10. Ibid., p. 385.

11. François Raguenet, *A Comparison between the French and Italian Musick and Opera's. Translated from the French; With Some Remarks. To Which is added a Critical Discourse upon Opera's in England, and a Means proposed for their Improvement* (London, 1709; facs. ed. of the Cambridge University copy of the work, Farnborough, England, 1968).

12. Ibid., pp. 85–86.

13. Ibid., p. 86.

14. See above, note 11.

15. Ibid., pp. 17, 70.

16. Ibid., p. 64.

17. Ibid., p. 65.

18. Ibid., p. 86.

19. *The Tatler*, ed. George A. Aitken, 1 (London, 1898; repr. ed., Hildesheim, 1970):40 (April 19, 1709): "Letters from the Haymarket inform us, that on Saturday night last the opera of 'Pyrrhus and Demetrius' [Scarlatti] was performed to great applause. This intelligence is not very acceptable to us friends of the theater; for the stage being an entertainment of the reasons and all our faculties, this way of being pleased with the suspense of them for three hours together, and being given up to the shallow satisfaction of the eyes and ears only, seems to arise rather from the degeneracy of our understanding, than an improvement of our diversions."

20. Nicola Grimaldi (1673–1732), Italian male contralto who arrived in London in 1708. See *Grove's Dictionary of Music and Musicians* 6 (1954):81–82.

21. *The Spectator* 1:22–23 (March 8, 1711).

22. *Essays Literary, Moral, and Political* (1741–42; repr. ed., London, n.d.).

23. Ibid., p. 147.

24. Facsimile of third ed. (1780), ed. Walter J. Hipple, Jr. (Gainesville, Fla., 1963). Biographical information is included in the "Introduction," pp. v–xxviii; see also Darenberg, *Studien*, p. 29.

25. Gerard, *An Essay of Taste*, p. 247.

26. Ibid., p. 268.

27. Avison (1709–1770) was an English composer and theorist whose *Essay* is said to be "the first serious attempt at musical criticism on the part of an English composer"; see *Grove's Dictionary of Music and Musicians* 1 (1954):275.

28. Avison, *Essay on Musical Expression*, pp. 43–44.

29. Beattie, *Essays on Poetry and Music* (London, 1776; Third ed., 1779), p. 170.

30. Ibid., p. 180.

31. H. Edmund Poole, ed., *Music, Men, and Manners in France and Italy (1770): Being the journal written by Charles Burney, Mus. D., during a Tour through those Countries* (London, 1969). On Burney's journey, see Romain Rolland, "A Musical Tour across Europe in the Eighteenth Century," in: *A Musical Tour through the Land of the Past* (London, 1922).

32. Poole, *Music, Men, and Manners*, p. 220.

33. On the beginnings of musical journalism in Germany, see F. Krome, *Die Anfänge des musikalischen Journalismus in Deutschland* (Leipzig, 1896).

34. In 1713–1714, Mattheson had published a series of translations and adaptations of articles from the *Tatler* and *Spectator*. See Beekman C. Cannon, *Johann Mattheson: Spectator in Music* (New Haven, Conn., 1947; repr. ed., 1968), p. 76.

35. Hans Gunter Hoke, "Marpurg," *MGG* 8 (1960), col. 1671.

36. Cannon, *Johann Mattheson*, p. 131.

37. Mattheson, *Das neu-eröffnete Orchestre* . . . (Hamburg, 1713), p. 231: "Ein Frantzose/Nahmens le Sieur de Vieuville soll zwar an dē Abbé Raguenet Antworten geschrieben haben/so er nennet: *Comparaison de la Musique Francoise & Italienne*; alleine ich habe biss dato noch nichts davon auffstäuben können."

38. Mattheson, *Critica musica* (Hamburg, 1722–1725; facs. ed., Amsterdam, 1964), pp. 91–231.

39. Ibid., p. 92: "Nicht nur dem Amte eines Uebersetzers/sondern auch zugleich dem Caractère eines *Critici* . . . ."

40. Ibid., p. 230.

41. Ibid., p. 310: "Der ungenannte *Autor* der drey letzten Bände/von der Histoire de la Musique . . . ."

42. Johann Gottfried Walther, *Musicalisches Lexicon oder musicalische Bibliothec* (Leipzig, 1732; facs. ed., Kassel, 1953), p. 634: "Vieuville, (de la) ein Frantzose, hat eine *Dissertation sur le bon gout de la Musique d'Italie, de la Musique Françoise & sur les Opera*, d. i. eine Rede über den guten Geschmack an der Italiänischen Music, an der Französischen Music, und über die Opern, geschrieben; solche hat jemand an 1712 in Form eines Briefes dem Hrn. Bonnet, zugesandt . . . woselbst sie das 12te Capitel ausmacht."

43. Howard J. Serwer, "Friedrich Wilhelm Marpurg (1718–1795): Music Critic in a *Galant* Age" (Ph.D. dissertation, Yale, 1969), pp. 5–6.

44. Marpurg, *Der critische Musicus an der Spree* 1 (Berlin, 1750):109–112, 117–119, 125–28, 133–36, 165–68, 183–85, 191–94, 199–201.

45. *Der critische Musicus an der Spree* 1 (1750):319–49.

46. Marpurg, *Historisch-kritische Beyträge zur Aufnahme der Musik*, 5 vols. (Berlin, 1754–1778), 1:550–59, 2:145–79.

47. Serwer, "Friedrich Wilhelm Marpurg," p. 237. In another place Marpurg translated the term as *"toller"* (senseless, absurd); see Serwer, p. 134.

48. Marpurg, *Kritische Briefe über die Tonkunst* (Berlin, 1760–1763), 1:65–71, 89–94, 113–18, 398–403, 405–6 (Raguenet), 1:406–11, 413–18, 421–23 ("Dissertation" from *Mercure*, 1713, attributed to Lecerf).

49. Marpurg, *Historisch-kritische Beyträge* 1 (1754):57–68.

50. Ibid., p. 146: "Jeder blieb den seiner Meinung, nachdem man sich müde geschimpfet hatte. Eine Parten ist öfters nicht birgsam genug, Lehren anzunehmen, und die andere nicht tonkündig genug, Lehren zu geben. Vielleicht kömmt es einer dritten Nation zu, den Ansspruch zu thun. Aber können sich auch nicht unter dieser Partenische finden, die nach eingesuchten vorgefussten Meinungen urtheilen, oder die aus Eigensinn nur das Böse einer Nation, nicht aber ihr Gutes erkennen wollen? Diejenige Musik verdienet allezeit den Preiss vor andern, in der mit dem Geschmack des Landes und der Zeit, die ächte Reinigkeit der Harmonie im Satze glücklich verbunden worden. Ohne diese ist keine Musik gut; einer herrschenden gewohnheit sich aber widersetzen wollen, ist thöricht. Aber jedes Land hat die seinige, und hält diese allezeit für die beste."

51. On Thomasius, see Paul Böckmann, *Formgeschichte der deutschen Dichtung* (Hamburg, 1949), pp. 483ff.

52. Fritz Martini, "Von der Aufklärung zum Sturm und Drang," in: *Annalen der deutschen Literatur*, ed. Heinz Otto Burger (Stuttgart, 1952), pp. 408ff.

53. On Gottsched and his circle, see J. Birke, "Gottsched's Opera Criticism and its Literary Sources," *Acta Musicologica* 32 (1960):194; *idem.*, *Christian Wolffs Metaphysik und die zeitgenössische Literatur und Musiktheorie: Gottsched, Scheibe, Mizler* (Berlin, 1966); Arnold Schering, *Musikgeschichte Leipzigs* 3 (Leipzig, 1941):274–76, 316–19; Walter Serauky and Hans Haase, "Gottsched," *MGG* 5 (1956), cols. 573–81.

54. Johannes Crüger, ed., *Johann Christoph Gottsched und die Schweizer, Johann Joseph Bodmer und Johann Joseph Breitinger*, Deutsche National-Literatur: Historisch-kritische Ausgabe, vol. 42 (Berlin, n.d.).

55. Gottsched, *Versuch einer critischen Dichtkunst*, in: *Ausgewählte Werke*, 6/1 (Berlin, 1973):176: "Derjenige Geschmack ist gut, der mit den Regeln übereinkömmt, die von der Vernunft . . . allbereit fest gesetzet worden."

56. Ibid., 6/2:366: "Die Oper sey das ungereimteste Werk, das der menschliche Verstand jemals erfunden hat. . . ."

57. Ibid., p. 368: "Was nur den Augen und Ohren gefiele, das wäre schon gut: und man müsste die Vernunft hier schweigen heissen, wenn sie uns dieses Vergnügens durch ihre critische Anmerkungen berauben wollte. . . . So wird die Weichlichkeit von Ju-

gend auf in die Gemüther der Leute gepflanzet, und wir werden den weibischen Italienern ähnlich, ehe wir es inne geworden, dass wir männliche Deutsche seyn sollten."

58. Ibid., p. 369: "So ist die Oper ein blosses Sinnenwerk: der Verstand und das Herz bekommen nichts davon. Nur die Augen werden geblendet; nur das Gehör wird . . . betäubet: die Vernunft aber muss man zu Hause lassen, wenn man in die Oper geht . . . ."

59. Johann Friedrich Doles (1715–1797), composer of sacred works and successor to J. S. Bach in Leipzig; Doles had studied with Gottsched as a student at the University of Leipzig. See Friedrich Blume, "Doles," *MGG* 3 (1954):627–39.

60. Schering, *Musikgeschichte Leipzigs* 3:318.

61. J. N. Forkel, *Allgemeine Literatur der Musik* (Leipzig, 1792; facs. ed., Hildesheim, 1962), p. 442.

62. Scheibe, *Critischer Musikus*; (Leipzig, 1737–1740; facs. ed., Hildesheim, 1970), pp. 375–76: "Weil ich nun zugleich in diesem Blatte den Musikverständigen und Musikanten zeigen wollte, wie genau die Dichtkunst und die Musik mit einander verwandt sind, und dass die Regeln der ersten auch in der letztern gelten, und weil ich sie ferner auf die Nachahmung der Natur führen, und ihnen solche Materien vorlegen wollte, die man fast noch gar nicht, oder doch nur sehr kaltsinnig, oder undeutlich, abgehandelt hat, ungeachtet sie doch zur Beförderung des guten Geschmackes allerdings nöthig sind: so war auch ein so wichtiges Unternehmen, nicht ohne die Vortheile auszuführen, welche uns eine vernünftige Critik allemal entdecket. Weil nun also meine Absichten zum Theil mit den Absichten des Herrn Professor Gottsched überein kamen, indem ich einigermassen nach der Art, wie dessen critische Dichtkunst eingerichtet war, von der Musik schreiben wollte . . . so gab ich auch meinen Blättern den Titel: Der critische Musikus."

63. Eugen Reichel, in his article "Gottsched und Johann Adolph Scheibe," *Sämmelbände der Internationalen Musikgesellschaft* 2 (1900–1901):654–68, includes a number of excerpts from the *Critische Dichtkunst* juxtaposed with their echoes in the *Critischer Musikus*. Also see Imanuel Willhelm, "Johann Adolph Scheibe: German Musical Thought in Transition" (Ph.D. dissertation, University of Illinois, 1963), pp. 1–18.

64. Scheibe's quarrel with Bach and its underlying aesthetic premises have been clarified in George J. Buelow's article, "In Defence of J. A. Scheibe against J. S. Bach," *Proceedings of the Royal Music Association* 101 (1977):85–100.

65. *Das neu-eröffnete Orchestre, oder Universelle und gründliche Anleitung/Wie ein Galant Homme einen volkommenen Begriff von der Hoheit und Würde der edlen MUSIC erlangen/seinen GOUT darnach formiren/die Terminos technicos verstehen und geschichtlich von dieser vortrefflichen Wissenschaft raisonniren mögt.*

66. Mattheson quite self-consciously took the side of the proponents of the senses as opposed to those of reason in his choice of the pseudonym "Aristoxenus." To Mattheson this ancient musician was "the champion of the senses and opposed to the scientific rationalism of the Pythagoreans" (Cannon, *Johann Mattheson*, p. 200, n. 176).

67. Mattheson, *Das neu-eröffnete Orchestre*, pp. 202–3: "Die Italiäner/welche heutiges Tages/theils durch die wesentliche Schönheit ihrer Wercke/theils auch durch die übertünchte und insinuante Kunst-Griffe in der *Composition*, den Preis vor allen anderen *Nationen* davon zu tragen scheinen/und den generalen GOUT mehrentheils auff ihrer Seiten haben/sind nicht nur in ihrem *Stylo* von den Frantzösen/Teutschen und Engelländern; sondern in gewissen Stücken unter sich selbst mercklich unterschieden."

68. See above, note 37.

69. Fux, *Gradus ad Parnassum*, trans. Lorenz Christoph Mizler as *Anführung zur regelmässig musikalsichen Composition* (Leipzig, 1742; facs. ed., Hildesheim, 1974), p. 178: "... me mea delectant, te tua, quemque sua ... ingleichen: de gustibus non est disputandum, nemo sit iudex in propria causa . . . ."

70. Ibid., pp. 179–80: "Ich sage also, dass diejenige Composition von guten Geschmack sey, und den Vorzug verdiene, welche sich auf die Regeln gründet, sich der gemeinen und ausschweisenden Gedancken enthält, was ausgesuchtes edles und erhabenes in sich hält, alles in natürlicher Ordnung vorbringt, und auch Musikverständigen ein Vergnügen zu machen fähig ist. . . . Das leichte ist schwer. Und auf diese schwere Leichtigkeit gründet sich das treffliche des guten Geschmacks, und das niedliche." Note the similarity in the last line to the idea expressed by the père André, Chapter V, note 53.

71. Ibid., p. 181: "Da aber die verschiedene Schreibart, und verschiedene Gattungen der Composition, auch einen verschiedenen Geschmack erfordern, so ist nun von der Verschiedenheit des Styls, als wornach sich hauptsächlich unsere Arbeit richten muss zu handeln. . . ."

72. Heinichen, *General-Bass*, pp. 20–24 (note); see also George J. Buelow, *Thorough-Bass according to Johann David Heinichen* (Berkeley and Los Angeles, 1966), pp. 273–4.

73. Heinichen, *General-Bass*, p. 10 (note): "Manche Nation suchet ihre grösste Kunst in Lauter *intricanten Musicalischen* tiff, taff, und gedrechselten Noten-Kunsteleyen. Die andere hingegen *appliciret* sich mehr auff den *Gout*, und nimet jenen dadurch den *Universal Applausum* hinweg, die Pappierene Künstler hingegen bleiben mit allen ihren Hexereyen in *obscuro*, u. werden noch wohldazu vor *Barbari* angeschrien, da sie es doch andern Nationen blindlings nachtun könten, wo fern sie sich, gleich jenen mehr auff den *Gout* und das Brillant der *Music* als auff unfruchtbare Künste *appliciren* wollen."

74. See above, p. 124.

75. Heinichen, *General-Bass*, pp. 10–11 (note): "Ein vornehmer ausländischer Componist gab einsmahls wieder die Gewohnheit seines Landes dieses offenhertzige *Raisonnement* von dem Unterschiede der *Music* zweyer Nationen. Unserer Nation sagete er: (damit ich seine eigene Worte in unsere Sprach *vertire*) inclinirt von Natur mehr zur *Dolcezza* (Anmuth, *tendresse*) der Music, so gar, dass sie sich offt hüten muss, nicht dadurch in eine Schläffrigkeit zu verfallen; die meisten *Tramontani* hingegen incliniren von Natur fast allzuviel zur *Vivacité* der Music, wodurch sie gar leicht in Barbarismum verfallen: wenn aber selbige sich die Mühe geben wollen uns unsere *Tendresse* der

Music zu rauben, und mit ihrer gewöhnlichen *Vivacité*, zu vermischen, so würde ein Tertium heraus kommen, welches nicht anders als aller Welt gefallen könte. Ich will meine damahls hierüber gemachte *Glossen* verschweigen, und nur dieses gestehen, dass mich dieser *Discurs* zum erstenmahl auff die Gedancken gebracht, dass eine glückliche Melange vom Italienischen und Französischen *Gout* das Ohr am meisten *frappieren*, und es über allen anderen besondern *Gout* der Welt gewinnen müsse.

76. Scheibe, *Compendium musices*, in Peter Benary, *Die deutschen Kompositionslehre des 18. Jahrhunderts* (Leipzig, 1960), p. 85: "Wird nun ein Anfänger alles bisshero in diesen *Compendio* angeführtes wohl in acht nehmen, so wird er auch endlich *Gout* erlangen, und dadurch überall durchgängigen Beyfall finden. *Gout* erlangt aber niemand eher, als biss er alle in der ersten und andern Abtheilung beschriebene Grund Regeln gefasst hat, ferner sich einen *fermen Stylum* erwehlet, alle übrigen Sorten des *Styli* nach ihren innerlichen und äusserlichen Wesen wohl kennet, die *Affecten* und alles übrige wohl ausdrücket, Zeit und Orth und Zuhörer wohl beurtheilet, von unterschiedenen üblichen *Instrumenten* eine Käntniss besizet, eine *judicieuse* Abwechselung und Veränderung und in allen Sachen ein überall herrschendes *Cantabile* blicken läst. . . ."

77. Ibid., p. 76: "Denn die Arten wie jeder *Componist* seine Gedancken vorträgt, nicht weniger auch das innere Wesen derselben an sich selbst, sind durchgehends von einander unterschieden, nichts desto weniger haben aber doch alle insgesammt *Gout*."

78. Ibid.: "Man muss sich auch in Ansehung der *Music* selbst, ob man in Französischen *Italien*ischen oder teutschen *Stylo* arbeitet, wohl vorsehen, damit man nicht einen mit den andern vermische, denn die Deutlichkeit des *Styli* muss so gut als die Ausdrückung der Sache selbst beobachtet werden."

79. From a letter to Johann Mattheson, quoted in Cannon, *Johann Mattheson*, p. 89; see also Hans T. David and Arthur Mendel, *The Bach Reader* (New York, 1945), p. 240, and Buelow, "In Defence of J. A. Scheibe," pp. 90–91.

80. Scheibe, *Critischer Musikus*, pp. 598–99: "Man betrachte hingegen die Symphonien in ihrer itzigen Gestalt: Gewiss, man wird weit andere Vorzüge erblicken. Da man einer fliessenden, einer ausdrückenden und lebhaften Melodie folget, die allein die Natur zur Mutter hat: so zeigen sich weit andere und weit angenehmere Wirkungen. . . . Die Melodie ist es also, wodurch man allerley Affecten und Leidenschaften erregen und ausdrücken kann."

81. Ibid., p. 3: "Der gute Geschmack beginnet zu herrschen, und dadurch fangen wir an, zu empfinden, wie glücklich diejenigen sind, welche der Vernunft und der Natur in einer wohlgeprüften Beurtheilungskraft folgen."

82. Ibid., p. 6: "Das von den Schönheiten der italienischen Musik gefasste Vorurtheil hat so gar viele deutsche Componisten und Musikanten mit Verführet. Aber was sollten sie anders thun? Der Geschmack war nur bey solchen Leuten, die doch keinen Begriff vom guten Geschmacke hatten. . . ."

83. Taste and style, though separated by Scheibe, retain a certain relationship, for he stipulates that taste is a necessary requirement for determining the proper style of a piece, and a knowledge of styles is essential before a composer can have good taste:

"But can one attain good taste in music if one has no conception of the good styles or if one considers them unnecessary or superfluous?" ("Kann man aber wohl den guten Geschmack in der Musik erreichen, wenn man keine Begriffe von den guten Schreibarten hat, oder wenn man sie wohl gar für unnöthig, oder für überflüssig hält?"), *Critischer Musikus*, p. 394.

84. Ibid., p. 201, n. 3: "Ein blosses Urtheil der Sinne, ohne Absicht auf den Verstand, ist keineswegs der gute Geschmack. Es ist wahr, dass wir in der Musik den Sinn des Gehöres, der Empfindung wegen, nöthig haben; allein, müssen wir auch nicht durch eben diesen Sinn die allerverborgensten Fehler, wie auch die feinsten Schönheiten eines Stückes erfahren? . . . Wenn wir aber die Empfindung gesunder Sinne mit der Fähigkeit des Verstandes verbinden: so werden wir dasjenige Urtheil, welches hieraus entsteht, den guten Geschmack nennen können."

85. Ibid., pp. 750–95: "Abhandlung vom Ursprunge, Wachsthume und von der Beschaffenheit des itzigen Geschmacks in der Musik." A comparison of this essay with Gottsched's essay on good taste (see above, note 55) reveals many similarities, though Scheibe is more liberal in admitting sensual perception to artistic judgment.

86. Ibid., p. 767: "Der Geschmack ist eine Fähigkeit des Verstandes, das jenige zu beurtheilen, was die Sinne empfinden."

87. Ibid., p. 795: "Diess ist es also, was ich voritzo vom itzigen Geschmacke in der Tonkunst anzumerken für nöthig erachtet habe. Meine Leser können nunmehro ganz leicht urtheilen, dass diejenigen Componisten, welche den Eigenschaften des guten Geschmacks zuwider, weder regelmässig noch scharfsinnig sind, elende Stümper in der Musik sind. . . . Männer aber, die, wie Hasse, Graun, Telemann und Händel, mit einer gesunden Einbildungs-und Erfindungskraft schreiben, und in deren Werken eine geläuterte Vernunft herrschet, und die in allen Noten Regel und Witz zeigen, solche Männer sind es, die den guten Geschmack besitzen. . . . Wir sind also nicht mehr Nachahmer der Italiener; vielmehr können wir uns mit Recht rühmen, dass die Italiener endlich die Nachahmer der Deutschen geworden sind."

88. Marpurg, *Der critische Musicus an der Spree*, p. 354: "Endlich nährte sich Deutschland dem glücklichen Perioden, da sein Geschmack vollkommen, und selbst den Ausländern zum Muster dienen sollte."

89. Ibid., pp. 37–38: "Wo die elendest Harmonie den gemeinsten und leichtsinnigsten Gesang begleitet . . . ."

90. *Historisch-kritische Beyträge*, 1:32: "Er will vor Süssigkeit vergehen."

91. Ibid., 1:1–41.

92. On Krause, see Heinz Becker, "Krause," *MGG* 7 (1958), cols. 1717–21.

93. Marpurg, *Historisch-kritische Beyträge*, p. 37: "Der ietzige Geschmack bey uns ist ja niemals in Italien bekannt gewesen. Die Vorwürfe, die St. Evremond und andere Franzosen, der welschen Musik, und zwar zu einer Zeit gemachet haben, da sie es

weniger als heutiges Tages verdiente, passen nicht auf den geläuterten Geschmack der Musikart bey uns."

94. "Wie ein Musikus und eine Musik zu beurtheilen sey," *Versuch einer Anweisung die Flöte traversiere zu spielen* (Berlin, 1752; facsimile of the 1789 ed., Kassel, 1968), pp. 275–334. On the aesthetics of the *Versuch*, see Rudolf Schäfke, "Quantz als Ästhetiker," *Archiv für Musikwissenschaft* 6 (1924):213–42.

95. Ibid., pp. 223–24: ". . . uneingeschränkt, prächtig, lebhaft, ausdrückend, tiefsinnig, erhaben in der Denkart, etwas bizarr, frey, verwegen, frech, ausschweifend, im Metrum zuweilen nachlässig . . . singend, schmeichelnd, zärtlich, rührend, und reich an Erfindung." Translation by Edward R. Reilly, *On Playing the Flute* (London, 1966), p. 334.

96. Ibid: ". . . zwar lebhaft, ausdrückend, natürlich, dem Publikum gefällig und begreiflich, und richtiger im Metrum . . . weder tiefsinnig noch kühn; sondern sehr eingeschränket, sklavisch, sich selbst immer ähnlich, niedrig in der Denkart, trocken an Erfindung . . . ." Translation by Reilly, p. 334.

97. Reilly, in his translation of this passage (*On Playing the Flute*, p. 341) identifies this composer as Hasse.

98. Quantz, *Versuch*, p. 333: ". . . wenn ferner die *Italiäner* und die *Französen* den Deutschen in der Vermischung des Geschmackes so nachahmen wollten, wie die Deutschen ihnen im Geschmacke nachgeahmet haben; wenn dieses alles, sage ich, einmüthig beobachtet würde: so könnte mit der Zeit *ein allgemeiner guter Geschmack in der Musik* eingeführet werden. Es ist auch dieses so gar unwahrscheinlich nicht: weil weder die Italiäner, noch die Französen, doch mehr die Liebhaber der Musik, als die Tonkünstler unter ihnen, mit ihrem puren Nationalgeschmacke selbst mehr recht zufrieden sind; sondern schon seit einiger Zeit, an gewissen ausländischen Compositionen mehr Gefallen, als an ihren inländischen, bezeiget haben."

99. See above, note 75.

100. Cassirer, *The Philosophy of the Enlightenment*, p. 176.

101. The relationship of the German *style galant*, national styles, good taste, and French classicism remains to be explored thoroughly. David Sheldon, in his article "The Galant Style Revisited and Re-evaluated," *Acta Musicologica* 47 (1975), p. 261, notes Mattheson's actual definition of galant as "le bon goût" (see also above, note 65), but points out that "this association of *galant* with 'good taste' seems surprisingly unique in the eighteenth-century musical literature." For whatever reason, it seems that taste and *style galant* were generally related to one another not directly, but through the common denominator of national styles. This assessment is borne out in the standard literature on *style galant*, including—besides Sheldon's article—Lothar Hoffman-Erbrecht, "Der Galante Stil in der Musik des 18. Jahrhunderts," *Studien zur Musikwissenschaft* 25 (1962):252–60; Serwer, "Friedrich Wilhelm Marpurg," pp. 246–81; Ernst Bücken, "Der Galante Stil," *Zeitschrift für Musikwissenschaft* 6 (1924):418–30; Arnold Schering, "Die Musikästhetik der deutschen Aufklärung," *Zeitschrift der Internationalen Musikgesellschaft* 8 (1906–1907):265–71.

102. See, for example, Mattheson's *Der vollkommene Capellmeister* (Hamburg, 1739; facs. ed., Kassel, 1954), p. 8. In the same work (p. 140) Mattheson includes *Leichtigkeit* (ease, freedom) as one of the four recommended qualities of melody; setting "nature" (*Natur*) above "art" (*Kunst*), Mattheson advises that "the French are to be imitated in this matter more than the Italians" ("Den Franzosen soll hierin mehr als den Welschen, nachgeahmet werden").

103. The terms are those listed by Schäfke, "Quantz als Ästhetiker," p. 219, in his list of "*galante*" adjectives which he opposes to a list of "*gearbeitete*" adjectives.

104. See above, Chapter V, note 12.

Bibliography

Sources Before 1800

Addison, Joseph, Richard Steele, *et al. The Spectator*. London: 1711–1714. Edited by Donald F. Bond. 5 vols. Oxford: Oxford University Press, 1965.

André, Yves-Marie (père). *Oeuvres*. 4 vols. in 1. Facsimile reprint of 1766–1767 ed. Geneva: Slatkine, 1971.

————. *Oevures philosophiques de père André*. Edited by Victor Cousin. Paris: Charpentier, 1843.

Aristotle. *The Works of Aristotle* (384–322 B.C.). Edited by W. D. Ross. 12 vols. Oxford: Oxford University Press, 1928–1952.

Avison, Charles. *Essay on Musical Expression*. London: C. Davis, 1752.

Bacilly, Bénigne. *L'art de bien chanter*. Paris, 1668. Translated by Austin Caswell as *A Commentary upon the Art of Proper Singing*. Musical Theorists in Transition, vol. 7. New York: Institute of Medieval Music, 1968.

Bardi, Giovanni de'. *Discorso . . . sopra la musica antica, e'l cantar bene*, in: *Lyra Barbarina*. Edited by Giovanni Battista Doni, Florence, 1763. Facsimile reprint. Bologna: Forni, 1974.

Batteux, Charles (abbé). *Les beaux arts réduits à un même principe*. Paris, 1743. Facsimile reprint of the 1747 ed. New York: Johnson Reprint Corp., 1970.

Blainville, Charles H. *L'esprit de l'art musical ou réflexions sur la musique*. Geneva: n.p., 1970.

Boileau-Despréaux, Nicolas. *Oeuvres poétiques de Boileau-Despréaux*. Paris: Charpentier, 1855.

Bollioud de Mermet, Louis. *De la corruption du goust dans la musique française*. Lyon: Delaroche, 1746.

Bouhours, Dominique (père). *Les entretiens d'Ariste et Eugène*. Paris, 1671. Edited by Ferdinand Brunet. Paris: Librairie Armand Colin, 1962.

————. *La manière de bien penser dans les ouvrages d'esprit*. Paris, 1715. Facsimile reprint. Brighton: Sussex Reprints, 1971.

Bonnet-Bourdelot, Jacques. *Histoire de la musique et de ses effets depuis son origine jusqu'à présent . . . .* Paris, 1715. Second ed. (4 vols., containing Lecerf's *Comparaison*), Amsterdam, 1721. Facsimile reprint of the third ed., Amsterdam, 1725. Graz: Akademische Druck-u. Verlagsanstalt, 1966.

Brossard, Sébastien de. *Dictionnaire de musique*. Paris, 1701. Facsimile of second ed. (1705). Hilversum, 1965.

Bruno, Giordano. *De gl'heroici furori*. Paris, 1585. Collezione di classici italiani, ser. 2, vol. 19. Turin: Unione tipografico-editrice torinese, 1928.

Bruny, Charles de. *Examen de ministère de M. Colbert*. Paris: D'Houry, 1774.

Burney, Charles. *A General History of Music from the Middle Ages to the Present Period*. London, 1789. Edited by Frank Mercer. 2 vols. London: G. T. Foulis, 1935.

―――――. *An Eighteenth-Century Musical Tour in France and Italy*. Edited by Percy A. Scholes. London: Oxford University Press, 1959.

―――――. *Music, Men, and Manners in France and Italy (1770): Being the Journal written by Charles Burney, Mus. D., during a Tour through those Countries*. Edited with introduction by H. Edmund Poole. London: Folio Society, 1969.

Callières, François de. *Histoire poëtique de la guerre nouvellement déclarée entre des anciens et des modernes*. Amsterdam: Pierre Savouret, 1688.

Cartaud de la Vilate, François. *Essai historique et philosophique sur le goût*. Amsterdam, 1736. Facsimile reprint. Geneva: Slatkine, 1970.

Castelvetro, Lodovico. *Poetica d'Aristotele vulgarizzata, e sposta*. Vienna, 1570. Facsimile reprint. Munich: Fink, 1968.

Castiglione, Baldassare. *Il libro del cortegiano*. Venice, 1528. Edited by Vittorio Cian. Florence: Sansoni, 1894.

Couperin, François. "Les goûts-réunis," Paris, 1724. In: "Les préfaces de F. Couperin." *Mélanges Couperin*. Paris: Picard, 1968.

Crousaz, Jean-Pierre de. *Traité du beau*. Amsterdam, 1715. Facsimile reprint. Geneva: Slatkine, 1970.

Dacier, André. *Preface to Aristotle's Art of Poetry*. From English translation of Dacier's *Poétique d'Aristote* (1692). London, 1705. Facsimile reprint. Los Angeles: William Andrews Clark Memorial Library, University of California, 1959.

Dacier, Anne. *Des causes de la corruption du goût*. Paris: Rigaud, 1714.

D'Alembert, Jean. *Oeuvres philosophiques, historiques, et littéraires de d'Alembert*. 18 vols. Paris: Bastien, 1805.

Dennis, John. *The Critical Works of John Dennis*. Edited by Edward Niles Hooker. 2 vols. Baltimore: Johns Hopkins Press, 1939–1943.

Descartes, René. *Compendium musicae*. Amsterdam, 1650. Translated by Walter Robert as *Compendium of Music*. n.p., American Institute of Musicology, 1961.

―――――. *Oeuvres*. Edited by Charles Adam and Paul Tannery. 12 vols. Paris: L. Cerf, 1897–1910.

Diderot, Denis. *Oeuvres complètes*. Edited by J. Asse´zat and Maurice Tourneux. 20 vols. Paris: Garnier frères, 1875–1877.

"Dissertation de Mr. L. T. sur la musique italienne et française," *Le Mercure*, November, 1713, pp. 38ff. Reprinted in Bonnet-Bourdelot, *Histoire de la musique*, pp. 291–317.

Doni, Giovanni Battista. *De praestantia musicae veteris libri tres*. Florence, 1647. Facsimile reprint. Bologna: Forni, 1970.

Dryden, John. "An Esay on Dramatic Poetry" (1668). In: *Criticism: The Major Texts*. Edited by Walter Jackson Bate. New York: Harcourt-Brace, 1952.

Du Bellay, Joachim. *Divers jeux rustiques*. Paris, 1568. Critical edition by V. L. Saulnier. Geneva: Droz, 1947.

Dubos, Jean-Baptiste (abbé). *Refléxions critiques sur la poësie et sur la peinture*. Paris, 1719. Sixth ed. Paris: Pissot, 1755.

Estienne, Henri. *Deux dialogues du nouveau langage françois italianizé*. Geneva, 1578. Facsimile reprint. Geneva: Slatkine, 1972.

―――――. *La precellence du langage françois*. Paris, 1579. Edited by Leon Feugère. Paris: Jules Delalain, 1850.

_____. *Principium monitrix musa*. Basel: n.p., 1590.

Fontenelle, Bernard le Bovier de. *Oeuvres de Fontenelle*. 5 vols. Paris: Salmon, 1825.

Forkel, J. N. *Allgemeine Literatur der Musik*. Leipzig, 1792. Facsimile reprint. Hildesheim: G. Olms, 1962.

Fux, Johann Joseph. *Gradus ad Parnassum*. Vienna, 1725. German translation by Lorenz Christoph Mizler, Leipzig, 1742. Facsimile reprint. Hildesheim: Olms, 1974.

Galilei, Vincenzo. *Dialogo della musica antica e della moderna*. Florence, 1581. Facsimile reprint. New York: Broude Bros., 1967.

Gentillet, Innocent. *Discours sur les moyens de bien gouverner. . . . Contre Nicolas Machiavel florentin*. Paris, 1576. Translated by Simon Patericke as *A Discourse upon the Means of Wel Gouverning*. London, 1602. Facsimile reprint. New York: Da Capo, 1969.

Gerard, Alexander. *An Essay of Taste*. Edinburgh, 1759. Facsimile of third ed., 1780. Edited by Walter J. Hipple, Jr. Gainesville, Fla.: Scholars' Facsimiles and Reprints, 1963.

Gottsched, Johann Christoph. *Versuch einer critischen Dichtkunst*. Leipzig, 1730. In: *Ausgewählte Werke*, vol. 6. Berlin: De Gruyter, 1973.

Goulas, Nicolas. *Mémoires*. Edited by Charles Constant. Paris: Renouard, 1879–1882.

Grandval, Nicolas Ragot de. *Essai sur le bon goust en musique*. Paris: P. Prault, 1732.

Gravina, Giovanni Vincenzo (abbate). *Delle tragedia*. Naples, 1715. In: *Scritti critici e teorica*. Bari: Laterza, 1973.

Grimm, Friedrich Melchior. *Correspondance littéraire, philosophique et critique*. Edited by Maurice Tourneux. 16 vols. Paris: Garnier frères, 1877–1882.

Guéret, Gabriel. *La guerre des auteurs anciens et modernes*. Paris, 1671. Reprint. Geneva: Slatkine, 1968.

Heinichen, Johann David. *Der General-Bass in der Composition*. Dresden: by the author, 1728.

Horace (Quintus Horatius). *The Works of Horace*. Translated by Sir Theodore Martin. 2 vols. Edinburgh and London: Blackwood, 1881.

Hume, David. "Of the Standard of Taste." In: *Essays Moral, Political, and Literary*. Edinburgh, 1741–1742. Edited by T. H. Green and T. H. Gross. London: Longmans, Green, and Co., 1898.

Huyghens, Constantin. *Musique et musiciens au XVIIe siècle. Correspondance de C. Huyghens*. Edited by Jonckbloet and Land. Leyden: E. J. Brill, 1882.

Jurgens, Madeleine, ed. *Documents du minutier central concernant l'histoire de la musique (1600–1650)*. 2 vols. Paris: S.E.V.E.N., n.d.

La Bruyère, Jean de. *Oeuvres complètes de La Bruyère*. 5 vols. Paris: Hachette, 1922.

La Fontaine, Jean de. *Oeuvres*. Edited by Henri Regnier. 11 vols. Paris: Hachette, 1883–1897.

La Mesnardière, Jules. *Poésies*. Paris: A. de Sommaville, 1656.

_____. *Lettre sur La Pucelle*. Paris: A. de Sommaville, 1656.

Lamy, Bernard. *Nouvelles réflexions sur l'art poétique*. Paris: A. Pralard, 1668.

La paix de l'opéra, ou parallèle impartial de la musique françoise et de la musique italienne. Amsterdam: n.p., 1753.

La Rochefoucauld, François VI, duc de. *Oeuvres*. 3 vols. in 4. Paris: Hachette, 1868–1883.

Laugier, Marc Antoine. *Apologie de la musique françoise, contre le sentiment de M. Rousseau*. Paris: n.p., 1754.

Lecerf de la Viéville, Jean-Laurent. *Comparaison de la musique italienne et de la musique française*. Brussels, 1704–1706. Facsimile reprint of the 1706 edition. Geneva: Minkoff, 1972.

    Reviews of first ed. (Brussels: F. Foppens, 1704) in:
    Journal des savants, August, 1704, pp. 508–509.
    Memoires de Trévoux, November, 1704, pp. 1881–1896.

Review of third ed. (Brussels: F. Foppens, 1706) in: *Journal des savants*, April, 1706, pp. 219–222.

―――――. *L'art de décrier ce qu'on n'entend point, ou le médecin-musicien.* Brussels: F. Foppens, 1706. Reviewed in *Journal des savants*, August, 1706, pp. 481–88.

Lecerf de la Viéville, Dom Philippe. "Lettre d'un réligieux benedictin de la congrégation de Saint-Maur à un de ses amis." *Mercure de France*, April, 1726, pp. 677–90.

Le Gallois, Pierre. *Lettre à Mlle. Regnault de Solier touchant la musique.* Paris: E. Michallet, 1680.

Lemaire de Belges, Jean. *La concorde des deux langages.* Paris, 1513. Edited by Jean Frappier. Paris: Droz, 1947.

"Lettre de M. X.*** à Mlle. X*** sur l'origine de la musique." *Le Mercure*, May, 1734, pp. 863–69.

Limojon de St.-Didier, Alexandre Toussaint. *Histoire de la ville et république de Venise.* Amsterdam: P. Mortier, 1697.

Le Moyne, Pierre. *Dissertation de poème héroïque.* Paris: L. Billaine, 1671.

Loret, Jean. *La muze historique.* Paris, 1650–1665. Edited by J. Ravenel and E. V. de La Pelouze. 4 vols. Paris: P. Jannet, 1857–1878.

Lully, Jean-Baptiste. *Oeuvres complètes.* Edited by Henry Prunières. Paris: Editions de la *Revue musical*, 1930–1939.

Malcolm, Alexander. *A Treatise of Music: Speculative, Practical and Historical.* Edinburgh, 1721. Reprint. New York: Da Capo, 1970.

Marolles, Michel de. *Mémoires.* Amsterdam, n.p., 1755.

Marot, Jehan. *Le voyage de Gênes.* Paris, 1532. Edited by Giovanna Trisolini. Geneva: Droz, 1974.

Marpurg, Friedrich Wilhelm. *Der critischen Musicus an der Spree.* 1 vol. Berlin: A. Haude and J. C. Spener, 1750.

―――――. *Historisch-kritische Beyträge zur Aufnahme der Musik.* 5 vols. Berlin: G. A. Lange, 1754–1778.

―――――. *Kritische Briefe über die Tonkunst. . . .* 3 vols. Berlin: F. W. Birnstiel, 1760–1763.

Mattheson, Johann. *Critica musica.* Hamburg, 1722–1725. Facsimile reprint. Amsterdam: F. A. M. Knuf, 1964.

―――――. *Das neu-eröffnete Orchestre. . . .* Hamburg: B. Schiller's widow, 1713.

―――――. *Der vollkommene Capellmeister.* Hamburg, 1737. Facsimile reprint of 1739 ed. Kassel: Bärenreiter, 1954.

Maugars, André. *Response faite à un curieux sur le sentiment de la musique d'Italie.* Rome, 1639. Edited by Antoine E. Roquet in *Maugars, célèbre joueur de viole, musicien du cardinal Richelieu . . . sa biographie suivie de sa "Response fait à un curieux. . . ."* Paris, 1865. Reprint. Geneva: Minkoff, 1972.

Mei, Girolamo. *Letters on Ancient and Modern Music to Vincenzo Galilei and Giovanni Bardi.* Edited and annotated by Claude Palisca. n.p.: American Institute of Musicology, 1960.

Ménestrier, Claude François. *Des représentations en musique anciennes et modernes.* Paris, 1681. Facsimile reprint. Geneva: Minkoff, 1972.

Mersenne, Marin. *Correspondance du père Marin Mersenne.* Edited by Cornelis de Waard. Paris: G. Beauchesne, 1932–.

―――――. *Harmonie universelle.* Paris, 1636. Facsimile reprint edited by François Lesure. 3 vols. Paris: Centre national de la recherche scientifique, 1963.

―――――. *Quaestiones celebrerrimae in Genesim.* Paris: Sebastian Cramoisy, 1623.

Michaud, Joseph, and Jean Poujoulat, eds. *Nouvelle collection des mémoires pour servir à l'histoire de France, depuis le XIIIe siècle jusqu'à la fin du XVIIIe.* 32 vols. in 34 (issued in 3 series). Paris: Chez l'éditeur du commentaire analytique de code civil, 1836–1889.

Michele, Agostino. *Discorso in cui si dimostra come si possono scrivere le commedie e le tragedie in prosa.* Venice: G. B. Ciotti, 1592.

Minturno, Sebastiano. *Arte poetica.* Venice, 1563. Facsimile reprint from the 1564 ed. Munich: Fink, 1971.

Misson, Maximilien. *A New Voyage to Italy.* Translated anonymously. London: printed for R. Bently *et al.*, 1699.

Molière, Jean-Baptiste Poquelin. *Oeuvres de Molière.* Edited by Eugène Despois. 13 vols. Paris: Hachette, 1875–1927.

Monteverdi, Claudio. *Claudio Monteverdi: Lettere, dediche e prefazione.* Edited by Domenico de'Paoli. Rome: De Santis, 1973.

Moreau, Célestin, ed. *Choix de Mazarinades.* 2 vols. Paris: Renouard, 1853.

Parran, Antoine (père). *Traité de la musique théorique et pratique contenant les préceptes de la composition.* Paris, 1639. Facsimile reprint. Geneva: Minkoff, 1972.

Perrault, Charles. *Critique de l'opéra ou examen de la tragédie intitulée: Alceste ou le Triomphe d'Alcide.* Paris: Barbin, 1674.

_____. *Mémoires de ma vie.* Paris, 1759. Paris: H. Laurens, 1909.

_____. *Parallèle des anciens et des modernes en ce qui regarde les arts et les sciences.* Paris, 1688–1697. Facsimile reprint. Theorie und Geschichte der Literatur und der schönen Künste, vol. 2. Munich: Eidos Verlag, 1964.

_____. *Le siècle de Louis XIV.* Paris: Coignard, 1687.

Perrault, Claude. "De la musique des anciens." In: *Essais de physique*, vol. 2. Paris: Coignard, 1680–1688. Reprint. 1721.

Perrin, Pierre. "Lettre écrite à Monseigneur l'archevesque de Turin." In: *Les oeuvres de poésie de Mr. Perrin.* Paris: Loyson, 1661.

Plato. *The Dialogues of Plato.* Translated by Benjamin Jowett. 5 vols. New York: Random House, 1892.

Pluche, Noël Antoine (abbé). *Le spectacle de la nature.* 7 vols. Paris, n.p., 1731–1747.

Plutarch. *Works.* Edited by K. Ziegler. Leipzig: B. J. Beubner, 1959.

Quantz, Johann J. *Versuch einer Anweisung die Flöte traversiere zu spielen.* Berlin, 1752. Facsimile reprint. Kassel: Bärenreiter, 1953. Translated by E. R. Reilly as *On Playing the Flute.* New York: Free Press, 1966.

La querelle des bouffons. Paris and The Hague, 1752–1754. 3 vols. Collected and reprinted. Geneva: Minkoff, 1971.

Rabutin, Roger de, comte de Bussy. *Correspondance.* 6 vols. Paris, 1858–1859. Reprint. Farnborough, England: Gregg International Publishers, 1972.

Raguenet, François. "A Comparison between the French and Italian Music." Translated by Oliver Strunk. *The Musical Quarterly* 22 (1946):411–36.

_____. *Défense du Parallèle des Italiens et des Français en ce qui regarde la musique et les opéra* (Paris, 1705). Facsimile reprint. Geneva: Minkoff, 1976 (cf. below; also includes the *Parallèle*).
Reviews of the *Défense* in:
Journal des savants, December, 1705, pp. 684–86.
Memoires de Trévoux, May, 1706, pp. 856–64.

_____. *Parallèle des Italiens et des Français en ce qui regarde la musique et les opéras.* Paris, 1702. Facsimile reprint. Geneva: Minkoff, 1976 (cf. above; also includes Raguenet's *Défense*).

Reviews of the *Parallèle* in:
Journal des savants, March 1702, pp. 186–9.
Memoires de Trévoux, July, 1702, pp. 341–50.

Rapin, René. *The Critical Works of Monsieur Rapin*. Translated by Basil Kennet. 2 vols. London, 1705. Second ed. London: printed for R. Bonwick, Richard Wilkin, *et al.*, 1716.

Ricci, Bartolomeo. *De imitatione libri tres*. Venice: by the author, 1541. 2nd ed. 1549.

Riccoboni, Antonio. *Poetica Aristotelis latine conversa*. Padua, 1587. Reprint. Munich: Fink, 1970.

Ronsard, Pierre. *Oeuvres complètes*. Edited by Paul Laumonier. Paris: Hachette, 1914–.

Rousseau, Jean-Jacques. *Oeuvres complètes de Jean-Jacques Rousseau*. 21 vols. Paris: E. A. Lequien, 1820–1823.

Sadoleto, Jacopo. *Sadoleto on Education: A Translation of the "De pueris recte instituendis."* Translated and introduced by E. T. Campagnac and K. Forbes. London: Oxford University Press, 1916.

Saint-Evremond, Charles Margaretel de St. Denis. *Oeuvres en prose*. Edited by René Ternois. Paris: Didier, 1962–.

Scheibe, Johann Adolph. *Compendium musices theoretico-practicum*. 1736. In: Peter Benary, *Die deutsche Kompositionslehre des 18. Jahrhunderts*. Leipzig: Breitkopf und Härtel, 1961.

————. *Critischer Musicus*. Leipzig, 1737–1740. Facsimile reprint. Hildesheim: G. Olms, 1970.

Sénecé, Antoine Bauderon de. *Oeuvres choisies de Sénecé*. Edited by Emile Chasles and P. A. Cap. Paris: P. Jannet, 1855.

Serré de Rieux. *Les dons des enfants de Latone*. Paris: P. Prault, 1734.

Swift, Jonathan. *The Prose Works of Jonathan Swift*. Edited by Temple Scott. 12 vols. London: G. Bell and Sons, 1900–1914.

Tallemant de Réaux. *Historiettes*. Paris, 1833. 10 vols. Reprint. Paris: Garnier, 1919.

Tassoni, Alessandro. *Dai pensieri diversi*. Modena, 1612. In: *Prose politiche e morali*. Scrittori d'Italia, vol. 2. Rome: Bari, 1930.

The Tatler. London, 1709–1711. Reprint of London, 1898–1899 ed. Edited by George A. Aitken. Hildesheim: G. Olms, 1970.

Temple, Sir William. "An Essay upon the Ancient and Modern Learning." In: *Critical Essays of the Seventeenth Century*, vol. 3. Edited by Joel E. Spingarn. Oxford: Clarendon Press, 1909.

Vicentino, Nicola. *L'antica musica ridotta alla moderna prattica*. Rome, 1555. Facsimile reprint. Kassel: Bärenreiter, 1959.

Walther, Johann Gottfried. *Musicalisches Lexicon oder musicalische Bibliothec*. Leipzig, 1732. Facsimile reprint. Kassel: Bärenreiter, 1953.

Vida, Marco Girolamo. *The "Arte poetica" of Marco Girolamo Vida*. Edited and translated by Ralph G. Williams. New York: Columbia University Press, 1976.

Wotton, William. "Reflections upon Ancient and Modern Learning." In: *Critical Essays of the Seventeenth Century*, vol. 3. Edited by Joel E. Spingarn. Oxford: Clarendon Press, 1909.

Vossius, Isaac. *De poematum cantu et viribus rhythmi*. Oxford: Scott, 1673.

Wallis, John. *Claudii Ptolemaei harmonicorum libri tres*. Oxford: Theatro Sheldoniano, 1682.

Zarlino, Gioseffo. *Le istitutioni harmoniche*. Venice, 1558. Facsimile reprint. New York: Broude Bros., 1965.

Sources After 1800

Adam, Antoine. "Baroque et préciosité." *Revue des sciences humaines*, April–June, 1949, pp. 208–24.

_____. *Grandeur and Illusion: French Literature and Society, 1600–1715.* Translated by Herbert Tint. London: Weidenfeld and Nicolson, 1972.

_____. *Histoire de la littérature francaise au XVIIe siècle.* 4 vols. Paris: Editions mondiales, 1962.

Allen, Dwight. *Philosophies of Music History: A Study of General Histories of Music 1600–1960.* n.p.: American Book Co., 1939. Second ed. New York: Dover, 1962.

Anthony, James. *French Baroque Music from Beaujoyeulx to Rameau.* New York: Norton, 1974. Second rev. ed. 1978.

Augé-Chiquet, Mathieu. *La vie, les idées et l'oeuvre de Jean-Antoine Baïf.* Paris: Hachette, 1909.

Barthélemy, Maurice. "L'opéra français et la querelle des Anciens et des Modernes." *Lettres romanes* 10 (1956): 379–91.

Bailly, A. *François Ier, restaurateur des lettres et des arts.* Paris: A. Fayard, 1954.

Batiffol, Louis. *Marie de Médicis and the French Court in the Seventeenth Century.* Translated by Mary King. London: Chatto & Windus, 1908.

Benary, Peter. *Die deutsche Kompositionslehre des 18. Jahrhunderts.* Leipzig: Breitkopf & Härtel, 1961.

Birke, J. *Christian Wolffs Metaphysik und die zeitgenössische Literatur-und Musiktheorie: Gottsched, Scheibe, Mizler.* Berlin: De Gruyter, 1966.

_____. "Gottsched's Opera Criticism and its Literary Sources." *Acta Musicologica* 32 (1960):194.

Bjurström, Per. *Giacomo Torelli and Baroque Stage Design.* Stockholm: Almquist & Wiksell, 1961.

Bobillier, Marie [Michel Brenet]. *Les concerts en France sous l'ancien régime.* Paris, 1900. Reprint. New York: Da Capo, 1970.

_____. *Notes sur l'histoire du luth en France.* Turin, 1899. Reprint. Geneva: Minkoff, 1973.

Böckmann, Paul. *Formgeschichte der deutschen Dichtung.* Hamburg: Hoffman und Campe, 1949.

Borgerhoff, Elbert Benton Op't Eynde. *The Freedom of French Classicism.* Princeton: Princeton University Press, 1950.

Borrel, Eugène. "L'interpretation de l'ancien récitatif français." *Revue de musicologie* 12 (1931):13–21.

_____. "Raguenet." *MGG* 10 (1962), cols. 1870–72.

Bosanquet, Bernard. *A History of Aesthetic.* London, 1892. Reprint of the second ed. New York: Meridian Books, 1957.

Bourgoin, Auguste. *Les maîtres de critique au XVIIe siècle.* Paris, 1889. Reprint Genova: Slatkine, 1970.

Boyer, Ferdinand. "Giulio Caccini à la cour d'Henri IV (1604–1605)." *Revue musical* 7 (1926):241–50.

Boyer, Noel. *La guerre des bouffons et la musique française.* Paris: Les Editions de la nouvelle France, 1945.

Bray, René. *La formation de la doctrine classique en France.* Paris: Hachette, 1927.

_____. *La préciosité et les précieux, de Thibaut de Champagne à Jean Giraudoux.* Paris: A. Michel, 1948.

Brody, Jules. *Boileau and Longinus.* Geneva: Droz, 1958.

Brunet, Pierre. *L'introduction des théories de Newton en France au XVIIIe siècle.* Geneva: Slatkine, 1970.

Bücken, Ernst. "Der Galante Stil." *Zeitschrift für Musikwissenschaft* 6 (1924):418–30.

Buelow, George J. "In Defence of J. A. Scheibe against J. S. Bach." *Proceedings of the Royal Music Association* 101 (1977):85–100.

—————. *Thorough-Bass Accompaniment According to Johann David Heinichen.* Berkeley and Los Angeles: University of California Press, 1966.

—————, A. Cohen, et al. "National Predilections in Seventeenth Century Music Theory: A Symposium." *Journal of Music Theory* 16 (1972):2–71.

Bukofzer, Manfred. *Music in the Baroque Era.* New York: Norton, 1947.

Bury, J. B. *The Idea of Progress.* London, 1920. Reprint. New York: Dover, 1932.

Cabeen, C. W. *L'influence de Marino sur la littérature française de la première moitié du XVIIe siècle.* Grenoble: Allier, 1904.

Cannon, Beekman C. *Johann Mattheson, Spectator in Music.* New Haven, Conn.: Yale University Press, 1947.

Capefigue, Jean Baptiste Honoré Raymond. *Richelieu, Mazarin, la Fronde, et le règne de Louis XIV.* 8 vols. Paris: Dufey, 1835–1936.

Carapetyan, Armen. "The Concept of *Imitazione della natura* in the Sixteenth Century." *Journal of Renaissance and Baroque Music* 1 (1946):47–67.

Cassirer, Ernst. *The Philosophy of the Enlightenment.* Translated by Fritz C. A. Koeller and James P. Pettegrove. Princeton: Princeton University Press, 1951.

Charlez, J. F. *Grimm et la musique de son temps.* Caen: Le Blac et Aardel, 1872.

Christout, Marie-Françoise. *Le ballet de cour de Louis XIV, 1643–1672.* Paris: Picard, 1967.

Clark, Alexander Frederick Bruce. *Boileau and the French Classical Critics in England, 1660–1830.* Paris: Champion, 1925.

Clercx, Suzanne. "Le terme: Baroque. Sa signification. Son application à la musique." *Les colloques de Wégemont* 4 (1957):17–34.

Cohen, Alfred. "Survivals of Renaissance Thought in French Theory 1610–1670: A Bibliographical Study." In: *Aspects of Medieval and Renaissance Music, A Birthday Offering to Gustave Reese.* Edited by Jan La Rue, et al. New York: Norton, 1966.

Corte, Andrea della. *La critica musicale e i critici.* Turin: Unione tipografico-editrice torinese, 1961.

Cousin, Victor. *La jeunesse de Mazarin.* Paris: Didier, 1865.

Croce, Benedetto. *Storia dell'età barocca in Italia.* Bari: Laterza, 1946.

Crocker, Lester G. *Two Diderot Studies: Ethics and Esthetics.* The Johns Hopkins Studies in Romance Literature and Languages, extra vol. 27. Baltimore: Johns Hopkins Press, 1952.

Crüger, Johannes, ed. *Johann Christoph Gottsched und die Schweizer J. J. Bodmer und J. J. Breitinger.* Deutsche National-Literatur, edited by Joseph Kürschner, vol. 42. Berlin and Stuttgart: W. Spemann, n.d.

Cucuel, Georges. "La critique musicale dans les revues du XVIIIe siècle." *Année musicale* 2 (1912):127–201.

—————. *La Pouplinière et la musique de chambre au XVIIIe siècle.* Paris, 1913. Reprint. Geneva: Slatkine, 1970.

Dalka, LaVerne. "Luigi Rossi's *Orfeo*, Paris, 1647: A Documentary and Analytical Study." Ph.D. dissertation, Yale, forthcoming.

Dammann, Rolf. *Der Musikbegriff im deutschen Barock.* Cologne: A. Volk, 1967.

Darenberg, Karl. *Studien zur englischen Musikästhetik des 18. Jahrhunderts.* Hamburg: De Gruyter, 1960.

Dean, Winton. "Criticism." *Grove's Dictionary of Music and Musicians*. fifth ed. 2:521–36.

Demuth, Norman. *French Opera: Its Development to the Revolution*. Sussex, 1963. Reprint. New York: Da Capo, 1978.

Deschanel, Emile. *Boileau, Charles Perrault. Le romanticism des classiques*, vol. 4. Paris, 1886–1891. Reprint. Geneva: Slatkine, 1970.

Dethan, Georges. *The Young Mazarin*. Translated by Stanley Baron. London: Thames and Hudson, 1977.

Ecorcheville, Jules. *De Lulli à Rameau, 1690–1730: l'esthétique musicale*. Paris: Fortin, 1906.

Eitner, Robert. *Biographisch-bibliographisches Quellen-Lexikon der Musiker und Musikgelehrten*. 10 vols. Leipzig: Breitkopf und Härtel, 1898–1905. Reprint. New York: Musurgia, 1947.

Ellison, Mary Beeson. "The *Comparaison de la musique italienne et de la musique françoise* of Lecerf de la Viéville: An Annotated Translation of the First Four Dialogues." Ph.D. dissertation, University of Miami, 1973.

Evans, R. L. "Diderot et la musique." Ph.D. dissertation, Birmingham, 1932.

Ferrero, Giuseppe Guido, ed. *Marino e i marinisti*. La letteratura italiana: Storia e testi, vol. 37. Milan: R. Ricciardi, 1954.

Fétis, François J. *Biographie universelle des musiciens et bibliographie générale de la musique*. 8 vols. Brussels, 1835–1844. Second rev. ed. Paris: Firmin-Didot, 1870–1875.

Finch, Robert. *The Sixth Sense: Individualism in French Poetry, 1686–1760*. Toronto: University of Toronto Press, 1966.

Flaherty, Gloria. *Opera in the Development of German Critical Thought*. Princeton: Princeton University Press, 1978.

Folkierski, Wladyslaw. *Entre le Classicism et le Romanticism: Etude sur l'esthétique et les esthéticiens du XVIIIe siècle*. Cracow: Academie polonaise des sciences et des lettres, 1925.

France, Peter. *Racine's Rhetoric*. Oxford: Clarendon Press, 1965.

Franklin, Alfred, *Histoire de la bibliothèque Mazarin et du palais de l'Institute, 1640–1885*. Paris, 1901. Second ed. Amsterdam: Heusden, 1969.

Gaudefroy-Demombynes, J. *Les jugements allemands sur la musique française au XVIIIe siècle*. Paris: G. P. Maisonneuve, 1941.

Gérold, Théodore. *L'art du chant en France au XVIIe siècle*. Strasbourg: Librarie Istra, 1921. Reprint. New York: Burt Franklin, 1973.

Gillot, Hubert. *La querelle des anciens et des modernes en France*. Paris: Champion, 1914.

Girdlestone, Cuthbert. *Jean-Philippe Rameau: His Life and Work*. n.p.: by the author, 1957. Rev. ed. New York: Dover, 1969.

Goldschmidt, Hugo. *Die italienische Gesangsmethode des 17. Jahrhunderts*. Breslau: Schlesische Buchdruckerei, 1898.

——————. *Die Musikästhetik des 18. Jahrhunderts und ihre Beziehungen zu seinem Kunstschaffen*. Zurich and Leipzig: Rascher, 1890.

Graf, Max. *Composer and Critic: Two Hundred Years of Musical Criticism*. New York: Norton, 1946.

Gros, Etienne. *Philippe Quinault: sa vie et son oeuvre*. Paris: E. Champion, 1926.

Grout, Donald J. "The Music of the Italian Theater at Paris, 1682–1697." *Papers of the American Musicological Society* 20 (1941):158–70.

——————. *A Short History of Opera*. New York: Columbia University Press, 1947. Second ed. 1965.

——————. "Some Forerunners of the Lully Opera." *Music and Letters* 22 (1941):1–25.

Haar, James, ed. *Chanson and Madrigal 1480–1530: Studies in Comparison and Contrast.* Cambridge, Mass: Harvard University Press, 1964.

Hallays, André. *Les Perrault.* Paris: Perrin, 1926.

Hatin, Louis Eugène. *Histoire politique et littéraire de la presse en France.* 8 vols. Paris: Poulet-Malassis et De Broise, 1859–61.

Hirschberg, Eugen. *Die Enzyklopädisten und die französische Oper im XVIII. Jahrhundert.* Leipzig: Breitkopf & Härtel, 1903.

Hitchcock, H. Wiley. "The Latin Oratorios of Marc-Antoine Charpentier." Ph.D. dissertation, University of Michigan, 1954.

Hoffmann-Erbrecht, Lothar. "Der galante Stil in der Musik des 18. Jahrhunderts." *Studien zur Musikwissenschaft* 25 (1962):252–60.

Hoke, Hans Gunther. "Marpurg." *MGG* 8 (1960), cols. 1668–73.

Hope, Quentin M. *Saint-Evremond: The Honnête Homme as Critic.* Bloomington: Indiana University Press, 1964.

Hüschen, Heinrich. "Die Musik im Kreise der artes liberales." Kongressbericht, Gesellschaft für Musikforschung. Graz and Cologne: Böhlau, 1956.

Isherwood, Robert. *Music in the Service of the King.* Ithaca, N.Y.: Cornell University Press, 1973.

Jacquot, Jean. "Echoes anglais des controverses sur la musique française et italienne (1700–1750)." In: *Mélanges d'histoire et d'esthétique musicales offerts à Paul-Marie Masson,* vol. 2. Paris: Richard Masse, 1955.

—————. "Music's Monument de Thos. Mace et l'évolution du goût musical en Angleterre." *Revue de musicologie* 34 (1952):25–26.

Jansen, Albert. *Jean-Jacques Rousseau als Musiker.* Berlin: G. Reimer, 1884.

Jones, Richard Foster. *Ancients and Moderns: A Study of the Background of the Battle of the Books.* St. Louis, 1936. Second ed. Berkeley: University of California Press, 1965.

Jullien, Adolphe. *La musique et les philosophes au XVIIIe siècle.* Paris: J. Baur, 1873.

Katz, Erich. *Die musikalischen Stilbegriffe des 17. Jahrhunderts.* Charlottenburg: W. Flagel, 1926.

Kaufmann, Henry W. *The Life and Works of Nicola Vicentino, 1511–c.1576.* Musicological Studies and Documents, vol. 11. n.p.: American Institute of Musicology, 1966.

Kern, Edith G. *The Influence of Heinsius and Vossius upon French Dramatic Theory.* Baltimore: Johns Hopkins Press, 1949.

Kortum, Hans. *Charles Perrault und Nicolas Boileau: Der Antikstreit im Zeitalter der klassischen französischen Literatur.* Berlin: Hachette, 1913.

Krantz, Emile. *Essai sur l'esthétique de Descartes; rapports de la doctrine cartésienne avec la littérature classique française au XVIIe siècle.* Paris, 1882. Second ed. Paris: F. Alcan, 1898.

Kretzschmar, Hermann. "Die venetianische Oper und die Werke Cavalli's und Cesti's." *Vierteljahrsschrift für Musikwissenschaft* 8 (1892):1–76.

Krome, Ferdinand. *Die Anfänge des musikalischen Journalismus in Deutschland.* Leipzig: Pöschel & Trepte, 1896.

La Harpe, Jacqueline de. *Jean-Pierre Crousaz (1663–1750) et le conflit des idées au siècle des lumières.* University of California Publications in Modern Philology, vol. 47. Berkeley and Los Angeles, 1955.

La Laurencie, Lionel de. *Le goût musical en France.* Paris, 1905. Reprint. Geneva: Slatkine, 1970.

—————. *Les créateurs de l'opéra français.* Paris: F. Alcan, 1921.

—————. *Lully.* Paris: F. Alcan, 1911.

Le Moël, Michel. "Un foyer d'Italianisme à la fin du XVIIe siècle." *Recherches sur la musique française classique* 3 (1963):43–48.

Lesure, François, ed. *Ecrits imprimés concernant la musique*. Répertoire internationale des sources musicales, vol. B 6. Munich: Henle, 1971.

Levi, Anthony. *French Moralists: The Theory of the Passions, 1585–1649*. Oxford: Clarendon Press, 1964.

Lindberg, Dian Igor. "Literary Aspects of German Baroque Opera: History, Theory and Practice (Christian H. Postel and Barthold Feind)." Ph.D. dissertation, UCLA, 1964.

Locke, Arthur. "Descartes and Seventeenth-Century Music." *The Musical Quarterly* 21 (1935):423–31.

Lombard, Alfred. *La querelle des anciens et des modernes: l'abbé Dubos*. Paris: Hachette, 1913.

Lowens, Irving. "St.-Evremond, Dryden, and the Theory of Opera." *Criticism* 1 (1954):226–48.

McGowan, Margaret. *L'art du ballet du cour en France, 1581–1643*. Paris: Editions du centre national de la recherche scientifique, 1963.

————. "The Origins of French Opera." In: *The New Oxford History of Music*, vol. 5. London: Oxford University Press, 1975.

Machabey, Arnaud. *Traité de la critique musicale*. Paris: Richard-Masse, 1947.

Magendie, Maurice. *La politesse mondaine et les théories de l'honneté en France au XVIIe siècle de 1600–1660*. Paris: F. Alcan, 1925.

Maland, David. *Culture and Society in Seventeenth-Century France*. New York: Charles Scribner's Sons, 1970.

Marsan, J. *La pastorale dramatique en France*. Paris: Hachette, 1905.

Martini, Fritz. "Von der Aufklärung zum Sturm und Drang." In: *Annalen der deutschen Literatur*, edited by Heinz Otto Burger. Stuttgart: Metzlersche Verlagsbuchhandlung, 1952.

Masson, Paul-Marie. "L'humanisme musical en France au XVIe siècle." *Mercure musical et bulletin français de la Société international de musique*, 1907, pp. 333–66.

————. "French Opera from Lully to Rameau." In: *The New Oxford History of Music*, vol. 5. London: Oxford University Press, 1975.

————. "Lullistes et Ramistes." *Année musicale* 1 (1911):187–213.

————. "La 'Lettre sur *Omphale*.' " *Revue de musicologie* 27 (1945):1–19.

————. "Musique italienne et musique française: la première querelle." *Rivista musicale italiana* 19 (1912):519–45.

Maugain, Gabriel. *Boileau et l'Italie*. Paris: Champion, 1912.

Mellers, Wilfred. *François Couperin and the French Classical Tradition*. London, 1950. Reprint. New York: Dover, 1968.

Mornet, Daniel. *French Thought in the Eighteenth Century*. Translated by Lawrence M. Levin. New York: Prentice-Hall, 1929.

————. *Histoire de la littérature française classique, 1660–1700*. Paris: Armand Colin, 1940.

Newman, Joyce Edith Watkins. "Formal Structure and Recitative in the 'Tragédies Lyriques' of Jean-Baptiste de Lully." Ph.D. dissertation, University of Michigan, 1974.

————. *Jean-Baptiste de Lully and his Tragédies Lyriques*. UMI Research Press: Ann Arbor, 1978.

Newman, William L. *The "Politics" of Aristotle*. 4 vols. Oxford: Clarendon Press, 1887–1902.

Nisbet, Robert. *History of the Idea of Progress*. New York: Basic Books, 1980.

Oliver, Alfred Richard. *The Encyclopedists as Critics of Music*. New York: AMS Press, 1966.

Palisca, Claude. "The *Alterati* of Florence, Pioneers in the Theory of Dramatic Music." In: *New Looks at Italian Opera: Essays in Honor of Donald J. Grout.* Edited by William W. Austin. Ithaca, N.Y.: Cornell University Press, 1968.

_____. "The Artusi–Monteverdi Controversy." In: *The Monteverdi Companion*, edited by Denis Arnold and Nigel Fortune. New York: Norton, 1968.

_____. *Baroque Music.* Englewood Cliffs, N.J.: Prentice-Hall, 1968.

_____. "The Beginnings of Baroque Music, Its Roots in Sixteenth-Century Theory and Practice." Ph.D. dissertation, Harvard, 1954.

_____. "The 'Camerata Fiorentina': A Reappraisal." *Studi musicali* 1 (1972):203–236.

_____. *Girolamo Mei (1519–1594), Letters on Ancient and Modern Music to Vincenzo Galilei and Giovanni Bardi.* Musicological Studies and Documents, vol. 3. n.p.: American Institute of Musicology, 1960.

Pecchiai, Pio. *I Barberini.* Rome: Biblioteca d'arte editrice, 1959.

Pellisson, Maurice. *Les comédies-ballets de Molière.* Paris: Hachette, 1914.

Perkins, James Breck. *France under Mazarin with a Review of the Administration of Richelieu.* London: G. P. Putnam's Sons, 1886. Third ed. 1887.

Picot, Emile. "Les Italiens en France au XVIe siècle." *Bulletin italien de la Faculté des lettres de Bordeaux* 1 (1901):93–177.

Pintard, René. "Influences italiennes en France au XVIIe siècle." *Revue des études italiennes* 1 (1936):194–224.

Pougin, Arthur. *Les vrais créateurs de l'opéra français: Perrin et Cambert.* Paris: Charavay frères, 1881.

Prunières, Henry. *Cavalli et l'opéra vénitien au XVIIe siècle.* Paris: Rieder, 1931.

_____. *Le ballet de cour en France avant Benserade et Lulli.* Paris: H. Laurens, 1914.

_____. "Lecerf de la Viéville et l'esthétique musicale classique au XVIIe siècle." *Bulletin français de la Société internationale de la musique* 4 (1908): 619–54.

_____. "Les musiciens du cardinal Antonio Barberini." In: *Mélanges de musicologie offerts à M. Lionel de la Laurencie.* Paris: E. Droz, 1933.

_____. "Les véridiques avantures de Charles Dassoucy." *Revue de Paris* 6 (1922):105–37.

_____ and Lionel de la Laurencie. "La jeunesse de Lully." *Bulletin français de la Société internationale de la musique* 5 (1909):234–42 and 329–53.

Racek, Jan. "L'esthétique musicale de Descartes." *Revue de musicologie* 11 (1930):289–301.

Rathéry, Edme Jacques Benoit. *L'influence d'Italie sur les lettres françaises du XIIIe siècle au règne de Louis XIV.* Paris: Firmin-Didot frères, 1853.

Reese, Gustave. *Music in the Renaissance.* New York: Norton, 1954. Rev. ed. 1959.

Reichel, Eugen. "Gottsched und Johann Adolph Scheibe." *Sämmelbände der Internationalen Musikgesellschaft* 2 (1900–1901):654–68.

Reilly, Edward R. "Quantz on National Styles in Music." *The Musical Quarterly* 49 (1963):163–87 (translation of the portion of the *Versuch* on national styles).

Richebourg, Louisette. *Contribution à l'histoire de la querelle des bouffons.* Paris: Nizet & Bastard, 1937.

Rigault, Hippolyte. *Histoire de la querelle des anciens et des modernes.* Paris, 1859. Reprint. New York: B. Franklin, 1965.

Rizza, Cecilia. *Barocco francese e cultura italiana.* Genoa: Stabilimento tipegrafico editoriale SASTE, 1973.

Roe, Horton Lawrence. "The *Camerata da' Bardi* and the Foundations of Music Drama." Ph.D. dissertation, University of Wisconsin, 1951.

Rogerson, Brewster. " 'Ut musica poesis': The Parallel of Music and Poetry in Eighteenth-Century Criticism." Ph.D. dissertation, Princeton, 1946.

Rolland, Romain. *A Musical Tour through the Land of the Past.* Translated by Bernard Miall. London: H. Holt & Co., 1922.

————. *Musiciens d'autrefois.* Paris, 1913. Translated by Mary Blaiklock as *Some Musicians of Former Days.* Freeport, N.Y.: Books for Libraries Press, 1968.

————. "L'opéra au XVIIe siècle." *Encyclopédie de la musique et dictionnaire du conservatoire,* pt. 1, vol. 3. Paris: Delagrave, 1931.

Roquet, Antoine E. *Maugars, célèbre joueur de viole, musicien du cardinal Richelieu . . . sa biographie suivie de sa "Response faite à un curieux. . . ."* Paris, 1865. Reprint. London: H. Baron, 1965.

Rousset, J. *La littérature de l'âge baroque en France.* Paris: Corti, 1953.

Sadowsky, Rosalie. "Jean-Baptiste *Abbé* Dubos: The Influence of Cartesian and Neo-Aristotelian Ideas on Music Theory and Practice." Ph.D. dissertation, Yale, 1960.

Saintsbury, George. *A History of Literary Criticism and Literary Taste in Europe.* 3 vols. Edinburgh: Blackwood, 1900–1904. Second ed. 1949.

Saisseln, R. G. *Taste in Eighteenth-Century France: Critical Reflections on the Origins of Aesthetics.* Syracuse: Syracuse University Press, 1965.

Schäfke, Rudolf. *Geschichte der Musikästhetik in Umrissen.* Basel, 1934. Reprint. Tutzing: Schneider, 1964.

Schering, Arnold. "Die Musikästhetik der deutschen Aufklärung." *Zeitschrift der Internationalen Musikgesellschaft* 8 (1906–1907):265–71.

————. *Musikgeschichte Leipzigs.* 3 vols. Leipzig: F. Kistner & C. F. W. Siegel, 1926.

Schneider, Herbert. *Die französische Kompositionslehre in der ersten Hälfte des 17. Jahrhunderts.* Tutzing: Schneider, 1972.

Schueller, Herbert M. "The Quarrel of Ancients and Moderns." *Music and Letters* 41 (1960):313–30.

Schürr, Friedrich. *Barock, Klassizismus und Rokoko in der französischen Literatur: eine prinzipielle Stilbetrachtung.* Leipzig: B. G. Teubner, 1928.

Serwer, Howard Jay. "Friedrich Wilhelm Marpurg (1718–1795): Music Critic in a Galant Age." Ph.D. dissertation, Yale, 1969.

Shedlock, J. S. "André Maugars." In: *Studies in Music.* Edited by Robin Grey. London: Simpkin, Marshall, Hamilton, Kent and Co., 1901.

Sheldon, David A. "The Galant Style Revisited and Reevaluated." *Acta Musicologica* 47 (1975):240–70.

Silin, Charles I. *Benserade and his Ballets de Cour.* Baltimore: Johns Hopkins Press, 1940. Reprint. 1970.

Smith, James Harry, and Edd Winfield Parks. *The Great Critics: An Anthology of Literary Criticism.* New York: Norton, 1932. Third ed. 1951.

Snyders, Georges. *Le goût musical en France aux XVIIe et XVIIIe siècles.* Paris: Vrin, 1968.

Solerti, Angelo. "Un viaggio in Francia di Giulio Caccini (1604–1605)." *Rivista musicale italiana* 10 (1903):707.

Soriano, Marc. *Le dossier Charles Perrault.* Paris: Hachette, 1972.

Sozzi, Lionello. "La polémique anti-italienne en France au XVIe siècle." *Estratto dagli atti della Accademia delle scienze di Torino* 106 (1971–72):99–190.

Spingarn, Joel E. *A History of Literary Criticism in the Renaissance: With Special Reference to the Influence of Italy in the Formation and Development of Modern Classicism.* Columbia University Studies in Comparative Literature, vol. 2. New York: Columbia University Press, 1899.

Striffling, Louis. *Esquisse d'une histoire du goût musical en France au XVIIe siècle.* Paris: Delagrave, 1912.

Strunk, Oliver. *Source Readings in Music History from Classical Antiquity through the Romantic Era*. New York: Norton, 1950.

Tagliabue, Guido Morpurgo. *Il concetto del gusto nell'Italia del settecento*. Florence: Nuova Italia editrice, 1962.

Tapié, Victor. *The Age of Grandeur*. Translated by Audrey Ross Williamson. London, 1960. Second ed. New York: Praeger, 1966.

—————. *Baroque et classicism*. Paris: Plon, 1957.

Thorpe, Clarence de Witt. *The Aesthetic Theory of Thomas Hobbes, with Special Reference to his Contribution to the Psychological Approach in English Literary Criticism*. New York: Russell and Russell, 1940. Second ed. 1964.

Toynbee, Arnold. *A Study of History*. 12 vols. Oxford: Oxford University Press, 1934–1961.

Truinet, Charles Louis Etienne (pseud. Nuitter) and A. E. Roquet (pseud. Thoinan). *Les origines de l'opéra français*. Paris: Plon, 1886.

Van Tieghem, Philippe. *Les grands doctrines littéraires en France, de la Pléiade au surréalisme*. Eighth ed. Paris: Presses universitaires de France, 1968.

—————. *Les influences étrangères sur la littérature française (1550–1880)*. Paris: Presses universitaires de France, 1961.

Verchaly, André. "Le Cerf." *MGG* 8 (1960), cols. 425–26.

—————. "Les airs italiens mis en tablature de luth dans les receuils français du début de XVIIe siècle." *Revue de musicologie* 35 (1953):45–48.

Vial and Denise. *Idées et doctrines littéraires du XVIIIe siècle*. Paris: Delagrave, 1930.

Vischer, Dora Christa. *Der musikgeschichtliche Traktat des Pierre Bourdelot (1610–1685)*. Bern: Berner Veröffentlichung zur Musikforschung, 1947.

Von Stein, Heinrich. *Die Entstehung der neueren Ästhetik*. Stuttgart: Cotta, 1886.

Walker, D. P. "Musical Humanism in the Sixteenth and Early Seventeenth Centuries." *Music Review* 2 (1941):1–71.

Wangermée, Robert. "Lecerf de la Viéville, Bonnet-Bourdelot et l'"Essai sur le bon goust en musique' de Nicolas Grandval." *Revue belge de musicologie* 5 (1951):132–46.

Weinberg, Bernard. *A History of Literary Criticism in the Italian Renaissance*. Chicago: University of Chicago Press, 1961.

Wellek, René. "The Concept of Baroque in Literary Scholarship." *Journal of Aesthetics and Art Criticism* 5 (1946):77–109.

—————. *A History of Modern Criticism: 1750–1950*. Vol. 1: *The Later Eighteenth Century*. New Haven: Yale University Press, 1955.

Wellesz, Egon. "Cavalli und der Stil der venezianischen Oper vom 1640–1660." *Studien zur Musikwissenschaft* 1 (1913):1–103.

Wolff, Helmuth Christian. "Italian Opera 1700–1750." *New Oxford History of Music*, vol. 5. London: Oxford University Press, 1975.

Wright, G. H. C. *French Classicism*. Cambridge, Mass.: Harvard University Press, 1920.

Yates, Frances A. *The French Academies of the Sixteenth Century*. Studies of the Warburg Institute, vol. 15. London: Warburg Institute. University of London, 1947.

Zeller, Berthold. *Henri IV et Marie de Médicis*. Paris: Didier, 1877.

Index